Bangkok

WHAT'S NEW | WHAT'S ON | WHAT'S BEST

www.timeout.com/bangkok

Contents

Bangkok by Area

Essentials

Published by Time Out Guides Ltd
Universal House
251 Tottenham Court Road
London W1T 7AB
Tel: + 44 (0)20 7813 3000
Fax: + 44 (0)20 7813 6001
Email: guides@timeout.com
www.timeout.com

Managing Director Peter Fiennes
Editorial Director Ruth Jarvis
Business Manager Dan Allen
Editorial Manager Holly Pick
Assistant Management Accountant Ija Krasnikova

Time Out Guides is a wholly owned subsidiary of Time Out Group Ltd.

© Time Out Group Ltd
Chairman Tony Elliott
Chief Executive Officer David King
Group General Manager/Director Nichola Coulthard
Time Out Communications Ltd MD David Pepper
Time Out International Ltd MD Cathy Runciman
Time Out Magazine Ltd Publisher/Managing Director Mark Elliott
Production Director Mark Lamond
Group IT Director Simon Chappell
Marketing & Circulation Director Catherine Demajo

Time Out and the Time Out logo are trademarks of Time Out Group Ltd.

This edition first published in Great Britain in 2010 by Ebury Publishing
A Random House Group Company
Company information can be found on www.randomhouse.co.uk
Random House UK Limited Reg. No. 954009
10 9 8 7 6 5 4 3 2 1

Distributed in the US by Publishers Group West
Distributed in Canada by Publishers Group Canada

For further distribution details, see www.timeout.com

ISBN: 978-1-84670-147-4

A CIP catalogue record for this book is available from the British Library.

Printed and bound by Firmengruppe APPL, aprinta druck, Wemding, Germany.

The Random House Group Limited supports The Forest Stewardship Council (FSC), the leading
international forest certification organisation. All our titles that are printed on Greenpeace
approved FSC certified paper carry the FSC logo. Our paper procurement policy can be found
at www.rbooks.co.uk/environment.

Time Out carbon-offsets all its flights with Trees for Cities (www.treesforcities.org).

Bangkok Shortlist

The **Time Out Bangkok Shortlist** is one of a new series of guides that draws on Time Out's background as a magazine publisher to keep you current with what's going on in town. As well as Bangkok's key sights and the best of its eating, drinking and leisure options, the guide picks out the most exciting venues to have recently opened and gives a full calendar of annual events. It also includes features on the important news, trends and openings, all compiled by locally based editors and writers. Whether you're visiting for the first time, or you're a regular, you'll find the *Time Out Bangkok Shortlist* contains all you need to know, in a portable and easy-to-use format.

The guide divides Bangkok into seven areas, each of which contains listings for Sights & Museums, Eating & Drinking, Shopping, Nightlife and Arts & Leisure, with maps pinpointing all their locations. At the front of the book are chapters rounding up these scenes city-wide, and giving a shortlist of our overall picks in a variety of categories. We include itineraries for days out, plus essentials such as transport information and hotels.

Our listings give phone numbers as dialled within Bangkok. In Thailand, you must include the area code. The international code for Thailand is 66. To call from outside Thailand follow this with the number given, dropping the initial '0'. Some listed numbers are mobiles, and are indicated as such.

We have stipulated price categories for restaurants and hotels with one to four **B** signs (**B-BBBB**), representing budget, moderate, expensive and luxury. Major credit cards are accepted unless otherwise stated.

All our listings are double-checked, but places do sometimes close or change their hours or prices, so it's a good idea to call a venue before visiting. While every effort has been made to ensure accuracy, the publishers cannot accept responsibility for any errors that this guide may contain.

Venues are marked on the maps using symbols numbered according to their order within the chapter and colour-coded according to the type of venue they represent:

❶ Sights & Museums
❶ Eating & Drinking
❶ Shopping
❶ Nightlife
❶ Arts & Leisure

Map key	
Major sight or landmark	
Railway station	
Park	
College/hospital	
Neighbourhood	SIAM
Pedestrian street	
Main road	
Temple	⛩
Airport	✈

Time Out **Bangkok** Shortlist

EDITORIAL
Editor Philip Cornwel-Smith
Deputy Editor Edoardo Albert
Proofreader Mandy Martinez

DESIGN
Art Director Scott Moore
Art Editor Pinelope Kourmouzoglou
Senior Designer Henry Elphick
Graphic Designers Kei Ishimaru, Nicola Wilson
Advertising Designer Jodi Sher

Picture Editor Jael Marschner
Deputy Picture Editor Lynn Chambers
Picture Researcher Gemma Walters
Picture Desk Assistant Ben Rowe
Picture Librarian Christina Theisen

ADVERTISING
Commercial Director Mark Phillips
International Advertising Manager Kasimir Berger
International Sales Executive Charlie Sokol
Advertising Sales (Bangkok) Asia City Media Group Company

MARKETING
Marketing Manager Yvonne Poon
Sales & Marketing Director, North America & Latin America Lisa Levinson
Senior Publishing Brand Manager Luthfa Begum
Art Director Anthony Huggins

PRODUCTION
Production Manager Brendan McKeown
Production Controller Damian Bennett

CONTRIBUTORS
This guide was researched and written by Philip Cornwel-Smith, with Laurie Osborne, Jarrett Wrisley, Chami Jotisalikorn and Brian Mertens. The editor would like to thank contributors to previous Time Out Bangkok guides, on whose work parts of this book are based.

PHOTOGRAPHY
Photography by Mark Parren Taylor, except: pages 10, 19, 22, 24, 28, 31, 39, 40, 43, 44, 45, 51, 52, 58, 60, 63, 65, 66, 78, 82, 109, 113 (right), 117, 118, 122, 143, 145, 151, 153, 154, 155, 157 Heloise Bergman.

The following images were provided by the featured establishments/artists: pages 7, 72, 73, 148, 161, 164, 170, 171, 172.

Cover photograph: Floating market, Bangkok. Credit: Getty Images

MAPS
JS Graphics (john@jsgraphics.co.uk).

About **Time Out**

Founded in 1968, Time Out has expanded from humble London beginnings into the leading resource for those wanting to know what's happening in the world's greatest cities. As well as our influential what's-on weeklies in London, New York and Chicago, we publish nearly 30 other listings magazines in cities as varied as Beijing and Mumbai. The magazines established Time Out's trademark style: sharp writing, informed reviewing and bang up-to-date inside knowledge of every scene.

Time Out made the natural leap into travel guides in the 1980s with the City Guide series, which now extends to over 50 destinations around the world. Written and researched by expert local writers and generously illustrated with original photography, the full-size guides cover a larger area than our Shortlist guides and include many more venue reviews, along with additional background features and a full set of maps.

Throughout this rapid growth, the company has remained proudly independent, still owned by Tony Elliott four decades after he started Time Out London as a single fold-out sheet of A5 paper. This independence extends to the editorial content of all our publications, this Shortlist included. No establishment has been featured because it has advertised, and no payment has influenced any of our reviews. And, for our critics, there's definitely no such thing as a free lunch: all restaurants and bars are visited and reviewed anonymously, and Time Out always picks up the bill.
For more about the company, see www.timeout.com.

Don't Miss

JIM THOMPSON

Bangkok : Main Store 9 Surawong Road – Bangkok 10500 tel: 0 2632 8100
Siam Paragon – The Emporium – Isetan – Central World
The Jim Thompson House & Museum – Central Chidlom
The Oriental Hotel – Royal Orchid Sheraton Hotel – The Peninsula Hotel
Marriott Resort & Spa – Four Seasons Hotel – The Hotel Plaza Athénée
Sheraton Grande Sukhumvit Hotel

Pattaya – Hua Hin – Samui – Phuket   www.jimthompson.com

BACC p12

Sights & Museums

The capital of Southeast Asia's only uncolonised country, Bangkok retains much of its cultural depth. Despite relentless development, Krung Thep (the 'City of Angels') keeps true to itself, embracing every onslaught with its *mai pen rai* (never mind) nonchalance, trademark smile and pervasive sense of the sacred. But it remains so fascinating partly due to its endearing chaos. Accessing Siamese heritage isn't always straightforward, but the joy is in treating Bangkok as an expedition. In this vast metropolis of over ten million people, the majority of sights lie in the old town nucleus of Phra Nakorn, the preceding capital of Thonburi, Chinatown, Dusit and along the waterways. Yes, there are glorious landmarks, but much of what you'll remember happens serendipitously en route.

Museums

Bangkok lacks a museum (*phipitapan*) dedicated to the city itself. To glean its history, you must piece together fragments from specialist museums, palaces, temples and the 'living museum' of the city's communities, markets and festivals.

The new Museum Siam (p58) interactively portrays social, economic and ethnic aspects of 'Siamese' culture marginalised by the official narrative of 'Thainess'. This diversity is missing from the more conventionally displayed treasure hoard of the National Museum (p58), which focuses on the royal, religious, archaeological and high-culture patrimony of the state, but fails to communicate the context of what is Southeast Asia's biggest repository of artefacts.

Wat Suthat

The city's many distinct communities are beginning to get recognition. The Bangkokian Museum (p93) evokes mid-20th century life in the old Farang (Westerner) quarter. A museum of Thonburi's multi-ethnic Kudi Jeen neighbourhood is also mooted. Meanwhile an impressive new Chinatown Heritage Centre (p88) helps trace Bangkok's urban evolution through its crucial Chinese contributions.

Palaces & mansions

The seat of power for Bangkok's first century, the Grand Palace and its temple of the Emerald Buddha, Wat Phra Kaew (p53), are now a museum and ceremonial venue. It's the country's must-see sight and imposes strict codes of dress and etiquette. It is the principal *wang* (palace), but the plethora of royal descendants has bequeathed a wealth of palaces and aristocratic mansions throughout the capital.

The National Museum occupies remnants of the Wang Na, or front palace. Nearby, Silpakorn University (p59) contains parts of Tha Phra Palace. When King Rama V moved his court to Dusit Park (p75), he built the all-teak Wang Vimarnmek and mansions and throne halls that today exhibit aspects of royalty, such as King Bumibol's photography and Queen Sirikit's revival of court arts.

Redevelopment has caused the loss of countless of the city's heirloom buildings. Several of the lesser-known palaces are open, but to visit them most require a written application a week or two ahead of your visit, such as Wang Bangkhunprom (p78) and Ratcha Wang Derm (p70).

Some of Bangkok's teak stilt houses survive as museums, notably MR Kukrit Pramoj's Heritage Home (p106) and Jim Thompson's House (p112). Other mansions have new uses, like the restaurants Blue Elephant (p106), Café Siam (p107) or China House (p94), H Gallery (p108), the Oriental Spa and Authors Wing of the Oriental Hotel (p173), indie bars

Tak Sura (p125) and Lollipop (p69), and the shopping precincts of Silom Village (p97) and OP Garden (p95).

Historic communities

Several heritage areas – Phra Nakorn, Banglamphu, Samsen, Chinatown, Kudi Jeen in Thonburi (p70), and the Old Farang Quarter of Bangrak (p92) – retain vibrant communities in a lattice of lanes (*soi*). One cooler option – and a favourite experience of most visitors – is to explore by boat along the river and canals (see p40).

Old communities typically feature shophouses, some ornate, with narrow *sois* reaching densely packed houses of wood or cement. Indie bohemians led the colonisation of historic streets like Thanon Phra Arthit (p80), which are now undergoing restoration and gentrification. Canal areas retain a higher proportion of teak homes on stilts. The daily focus of old town life is the market (see p21), though the supermarket lifestyle of downtown districts is encroaching everywhere. Old areas also retain the most authentic Thai food outlets (see box p79).

Temples & shrines

Most communities have at least one *wat* (Theravada Buddhist temple). Their resident monks ambulate each morning to collect food alms. *Wats* hold periodic festivals (pp34-38) and may perform secular roles as schools, hospitals or orphanages to fairgrounds, lodgings or cinemas, as well as tourist sights. At all religious sites you should observe decorum in dress and behaviour.

Some visitors become aficionados of temple design, spotting swanlike *chofa* finials, ornate gables, roofs of green and orange tiles, crown-like windows, conical *chedi* (stupas) clad

S H O R T L I S T

Must-see sights
- Grand Palace (p53)
- Jim Thompson's House (p112)
- National Museum (p58)
- Wat Pho (p61)

New wave museums
- BACC (p111)
- Chinatown Heritage Centre (p88)
- Museum Siam (p58)
- TCDC (p134)

Best views
- The Dome (p93)
- Golden Mount (p66)
- Rama VIII Bridge (p78)
- BTS SkyTrain (p182)

Heritage houses
- Blue Elephant (p106)
- Dumnam (p87)
- Dusit Park (p75)
- MR Kukrit Pramoj's Heritage Home (p106)
- Phyathai Palace (p124)
- Wang Bangkhunprom (p78)

Top galleries
- 100 Tonson (p123)
- H Gallery (p108)
- Kathmandu (p97)
- Numthong (p146)
- Silom Galleria (p97)
- Gallery Ver (p99)

Sublime temples
- Wat Benchamabophit (p77)
- Wat Kalayanamit (p71)
- Wat Ratchabophit (p61)
- Wat Suthat (p67)
- Wat Trimit (p86)

Quirkiest shrines
- Erawan Shrine (p119)
- Kwan Im Shrine (p146)
- Chao Poh Seua Shrine (p65)
- Maha Uma Devi (p93)

DON'T MISS

in gold, stucco or ceramic mosaic, or leaf-shaped *sema* boundary stones around the *bot* (chapel). All stylistic periods of Buddha images can be seen in the cloister of Wat Benchamabophit (p77) as well as the National Museum.

Many Sino-Thais follow Mahayana Buddhism, as well as Taoism. Shrines outside Chinatown include Chao Poh Seua Shrine (p65) and Kwan Im Shrine (p146), with activity busiest at Chinese New Year (p34) and the Vegetarian Festival (p37).

Thais also revere Hindu gods notably at Devasthan (p65), Maha Uma Devi (p93) and the Erawan Shrine (p119). The latter is a glorified spirit house, a feature of every plot of land, where animist belief holds that the resident spirit must be placated with daily offerings. Two unusual spirit sites are the phallic Nai Lert Shrine (p118) and effigies of the ghost Mae Nark at Wat Maha But (p140).

Contemporary art

New ideas and individualism are weaning Thai art from religious subjects and revered masters' templates. Students still hail the Italian Silpa Bhirasri (born Corrado Ferroci) – designer of the Democracy Monument (p65) and Rama V statue (p76) – as the father of modern art, as he founded Silpakorn University (p59).

A neo-traditional, spiritual style emerged, and today it fills half of Bangkok's galleries. Curators at progressive galleries showcase a new generation of artists with reputations for conceptual art driven by folk, ethnic and pop culture. Photography gets exposure at Kathmandu (p97), Phranakorn Bar (p68), and the Foreign Correspondents Club of Thailand (0 2652 0580-1, www.fccthai.com).

The long-heralded Bangkok Art & Culture Centre (BACC, p111), while not without problems, now acts as a much-needed focus for exhibitions and festivals. More impressive still, the Thailand Creative & Design Centre (TCDC, p134) holds world-class exhibitions and events. The free map *Art Connection* (monthly) covers all art happenings.

Sightseeing tips

Cool hours have the best light and most local activity. However, traffic, humidity and obstacles make strolling a challenge. Take a hat, sunscreen, light bag, water and shoes that are easily removed at temples, palaces or houses.

Most state-funded museums have low entrance charges, close around 4pm and shut on Mondays. BACC, TCDC and Museum Siam are late-opening exceptions. Privately run sights open longer, charge more and offer broader services.

Mass tourism has spawned some 'edutainments'. These veer from sights like the Snake Farm (p100) and Siam Ocean World aquarium (p112) to dinner shows of traditional dance and the Siam Niramit cultural extravaganza (p150). Bigger malls have children's play areas, while Siam Paragon (p116) will open a role-playing KidZania theme park in late 2010.

Green space in the city is limited, but parks are increasing in number. Meanwhile, a semi-wild expanse lies just minutes from downtown across the river at Bang Kra Jao (p151).

Tour companies abound, but Bangkok Tourist Bureau (p187) runs some great walking tours. Spice Roads offers inspiring cycle tours (0 2712 5305, www.spiceroads.com). Those with a serious cultural interest can join Siam Society (p133) trips.

Red Sky p120

Eating & Drinking

Like its iconic green curry, Bangkok dining is a sophisticated, eclectic stew. The disparate cooking traditions, exacting chefs, ultra-fresh ingredients and demanding consumers have combined to forge a great world food city. There are intimate fine dining gems and excellent Italian trattorias, pierside Sino-Thai seafood halls and vendors who serve a single dish so well that locals travel across town to eat it.

The drinking scene is equally vibrant, though increasingly regulated (see p24). From streetside bars serving beer and bucket cocktails, to artsy holes-in-the-wall, chic cocktail lounges and towering rooftop hangouts (see box p96), you can quaff on a shoestring or an expense account.

From street to chic

Escape the de-spiced tourist menus. Eat local. Bangkok's position, between India and China, encouraged its cooks to borrow from both – and beyond. And yet, the Central Plains style of cooking remains singular in its style and complexity, and is served by most upscale Thai restaurants. This is Thailand's most elevated culinary form – making use of fresh local herbs, seafood and meats in piquant salads, spicy soups and that famed green curry (see p189).

Regional menus have their niches, especially the salads, grilled meats and sticky rice of Isaan, Thailand's northeast, at places like Isaan Rot Det (p125). Southern Thai dishes exhibit their pungent spiciness at Ruen (p137). *Lanna* (northern) food,

YOU KNOW WHO YOU ARE.
BANGKOK • 424/3-6 SIAM SQUARE SOI 11
662-251-0797 • HARDROCK.COM

Hard Rock
CAFE

influenced by Burma and Yunnan, is found at food markets, notably Or Tor Kor (p144).

The owner of suave Thai restaurant Ruen Urai (p101) suggests exploring Bangkok's culinary scene by context, from streetfood up to fine dining. Eating on plastic stools at stalls – Thailand's true dining room – is both safe and rewarding, whether at itinerant carts or permanent markets. Classic vendor dishes include noodles, *khao mun gai* (chicken rice), and *khao ka moo*, a braised pork shank so tender it slips lazily from bone to plate.

Shophouses are often *Raan Ahaan Tam Sang* (cook-to-order restaurants), which rustle-up dozens of dishes. The ever-rarer kitchens of the old town, like Chote Chitr (p67), gained fame for refined curries, salads and specialities. The riverside Kaloang (p79) is typical of Thai seafood influenced by migrant Chinese cooks, served in ramshackle surroundings.

More genteel restaurants in homes (*baan*) or gardens (*suan*) have book-sized menus and may serve Royal Thai Cuisine with fruit carving. Many think food quality declines as the decor improves, but Thai fine dining is gaining recognition, whether refined classics or fusions, combined with solicitous service, chic settings and the wonders of air-conditioning.

Hygiene is generally better than it looks, even on the street. Often food poisoning originates from poor refrigeration rather than stalls that seem crude, but buy, cook and sell the food within hours. Look for stalls with cleanliness certification stickers. Turnover and common sense are key guides – busy and clean means safe. Machine-made ice cubes (or hoops) are pure; shaved ice less so. Thais adjust their food with condiments and herbs, share

SHORTLIST

Best Thai restaurants
- Bo.lan (p134)
- Chote Chitr (p67)
- Ruen Mallika (p137)
- Ruen Urai (p101)
- Taling Pling (p107)

Best streetfood
- Or Tor Kor Market (p144)
- Nang Leong Market (p77)
- Sukhumvit Soi 38 (p79)
- Soi Texas (p89)

Best riverscapes
- Amoroso, Arun Residence (p167)
- Mandarin Oriental (p173)
- Supatra River House (p72)

Best European
- D'Sens (p100)
- Giusto (p135)
- Le Banyan (p130)
- Le Beaulieu (p130)

Best rooftops
- Dome (p93)
- Gazebo (p83)
- Phranakorn Bar (p68)
- Vertigo (p107)

Best design
- Bed Supperclub (p132)
- China House (p94)
- Hazara (p140)

Best nostalgia
- Café Siam (p107)
- Le Dalat Indochine (p136)

Best fusion
- Eat Me! (p100)
- Greyhound (p135)
- Kuppa (p136)

Best cocktails
- Distil (p93)
- Hu'u (p107)
- Long Table (p136)

most Thai dishes, and eat with fork and spoon. They use chopsticks only for noodles and Chinese food.

Time & place

Food is integral to Thai culture, so people eat many times a day. Bangkokians constantly nibble on 'empty food' (*aahan waang*) like snacks, sweets (*khanom*) or, increasingly, fast food. Meanwhile, food choice changes with the hours.

Thais rise early for a breakfast (*aahan chao*) of fried bananas, rice porridge, Chinese buns or savoury dishes. They lunch at noon sharp (*aahan thiang*) at noodle stalls or curry and rice shops (*raan khao kaeng*). Shophouses keep eccentric hours and some stay open till rush-hour dinner time (*aahan yen*). Smarter restaurants open at lunch and 6-9pm, or later in places serving Westerners. After hours, people eat 'drinking food' at bars (*kub klaem*), rice soup (*khao tom*) and can dine at Mid Night Kai Ton (p123) or Nana's Arab cafés. Markets will bag portions to take-away.

International

Bangkok has become one of Asia's most cosmopolitan dining destinations. For centuries a hub of trade, migration and (more recently) tourism, it has pockets of authentic ethnic food: from Paruhat's basic Indian curry houses to Nana's regal North Indian restaurants; and Japanese Izakaya dives to artful sushi bars around Soi Thaniya and Phrom Phong. Sukhumvit is the hotbed of foreign food, with its own Koreatown (Sois 12-15) offering sizzling beef and ice-cold *sochu*. A maze of Arabic restaurants (Sois 3-5) offers the best from Beirut to Baghdad.

French bistros and Gallic fine dining abound, and there are so

Bo.lan p134

many Italian restaurants, some world class, that an Italian Chefs Association boasts hundreds of members. Some of Bangkok's most accomplished food is found in hotels (see box p131).

Vegetarian

Bangkok can frustrate the meat-averse. Most vegetable (*pak*) dishes conceal ingredients like fish sauce, pork or prawn. Banglamphu has the best of the few veggie restaurants. Some cooks, as at Curries & More (p119), will cater to requests for *mangsawirat* (meat-free) or *jeh* (unspiced vegan). Indian and International menus have vegetarian options and some Chinese places serve mock meat. Yellow pennants indicate stalls, restaurants and hotels citywide that join in October's ten-day Chinese Vegetarian Festival (p37).

Fruit & hydration

Keep your eyes peeled for a Technicolor array of seasonal fruit. Much of it – from pineapple and papaya to guava and unripe mango – comes sliced and bagged with a bamboo skewer for B10, or served as juices or smoothies. Herbal drinks like bael fruit, Chinese plum, rozelle and lemongrass have made a retro comeback. Thais often eat or drink their fruit with salt (*gluea*) or chilli (*phrik*) plus sugar (*nam than*), partly for re-hydration. Specify how you like it.

Bottled water (*nam plao*) is sold everywhere. The ultimate electrolyte pick-me-up is coconut juice, sold chilled and fresh from the shell.

Cafés & bars

You can find fresh espresso even at market stalls, with plentiful local and foreign coffee chains. Old-style

Thai coffee (*kafae boran*) comes hot or iced from stalls, such as Baan Rai (p140), where it is brewed, strained and served usually with condensed milk and sugar. They may serve weak tea as a chaser, and brick-colour Thai tea, again with condensed milk. Ong's Tea (p116) lets you sample its gourmet Chinese leaves.

The Mandarin Oriental (p173) and Four Seasons (p177) host the best English high teas. Good hotel bakery-delis include the Conrad (p176), Grand Hyatt Erawan (p177) and JW Marriott (p178).

Alcoholic drinks tend towards beer and shared bottles of whisky with mixers in local-style bars. Vast beer gardens proliferate from November to January. More upmarket (and several impromptu bar stalls) have some wines, spirits and cocktails. To sup ales, cider, Guinness and imported lagers, join expatriates at pubs emitting English, Irish, German, Aussie or American accents. The hippest bars have the most refined drinks lists, but wine bars are rare (see p125 Wine Pub and p95 V9) due to sticker shock from high duties. Nearly every bar serves food.

Service & price

Hotels and smart restaurants often add a ten percent tip (keeping half), but Thais generally leave B20-B40, unless staff are outstanding. Service is friendly but not necessarily fast. Thai dishes trickle in as the kitchen completes them. Specify if you want Western dishes in order. It's wise to book notable restaurants, especially on weekends.

We classify restaurants by price, excluding alcohol: **B** is cheap (under B250 per person for three courses), **BB** moderate (B250-B750), **BBB** expensive (B750-B1,250) and **BBBB** premium (over B1,250).

Siam Paragon p22

Shopping

At times, Bangkok feels like one long, uninterrupted bazaar. Market-going infuses the culture, and Thais' faddish tastes ensure a constantly refreshed variety of goods and retail experiences, with endless fairs, promotions, festivals and entertainments. As with their food, Thais like their shopping spicy.

Thais prize convenience, so not only do retail outlets proliferate beyond any imaginable demand, but shops come to you, in the form of itinerant vendors. As tastes and incomes change, however, so shopping goes up-market.

Bangkok now boasts luxury malls, global branded stores, homegrown boutique labels (see box p115) and world-class design. Yes, prices have risen, but they still remain good value. In Thai retail slang, the city stocks everything 'from pestles to warships'.

Mall-going

In this hot, humid city, shopping is increasingly divided between outdoor and indoor. Markets and stand-alone shops appeal for their character and craft, but officials and developers increasingly restrict informal vending, partly to relieve congestion, piracy, extortion and the charming chaos of it all. As branding power spreads, all-in-one complexes come to resemble artificial towns. Most malls are anchored by department stores, and have cinemas, bowling alleys, children's play zones, gyms, supermarkets, food courts, restaurants, exhibition halls and basement services like dry-cleaning, key-cutting, sewing and shoe repair.

The showpiece malls line a three-kilometre (two-mile) 'Ratchaprasong Shopping Street' retail corridor (see

Whatever your carbon footprint, we can reduce it

For over a decade we've been leading the way in carbon offsetting and carbon management.

In that time we've purchased carbon credits from over 200 projects spread across 6 continents. We work with over 300 major commercial clients and thousands of small and medium sized businesses, which rely upon our market-leading quality assurance programme, our experience and absolute commitment to deliver the right solution for each client.

Why not give us a call?

T: London (020) 7833 6000

p118) along Thanons Rama I and Ploenchit, and extending down Sukhumvit (p127); most are linked to BTS elevated walkways. At one end, the micro-boutiques of Siam Square (p109) act as the hub of Thai fashion and trendspotting.

Markets & hawkers

Talad (markets) and *rot khen* (roving carts) garnish Bangkok in the purest expression of the sensual Thai culture, with their kaleidoscope of scents (jasmine garlands, musty puddles, durian), sounds (yelping hawkers, booming techno), sights (sleeping children, slithering eels, temple fairs), touch (antique silk, fake fur) and tastes (many unique to Thailand). Markets often integrate into their community, like Talad Banglamphu (p82) or Sampeng Lane Market (p87) in Chinatown. Temporary markets endow festivals with local or seasonal treats, traders vary in shifts at particular spots, and Chatuchak Weekend Market (p144) sells just about everything.

Like the floating markets from which they derive (p73 and p152), cart vendors remain fluid. No amount of campaigns to restrain their trading or encroachment on crowded roads or pavements ever lasts long. Colonising any spare space by pedal or paddle, motor or manpower, they congregate at already congested places, such as *soi* mouths, shopping strips and tourist haunts. Most recently they swamped Siam Square by night with youth fashion. Food comprises half of what is peddled; for streetfood hotspots, see box p79. Monday is a designated rest day for street vendors, though daily markets remain open and others operate at specific times. Beware of pick-pockets, generally feel free to touch merchandise, and smilingly decline persistent touting.

DON'T MISS

S H O R T L I S T

Best Thai fashion
- Fly Now (p121)
- Issue (p114)
- Sretsis (p122)
- Siam Centre (p116)
- Siam Square (p109)

Best Thai design
- BIG Fair, IMPACT (p151)
- Panta (p116)
- Propaganda (p116)
- Reflections (p179)
- Siam Discovery (p116)
- Bangkok Design Festival (p37)

Best markets
- Chatuchak Weekend Market (p144)
- Pahurat Market (p91)
- Pak Khlong Talad (p69)
- Sampeng Lane (p87)
- Suan Lum Night Bazaar (p107)
- Thanon Khao San (p80)
- Trok Itsaranuphap (p90)

Best tailors
- Art's Tailors (p102)
- Kai Boutique (p121)
- Sequin Queen, Pratunam Market (p124)

Best Thai silk
- Almeta (p138)
- Baan Khrua (p50)
- Jim Thompson (p102)

Flashiest malls
- Central World (p121)
- Emporium (p138)
- Gaysorn (p121)
- Siam Paragon (p116)

Best souvenirs
- Monk's Bowl Village (p49)
- OTOP Fairs, IMPACT (p151)
- Silom Night Bazaar (p102)
- Triphum (p116)

Markets p21

Updating tradition

Once famed for its exotic crafts, silk and copy goods, Bangkok has reconfigured traditional crafts into a neo-Thai design aesthetic (see p47) with indigenous materials, tropical colours and pared-down Thai forms. You can see this elegant style applied across clothing, decor, accessories and home spa products. 'Original' is gradually displacing 'copy' as Bangkok's retail mantra.

Asian objet d'art is a major niche. Antiques shops spread around Thanon Charoen Krung into Silom and Surawong Roads, River City (p95) and Chatuchak Weekend Market (p144), though these tend now to be more from surrounding countries. And some antiques are newer than they look due to the accelerated ageing techniques of wily carvers.

Antique treasures (and even reproduction Buddha images) are prohibited from export without a licence from the Fine Arts Department's Office of Archaeology (81/1 Thanon Si Ayutthaya, 0 2628 5033/5021 ext 306). Most shops and antiques dealers offer to arrange shipping.

Chatuchak, Khao San Road and Sukhumvit's Nana areas also brim with souvenir crafts, while Paragon Passage at Siam Paragon (p116) and Exotique Thai at Emporium (p138) offer higher quality Siamese collectibles. Items bearing the OTOP logo are state-marketed village goods. Traditional crafts include: forged steel cutlery by knifemaker NV Aranyik (p122); nielloware (etched two-tone metal); pewterware; *benjarong* (five-colour gilded ceramic); Celadon (green crackle-glazed crockery and vases); woodcarving; brassware; puppets (at Thai Puppet Theater, p108); lacquerware; handwoven textiles, often loomed by tribesfolk, and Thai silk, a heavy, coarse, lustrous fibre made famous by Jim Thompson (p102) and now made to order by Almeta (p138).

You can still buy crafts from their source. Artisans working in and around Bangkok include weavers at Ban Khrua Thai Silk (p50), metalbeaters at the Monk's Bowl Village (p49), goldsmiths at Tang Toh Kang (p87) and bronze foundry workers in the lane beside Wat Suwannaram (p72).

Tailors

Haberdasheries crowd tourist areas, especially Sukhumvit Sois 3-11, Thanon Khao San, Thanon Charoen Krung (between Silom and River City) and malls. Typically run by Thai-Indians, they can tailor bespoke suits and dresses for bargain prices. For optimum quality and service, dismiss the '24-hour with free kimono' packages. Most respond professionally to customers who are thorough about cut, cloth and detailing. Give them a pattern or choose from their catalogues and magazine cuttings. Insist on at least two fittings over several days.

Modus shoperandi

Shopping is flexible due to late closing. Shops open from 10am till 6pm or later in tourist areas, but some close on Sundays. Malls and department stores stay open daily till 8pm, often 10pm, even having 'Midnight Sales'.

The metric system predominates in weights, volumes, distance and fabric. Thai Baht is the only currency needed, although some antiques are priced in US dollars.

Many retailers rely on tourists, and assistants often follow you. Don't be offended; they're keen to serve and are on commission. They'll take your selection with cash (or card) and return from the till with bagged goods, change and a receipt. Otherwise, say: *'Khor doo dai maii?'* ('Can I just look?').

Prices & bargaining

Generally fixed, shop prices are low by world standards, and discounted in frequent sales, end-of-month promotions, and during each Thailand Grand Sale (June-July and December-January). Department stores often give instant five per cent discounts for tourists (show your passport) or for certain credit cards. Some services, like travel agents, add on credit card fees. Some of the best bargains are at the busy public weekend days of trade fairs, typically held at IMPACT (p151).

Bargaining is normal at markets (however, note that this does not apply to cooked food), though the mark-up is less than the Asian average; most can't discount more

Sretsis p21

than 20 per cent. Pre-armed with shop prices, you must remain polite and honour any bid they accept. Asking in Thai can lower the starting price, and walking away from an impasse may reveal the 'best price'.

New consumer laws may change the no-exchange norm, and reduce the number of scams, though rip-offs are largely confined to touts, freelance traders, gems, and too-good-to-be-true scenarios. Some shops might refund or exchange faulty goods (unlikely if you lose your temper). Refer complaints to the Office of the Consumer Protection Board (hotline 1166, www.ocpb.go.th) or the Food & Drug Administration (hotline 1556, www.fda.moph.go.th).

Crackdowns and changing trends are marginalising counterfeit goods, though they keep reappearing. Potential buyers should consider increasingly stringent laws against bringing pirated goods into their countries.

Bed Supperclub p132

WHAT'S BEST
Nightlife

Bangkok's nightlife has outgrown its go-go and cover band notoriety through new nocturnal scenes, from quirky dens to models' bars to star DJs. And open-air cocktail nests atop skyscrapers (see box p96) put BKK on the jet-set map. Ever-sleeker clubs attract varying Thai:foreign ratios, while the indie scene thrives on peripatetic party nights (see box p149); live music is never far away, and after-hours venues keep shifting. The city never stops partying – what else to expect from the home of Red Bull?

A 'social order' campaign demarcated just three nightlife zones, ignoring most bar strips, yet matching the sex trade haunts. The Patpong Zone includes go-go bars (see box p104), the half-gay bar strip Silom Soi 4 and all-gay Silom Soi 2 (p99). The Ratchadaphisek Zone harbours massage parlours, the down-market disco barns of Ratchada Sois 4 and 8. The adjacent Phetchaburi Zone has more massage joints and bars for the hipper youth at Royal City Avenue (RCA).

Outside the zones, rules on clubs prove unrealistic, so ambiguity reigns. Some areas seem devoid of nightlife, yet streets can burst into vogue, like unpretentious Thanon Kamphaengphet (p143), or the rich-kids playground of Thonglor-Ekamai (see box p140). Thanon Khao San (p80) has parallel scenes for backpackers and Thais, while Thanon Phra Arthit (p80) harbours indie hangouts. Nana is notorious for its go-go (p127), but Q Bar (p133) and Bed Supperclub (p132) have prompted so many chic rivals that a Sukhumvit Soi 11 Association has emerged (Facebook: Sukhumvit Soi 11). Pricey expatriate pubs focus on Phromphong, Nana and Saladaeng. Yet budget boozing can be done pretty well anywhere: down alleys, in markets, on piers, even in '70s-style suburbia. Cool-season beer gardens flourish, while Thanon Khao San and Nana have pavement bars set up around stalls or on open-top *tuk-tuks*.

DJs & bands

At local clubs revellers jiggle around tall tables, snacking and topping up their whisky-cokes while DJs talk over pop-dance requests. Downtown playlists are edgier, if often samey. Among homespun DJs, listen out for Spydamonkee, Dragon, Joeki, Arsit, Octo, indie veteran Seed, and DJ spin champions Oatawa and Kolor One.

Club investment has generally proved risky, but stalwarts like Club Culture (p126) or Narcissus (p138) diversify with themed nights, annual dance parties (www.culture-one-bkk.com) and import DJs (Tiësto, Qbert, Goldie, Oakenfold), burnishing Bangkok's credibility as an international party hub.

Taxis play *morlam*, the infectious, upbeat folk music from Isaan, Thailand's northeast, but try it live at Isaan Tawandaeng (p148). Meanwhile, Raintree (p126) hosts 'songs for life', a mix of Thai riffs and country rock. Jazz merges into blues here, as at Saxophone (p126), Brown Sugar (p103), Bamboo Bar (p97) or sometimes Rain Dogs (p108). Brick Bar (p82) and Bu-ngah serve up energetic ska. Even heavy metal has a home in Bangkok, at the Rock Pub (p126). Many clubs have house bands or gigs by Thai pop or indie acts.

Gay & lesbian

Since the 1990s a modern 'gay' identity has emerged, while *katoey* (ladyboys) remain highly visible.

SHORTLIST

Model playgrounds
- Bed Supperclub (p132)
- Koi (p136)
- Long Table (p136)

Best one nighter
- Club Soma (p149)
- DudeSweet (p149)

Best live music
- Arabian Night (p132)
- Brick Bar (p82)
- Brown Sugar (p103)
- Isaan Tawandaeng (p148)
- Raintree (p126)
- Saxophone (p126)

Most eccentric
- Rain Dogs (p108)
- Snop (p148)
- Tawandaeng German Brewhouse (p152)
- Wong's Place (p108)

Best gay
- Babylon (p107)
- DJ Station (p103)
- Telephone Pub (p105)
- Zeta (p149)

Top DJs
- 808 (p148)
- Bed Supperclub (p132)
- Club Culture (p126)
- Q Bar (p133)

Coolest indie hangout
- Happy Monday (p142)
- Lollipop (p69)
- Pla Dib (p144)
- Ratchada Night Market (p147)
- Tak Sura (p125)

Best expat pub
- Barbican (p100)
- Bull's Head (p134)
- Cheap Charlie's (p130)
- Molly Malone's (p101)
- Roadhouse BBQ (p101)

Get the local experience

Over 50 of the world's top destinations available.

Out venues have exploded from the all-gay Silom Soi 2 (p99) and part-gay Soi 4. Out youth flocks to Thanon Kamphaengphet's bars, like Fake (p146). Less affluent young locals jiggle in Saké Coffee Pub (p69) and distant Lamsalee (Ramkhamhaeng Soi 89/2), where decor, cabarets and beauty contests have a folky flavour. Saunas veer from luxury Babylon (p107) to all-night suburban steameries. Multi-day G-circuit dance parties draw mainly Asian visitors.

Lesbians are called *tom-dee* due to their accentuated butch-femme roles. They flock to Zeta (p119) and go online at www.lesla.com.

For more ideas about places to go in Bangkok, see www.utopia asia.com, www.dreadedned.com or www.fridae.com.

Soi Cowboy p139

Clubbing culture

Traffic means barhopping mostly happens within bar strips. And given the culture of hosting, Thais tend to settle in groups in one venue. Clubs therefore often have multiple functions: lounge, disco, karaoke, band, TV football, garden, rooftop and ever-present *kub klaem* (drinking food). Although some Thais divide bills, the host often pays, typically for a bottle of whisky with mixers to share, whether premium Scotch, cheaper blends or fiery local rums like Mekong or Saeng Som.

Thais also share beer, hence the large bottles and draft pitchers of local brews such as Singha, Chang and licensed Heineken, often drunk on the rocks. Cocktails, too, get shared, with Kamikaze coming in a jug or Saeng Som with Red Bull in a bucket and supped through several straws. Many clubs sell just whisky, beer and sodas by the bottle; others have limited spirits and wine. Some mixologists excel at

signature cocktails, like lemongrass mojitos or lychee martinis.

Dress codes are relaxed, but chic venues attract models and fashionistas. A few high-end bars prohibit sandals, men's shorts and (infamously at the Dome, p93) knapsacks and ripped denim.

Recreational drugs are banned. Clubs rarely search customers, but police roadblocks do stop people, with serious repercussions if drugs are found. Police raids with urine tests are however rare now. Air-con venues ban smoking, but many have outdoor smoker's zones. The minimum drinking age is 20, but many doormen demand state-issued picture ID however old you are. Take note of fire exits on arrival.

Venues in zones close at 2am; bars and music venues outside at 1am, but may extend on officials' whim. Inevitably, the social order clampdown fuelled an unregulated after-hours sub-culture. Taxi drivers, fliers, club scouts and fellow partiers can point the way.

Queen's Gallery p67

Arts & Leisure

Modern entertainments may increasingly eclipse traditional arts, but few images signify Thainess like glittering costumed court dance. Do try to see masters of dance, puppetry, music or, indeed, Muay Thai boxing, which shares this balletic and ritual heritage. Those seeking deeper arts insights can attend Siam Society events (p133) and the hands-on cultural programmes of Origin (p147).

Modern staged productions veer from orchestras and opera to musicals and ladyboy cabaret. Thai film has auteurs worth catching. And Thais sure know how to relax at sumptuous spas.

Thai dance-drama

Since classical dance-drama embodies sacred rites, performers face obstacles in developing these arts. Hence, many dancers and audiences have abandoned tradition for imported forms: Butoh, mime, physical theatre, contemporary dance. Most common are weak retreads of the official stereotype at tourist shows like those at Silom Village (p97) or Siam Niramit (see p150). You can see several forms at once at Sanam Luang on the King's Birthday (p38) and Queen's Birthday (p36) nights. Patravadi Theatre (p73) provides a vital stage for all forms: modern, traditional, imports and fusions.

Thai thespians believe they must succumb to their characters' spirit. Before every show, cast and crew convene for a *wai khru* rite to honour their masters. Many times daily, devotees thank the spirits at Lak Muang (p58) and the Erawan Shrine (p119) by commissioning resident dancers to do an excerpt of

DON'T MISS

Lakhon Chatri, a typically slow, mannered dance derived from the Malay-influence Manohra repertoire. No wonder Thai dance is so beguiling; it channels the gods.

The most intricate and venerated genre, *Khon* masked dance was once performed only for royalty. It relates the *Ramakien*, the Thai take on India's epic *Ramayana*. Only episodes are seen at rare productions and at weekly shows in Sala Chalermkrung (p91), with excerpts at Sala Thai restaurant (p131). Internationally lauded Phichet Kluncheun modernises Khon at festivals and at his distant Chang Theatre (Pracha Uthit Soi 59, 08 1985 0281, www.pklifework.com). There's a Khon Museum at Suan Pakkard Palace (p125).

Lakhon (drama) has two main threads. Rousing, melodramatic *Lakhon Nok*, formerly all-male, and the more refined *Lakhon Nai*, once an all-female court repertoire. One predictable staging is at Naris Day (p36), at the Baan Plainern palace of arts pioneer Prince Naris. Peeramon Chomthavat's authentic troupe Aporn Ngam appears at Bangkok Theatre Festival (BTF, p38) and Origin (p147) in tales like *Unarut* or *Inao*.

Likay, a brash folk opera, blends literature, fables and comedy. It's now limited to temple fairs, fusions with *morlam* music (p148) and topical interpretations by Makhampom at BTF and its Makhampom Studio (Saphan Kwai intersection, 0 2616 8473, www.makhampom.net).

Language is a barrier to appreciating Bangkok's progressive Stage Play companies, excepting those at Bangkok Community Theatre (www.bct-th.org) and some plays by Patravadi Theatre and Makhampom. But musicals have boomed since the opening of Muangthai Ratchadalai Theatre.

SHORTLIST

Best venues
- Aksra Theatre (p126)
- Muangthai Ratchadalai Theatre (p149)
- Patravadi Theatre (p73)
- Thailand Cultural Centre (p150)

Best traditional gurus
- Luang Pradit Pairoh Foundation (p146)
- Patravadi Theatre (p73)
- Thai Puppet Theatre (p108)

Best free dances
- Bangkok Theatre Festival (p38)
- Erawan Shrine (p119)
- Lak Muang (p58)

Best alternative arts
- BACC (p111)
- Fat Festival (p38)
- Gallery Ver (p99)
- Phiman Waterview (p169)
- Reflections (p179)

Kitschest cabaret
- Calypso (p126)
- Mambo (p152)
- Miss AC/DC (p38)

Best holistic
- Arima Onsen (p105)
- Bodhi (p139)
- Chi Spa (p172)
- Devarana Spa (p172)
- Divana Spa (p139)
- Nicolie Asian Massage (p97)
- Sareerarom Tropical Spa (p142)

Best sport
- Lumphini Boxing Stadium (p108)
- Lumphini Park (p99)
- Ratchadamnoen Boxing Stadium (p78)
- RBSC Horse Racing (p117)

Offset your
flight with
Trees for Cities
and make your
trip mean
something for
years to come

www.treesforcities.org/offset

Trees for Cities
Charity registration number 1032154

Puppetry

Thai dance and puppetry are indivisible. *Khon* derives its flat-stanced aesthetic from *Nang* (shadow puppetry); later, *Hun* (marionettes) emulated the glittery stylisation of *Khon*. At festivals you may see *Nang Yai*, outsize shadow puppets with no moving parts manoeuvred by dancers, or smaller, hinged *Nang Talung* animated by a satirical narrator. Small, painted *Hun Krabok* glove puppets have hands moved by sticks. At the Thai Puppet Theater (p108) and Aksra Theatre (p126), uncannily lifelike *Hun Lakhon Lek* involve toddler-sized puppets, each manipulated by three dancers.

Phiphat music

Hearing the discombobulating rhythms of a *Phiphat Wong* (Thai classical orchestra) is fascinating, but hard to find except at tourist dances. Scheduled recitals occur at BTF, Naris Day, and the National Theatre (5-7pm Sat, music; Sun, dance, Dec-Apr, B20; p62). You can hear (and join) weekend practice at Luang Pradit Pairoh Foundation (p146). The leading *phiphat* ensemble Fong Nam regularly plays at Tawandang German Brewhouse (p152).

Concert & cabaret

There are many Western classical events – by chamber groups, visiting ensembles and the Bangkok Symphony Orchestra (BSO; 0 2255 6617-8, www.bangkoksymphony. org), which plays free Concerts-in-the-Park in the cool season (p38). Bangkok Music Society (08 1648 7648) performs four concerts per year. Check www.bangkok concerts.org. Thailand Cultural Centre (p150) hosts ballet, opera,

Nicolie Asian Massage p29

DON'T MISS

musicals and the International Festival of Music & Dance (p36). Bangkok Opera (www.bangkok opera.com) reinterprets classics and premières operas by founder SP Somtow, who also assembled the Bangkok Sinfonietta.

Shows by lip-synching ladyboys (*kathoey*) tend to be commercial spectacles. Grittier, wittier and more inventive are the drag shows at gay clubs (p103).

Film

Thai film has gone from arthouse curio to global player, with lauded directors like Pen-ek Rattanaruang, Nonzee Nimibutr and Apichartpong Weerasethakul. Distributors also clamour for the action kickfests by Tony Jaa. However, Thais prefer nationalistic-historical epics, ghost tales and teen comedy. Hollywood remakes local thrillers (*Shutter*, *6ixtynin9*, *Bangkok Dangerous*) and uses Thailand for locations, as itself

(*The Beach, Elephant King*) or a lookalike (*Good Morning Vietnam, Tomorrow Never Dies*). For Thai film critiques read www.thaicinema.org, Wise Kwai (www.thaifilmjournal.blogspot.com) and Kong Rithdee in Friday's *Bangkok Post*.

Filmgoing is a treat, with cheap, superlative multiplexes, subtitling, IMAX (p117) and two arthouses, plus the Bangkok International Film Festival (p36), World Film Festival of Bangkok (Oct, p37) and Short Film & Video Festival (Aug, p36). Age ratings started in 2009, but censors can't stop interfering. For daily-changing times, check www.movieseer.com.

Sports

Thai traditional Kites fight over Sanam Luang each windy March, but many indigenous Thai games face decline. Meanwhile, *Muay Thai* kick boxing has become a global sport managed by the World Boxing Council (WBC) and World Muay Thai Council (0 2369 2213-5, www.wmcmuaythai.com). Many foreigners train with Thais at Fairtex, some winning titles at Lumphini Stadium (p108) or Ratchadamnoen Stadium (p78). All fighters must wear the sacred headband and armlet during the ritual dance to honour teachers before every fight, which a live band accompanies. Loinclothed, bound-fisted old styles have also revived, as at Baan Chang Thai (p142).

Takraw, an acrobatic foot-volley game using a woven rattan ball, is played in parks at dusk, but is losing popularity to football. TVs broadcast European league football everywhere, mostly for gambling purposes. Thais also have a flutter on horseracing at the RBSC (p117) and Royal Turf Club (p78).

Golf courses stripe the suburbs, notably the well-maintained

Vintage Club (549/1-4 Thanon Panvithee, Klongdan, 0 2707 3820, www.vintagethaigolf.com), challenging Bangsai Country Club (77/7 Moo 3, Thanon Samkoksena, Thangluang (Route 3111), Ayutthaya province, 0 3537 1494-7) and user-friendly, Royal Golf & Country Club (69 Moo 7, Sukhumvit Soi 77, 0 2738 1010, www.royalgolfclubs.com).

Information & tickets

Friday editions of the *Bangkok Post* and *Nation*, the free weekly *BK* (www.bkmagazine.com) and free monthly *Bangkok 101* carry listings. Thai TicketMajor (0 2262 3456, www.thaiticketmajor.com) sells tickets to shows, concerts and sports events, online and at booths in malls.

Massage & meditation

Thailand has become a world holistic centre with an Institute of Thai Traditional Medicine (0 2965 9683, www.ttmdf.com) supplementing the know-how of Wat Pho (p61), which teaches Thai massage in English. An unrivalled breadth of swish spas and budget massage houses dispense indigenous and imported therapies (see box p172).

Massage parlours proliferate, both polite 'ancient healing massage' (*nuad paen boran*) and something naughtier (*nuad*). Point out any medical conditions beforehand. Tip generously as masseurs get little pay.

Visitors can learn meditation in Bangkok at centres like Wat Mahathat (p60). Contact the World Fellowship of Buddhists (616 Soi Methiniwet, Sukhumvit Soi 24, 0 2661 1284-7, www.wfb-hq.org), where monks also give meditation talks in English (2-6pm, first Sunday of the month).

Calendar

Chinese New Year p34

Thais are an irrepressibly festive people, whether it's royal anniversaries, Buddhist rites (see box p35), arty showboating, youth culture (see box p37) or simply *sanuk* (fun). They even celebrate foreign festivals, from Halloween to Christmas. Malls often develop promotions into events with music, performance, exhibitions, fashion shows and, as at every function, food. For trade fairs, see p151 IMPACT.

What's going on reflects Bangkok's monsoon seasons. Outdoor activities favour the cool, dry 'winter' (Nov-Jan). Things happen more indoors in the hot season (Feb-May) and the erratic, humid early rainy season (May-Jun), with less happening all round from July to September due to frequent afternoon and evening storms. We've given future dates for lunar religious festivals. Dates highlighted in bold are public holidays. Advance information is often incomplete or changes suddenly, so check with venues, tourist offices (p187), listings media (p32) or online.

January

Ongoing **Concert in the Park** (see Dec); **Beer Gardens** (see Nov)

1 Jan **New Year's Day**
Thais make merit at shrines and *wats*.

2nd Sat in Jan **National Children's Day**
Doors usually closed to the public are opened (8.30am-4pm), including the inner Grand Palace, Defence Ministry and Government House. Zoos, theme parks and many other sights are free.

Jan & Feb **Bangkok Fringe Festival**
Patravadi Theatre
(www.patravaditheatre.com).
A showcase of dance, drama and music of East and West, in traditional, modern and fusion forms. The weekend evening shows are mostly intelligible to non-Thai speakers.

23 Jan 2012 **Chinese New Year**
Rites and festivities citywide by Thai-Chinese. Chinatown fills with lion and dragon dances, firecrackers, lanterns, Chinese opera and even more food stalls than usual. 2012 is a dragon year.

February

Ongoing **Concert in the Park** (see Dec)

4 Feb 2010, 3 Feb 2011 **Chinese New Year**
See Jan; 2010 is a tiger year, 2011 the year of the rabbit.

Late Jan or early Feb **Temple Fairs**
Wat Hualumphong, 728 Thanon Rama IV; Wat Phlubphlachai, 5 Thanon Mitreejit.
Two of the most central folk fairs occurring around Chinese New Year.

Feb **Elle Fashion Week**
Central World, p121 (Elle magazine 0 2240 3700 ext 1703).
Since 1999, Bangkok's original catwalk fest for emergent labels, now twice yearly at Central World. Some public runway seats are available.

28 Feb 2010, 18 Feb 2011 **Makha Bucha**
Thais circle temples at dusk to mark when the star Makha illuminated 1,250 disciples who gathered spontaneously to hear Buddha's last major sermon. Alcohol banned all day.

March

7 Mar 2012 **Makha Bucha** (see Feb).

Mid Mar **Bangkok International Fashion Week**
Siam Paragon, p116 (www.Thailandfashion.net).
Four days of catwalk shows by Thai designers, several of whom have international reputations. Some public seats are available, but only fashionistas get to crash the parties.

April

6 Apr **Chakri Day**
Royal rites at the Chakri dynasty pantheon, which is in Wat Phra Kaew, and also at the statue to King Rama I at Memorial Bridge.

13-15 Apr **Songkran**
The indiscriminate water throwing that goes on during the Thai New Year evolved from gentle bathings of reverence and purification, as still happens today with elder monks and Buddha images such as the Phra Buddha Sihing, which is brought to Sanam Luang. Thais also clean the house, make sand *chedi* in temples, crown Miss Songkran and party wildly with water, talc and booze. Officials try to confine excesses to peak areas like Patpong (p99) and Thanon Khao San (p80), where shows are staged. Bangkok is eerily empty.

Wat's happening

Likay

Eclecticism is the hallmark of Bangkok festivals. Thais mark New Year five times, officially according to the Western and Thai reckonings (p34 **Songkran**), and unofficially for the start of the Chinese, Indian and Mon calendars. Just as Thai altars include Hindu gods, Chinese deities and spirit shrines, so Thais outnumber Indians at **Navaratree Festival** (p37), flock to the Mon New Year following Songkran, and enthusiastically join **Chinese New Year** (p34), **Mid-Autumn Festival** (p36) and the **Vegetarian Festival** (p37). Thais even embrace Halloween and Christmas, though with more commercial glee than reflection.

But for a sense of indigenous Thai worship, the best approach is to attend a Theravada Buddhist holy day, when devotees ambulate the *bot* (chapel) clockwise three times bearing incense, candle and lotus stem to symbolise the cycle of life, while the monks chant from within. The rite is most serene at Wat Benchamabophit (p77), Wat Saket (p66), Wat Suthat (p67) and Wat Bowoniwet (p80). **Makha Bucha** (p34) marks the Buddha's last sermon, while his anniversary

of birth, enlightenment and death, **Visakha Bucha** (p36), is the focal day for Buddhists worldwide. Here, it lengthens into a week of events, focused on Sanam Luang (p59). **Asanha Bucha** (p36) marks the Buddha's first sermon after enlightenment. The next day, **Khao Phansaa**, begins the three-month rainy season lent with offerings of giant carved candles (symbolising monastic study). Lent ends with **Ork Phansa** (p37) and a month of Kathin robe donating and temple fairs (*ngan wat*) leading up to **Loy Krathong** (p38), an enchanting night of candlelit floral floats.

The template for many Thai festivals, *ngan wat* continue a tradition of festive merriment as a social pressure valve. There's much fun to be had, and flirting to be done, around entertainments like *likay* (p29), *luuk thung* folk tunes (p148), boxing (p32), roving film projections and beauty contests, plus speciality food stalls and fairground rides. Fairs are also a way of drawing secular people back into the *wat*. They are free and fun, but rarely publicised in English, so keep an eye open for the trademark lights and banners.

28-29 Apr Naris Day
Baan Plainoen, Thanon Rama IV
(0 2249 4280).
Descendants of King Rama V's brother Prince Naris – artist, architect and designer – commemorate his birth in 1863 by opening his traditional house for an afternoon of classical Thai dance followed by a free open day.

May

1 May **National Labour Day**

5 May **Coronation Day**

13 May 2010, **10** May 2011/12
Royal Ploughing Ceremony
Sanam Luang, p59.
Brahmin priests use sacred oxen to forecast the year's rainfall and harvest in costumed royal pageantry. Farmers then rush in to gather the blessed seeds. A holiday only for state workers.

28 May 2010, **17** May 2011
Visakha Bucha
Buddhism's holiest date commemorates the Buddha's birth, enlightenment and death. Devotees bring lunch to monks, then in the evening process around temples by candlelight. Alcohol banned all day.

June

4 Jun 2012 **Visakha Bucha**
(see May)

June **La Fête**
www.alliance-francaise.or.th
This French-backed, multi-venue arts festival includes Thai collaborations.

July

16-17 July 2010, **15-16** July 2011
Asanha Bucha & Khao Phansa
The anniversary of the Buddha's first sermon after attaining enlightenment is observed with temple rituals and giant candle offerings. Next day, Khao Phansa, the monks' three-month rainy season retreat begins, a time of many ordinations. Alcohol banned all day.

August

2-3 Aug 2012 **Asanha Bucha & Khao Phansa** (see July)

12 Aug **Queen's Birthday**
Citywide shrines, illuminations on Thanon Ratchadamnoen and candle-holding crowds in Sanam Luang celebrate Queen Sirikit on what is also Mother's Day.

Mid Aug **Short Film & Video Festival**
BACC, p111 (www.thaifilm.com).
An influential free showcase of Thai indie film that also has some global and gay programming.

September

22 Sept 2010, 12 Sept 2011, 30 Sept 2012 **Chinese Mid-Autumn Festival**
Mooncake promotions herald this Chinese festival, during which Chinatown fills with stalls.

Sept & Oct **International Festival of Music & Dance**
Thailand Cultural Centre, p150 (www.bangkokfestivals.com).
Bangkok's biggest annual arts festival stages top or second tier opera, dance, ballet, jazz and classical music.

Late Sept **Bangkok International Film Festival**
www.bangkokfilm.org
Run by TAT at various downtown multiplexes, this 10-day feast of film spans countries and tastes, with a major regional contingent. It's date keeps changing from year to year.

October

Ongoing **International Festival of Music & Dance** (see Oct)

Early Oct **World Gourmet Festival**
Four Seasons Hotel, p177.
For ten days, leading foreign chefs prepare feasts, classes and wine tastings.

Early Oct **Bangkok Design Festival**
www.bangkokdesignfestival.com
Citywide exhibitions, events, talks and sales, focusing on TCDC (p133) and BACC (p111).

Mid Oct **Elle Fashion Week**
(see Feb)

8 Oct 2010, 28 Sept 2011, 16 Oct 2012 **Navaratree Hindu Festival**
Maha Uma Devi, p93.
A Ganesha procession and Hindu rites precede the dramatic Uma procession, passing dozens of petal-carpeted shrines around Silom and Sathorn, with fevered rites, blessings, mediums and self-mortification. To fit in, you should wear white.

Oct **Vegetarian Festival**
Yellow pennants indicate food stalls and restaurants going veggie for this ten-day Chinese purge of meat and heating foods by white-clad devotees. Chinatown explodes with activity and Chinese opera around shrines, notably in Charoen Krung Soi 20.

23 Oct 2010, 12 Oct 2011, 30 Oct 2012 **Ork Phansa**
The rainy season officially ends, and with it the three-month Buddhist Lent, with *wat* rituals such as the shaving of monks' scalps and brows. It's followed by the Kathin month of robe giving and temple fairs.

23 Oct **King Chulalongkorn Day**
Royal Plaza, p76.
Thousands gather to worship at his equestrian statue.

Oct or Nov **World Film Festival of Bangkok**
www.worldfilmbkk.com
Run by the *Nation* newspaper, this major cinefest focuses on auteurship, Asian films and themes.

Oct or Nov **Bangkok Pride Festival**
This week of cabarets, parties and events around Silom has faded quite

Indy city

Bangkok lacks the rebellious underground found in some cities, but an emergent indy (independent) subculture is lending edge to Thai creative scenes. Indy Bangkok is like the Bauhaus, psychedelia, punk, postmodernism, sexual liberation, the internet and mass consumerism all happening at once, with a dose of Japanese 'cute'. Raised under democracy, open-minded and often foreign-educated, these *dek naew* (trend kids) seek stimulation and self-discovery in singer-songwriter music, avant-garde movies, art installations, extreme sports, provocative plays, individualist fashion and independent travel.

Emerging in mid-1990s alternative rock, indy Thais now have many venues like Lollipop (p69), Tak Sura (p125), Happy Monday (p142) and Dudesweet parties (p149). But they were once limited to Thanon Phra Arthit's 'art bars', such as Hemlock (p81), and festivals in its Santichaiprakarn Park (p83). It still hosts the **Bangkok Theatre Festival** (p38) and the **Indy Festival** (p38), featuring art, photography and self-recorded music, as well as critical media and handmade books. You can witness the full diversity of indy culture at November's **Fat Festival** (p38), which often holds a Fat T-shirt Festival spin-off in July.

Now indy is merging into Bangkok's nascent creative movement. Meet the new Thai wave at Petcha Kutcha nights, Lomography shows, BACC exhibitions (see box p112), film festivals (p36), **Bangkok Design Festival** (above) and, especially, **TCDC** events (p133).

badly, so 'Pink in the Park' at Lumphini Park pool and the closing parade may not happen in the future.

November

Nov-Jan Beer Gardens
Lager-laced al fresco fun with food stalls and live bands at plazas, bar strips and malls like Central World.

Nov Golden Mount Temple Fair
Bangkok's best loved fair rings Wat Saket for ten days around Loy Krathong. Other fairs during this period are less crowded.

26 Nov 2010, 10 Nov 2011, 28 Nov 2012 Loy Krathong
Thais crowd waterways to cleanse sins by offering the water spirit a delicate, candlelit Krathong float made from banana tree trunk, leaf, incense and flowers. This is a magical night, with many temple fairs.

1st weekend in Nov Fat Festival
0 2641 5234/www.thisisclick.com.
Run by Fat Radio, this effervescent indie gathering attracts youth tribes with dozens of bands, art installations and countless stalls of homemade books, art, music and fashion.

Nov Bangkok Theatre Festival
www.lakorn.org
A charming mixture of modern and traditional performance at Santichaiprakarn Park and city venues. It's partly free and fairly accessible to non-Thais.

Late Sat in Nov Ploenchit Fair
Shrewsbury International School (www.ploenchitfair.com).
Huge expat charity event with funfair, bars and shows run by the British embassy since the 1950s.

Late Sun in Nov Bangkok Marathon
National Jogging Association (0 2628 8361/www.bkkmarathon.com).
Full, half and mini-marathons are run through the old town.

December

Ongoing Beer Gardens (see Nov)

2 Dec Trooping the Colours
Royal Plaza, p76.
The Thai armed forces march past royalty arrayed in plumed dress uniforms of brilliant hues.

5 Dec King's Birthday
The Thai people's deep reverence for King Bhumibol is on display on what's also Father's Day (and a national holiday). The king addresses the crowds at Royal Plaza in the morning. Thousands light candles after dark in Sanam Lung, where fireworks, and traditional music and dance carry, on until late. There are decorations strewn along Thanon Ratchadamnoen and throughout the city.

10 Dec Constitution Day
Rites at Democracy Monument.

Early Dec Miss AC/DC Pageant
www.missacdc.com
Spoof drag queens 'represent' some 70 countries in 'national costumes', gowns, talents and philosophising. Resuming in 2010.

Dec to Feb Concert in the Park
www.bangkoksymphony.org
Free late-afternoon Sunday picnic concerts in parks by Bangkok Symphony Orchestra, with light folk, pop and classical tunes. Picnicking listeners can forage at various stalls.

Mid Dec Indy Festival
Santichaiprakarn Park (www.thaiwriternetwork.com).
This open-air 'free space' enables 'indy' youth to present their publications, music, artistry and short films.

31 Dec New Year's Eve
Say 'Sawatdee phi mai' at parties citywide, the Central World countdown or while watching the fireworks at Sanam Luang and riverside hotels. There are late bar hours and, a real help, the BTS/MRT run all night.

Itineraries

Wat Arun p71

Pier-to-Pier Sights

Visitors often regard boating as their most rewarding city experience, even though the 'Venice of the East' label barely applies any longer, since most Bangkok canals have been lost to road-building. Yet *khlongs* still thread through the **Thonburi** (p69) west bank and branch into the plantations of **Nonthaburi** (p150), stretching on throughout Thailand's Central Plains, connecting rivers, rice farms, towns, temples and floating markets (p153).

Exploring the waterways requires some strategy. The rule to bear in mind is that the longer you spend, the greater the value and rewards. A half-day enables you to see the mostly urban canals of Thonburi, now heavily scarred by concrete flood barriers, because this delta instinctively wants to overflow. A full day takes you upriver and into a rustic canalscape barely modernised – though riparian lifestyles are changing fast.

At a tourist-oriented *tha* (pier) – **Saphan Thaksin**, **Tha Oriental**, **River City**, **Tha Tien** (beside Wat Pho) or **Tha Chang** (by the Grand Palace) – it's hard to identify fixed price tours and touts often overcharge. They operate on a fast-turnover basis, cramming in riverside sights like **Wat Arun** (p71) that are cheaper and less rushed if seen separately, rather than using the time to delve deeper into Thonburi. The savvy hire a freelance boatman (easier with a Thai speaker) and negotiate a tailored route. Tours of one or two hours on a longtail boat cost from B500 per hour.

Tours of one hour limit you to a single canal, a couple of stops and souvenir-vendor boats floating-in-wait. Two hours gets you round the ear-shaped loop of **Khlong Bangkok Noi** and **Khlong Bangkok Yai**, which comprised the original meander of the river before a 17th-century shortcut widened into the majestic course girding Rattanakosin Island. You'll typically pause at the **Royal Barge Museum** (p70), **Wat Suwannaram** (p72), a fish-feeding spot and **Taling Chan Floating Market** (a static weekend eating place, p73). Some of the operators might detour down Khlong Bangluang Noi to see its exquisite temples, orchid farm and the debased Wat Sai Floating Market.

But the most relaxing day trip is to ply the river upstream, then explore the more rustic canals of Nonthaburi province. Hotels and tour firms run chartered tours, but you get the same experience and total flexibility by riding the Chao Phraya Expressboats, which connects to the BTS Skytrain at Tha Saphan Taksin. Alight and reboard at any pier for mere pennies. Some are designated Tourist Expressboats with English commentary, taking 45 minutes to reach the Nonthaburi terminus, overtaking convoys of dainty tugs pulling beetle-shaped barges.

Expressboats do travel a few stops downsteam, but the following points out the main sights heading upstream. Since Bangkok and Thonburi were originally built to face the water, you see beautiful frontages that neglect has helped preserve. After decades of focusing on road access, developers are starting to value river views, with ominous implications.

The shore of the Old Farang Quarter is particularly grand. Just beyond the **Shangri-La** hotel (p174) stand the classical edifices of Assumption College, EAC (Eastern Asiatic Company) and the **Oriental** hotel (p173), which runs the **Oriental Spa** (see box p172) and **Sala Rim Nam** restaurant (p98) on the western bank beside the soaring **Peninsula** hotel tower (p173). Historic edifices continue on

the east bank with the restored French Embassy and mouldering Italianate Customs House, slated for conversion into an Aman Resort hotel; and Wat Muang Khae, dwarfed by the green-glass slab of the Communications Authority Tower. Beyond the leaf-shaded Portuguese Embassy, the mouth of Khlong Phadung Krung Kasem is obscured by the overscaled Royal Orchid Sheraton Hotel and **River City** antiques mall (p95), a major ferry terminus. The saucer-topped tower on the Khlong San bank opposite houses the **Millennium Hilton** hotel (p173).

The dainty **Holy Rosary Church** (p86), the classical **Siam Commercial Bank** (p86) and ancient Chinese temples punctuate the shambles of Chinatown's waterfront. Those stilt shacks are the backs of *godowns*, still-functioning warehouses from when Sampeng was the principle port plied by junks and schooners.

Facing west, admire the mural-rich temples Wat Thong Noppakhun and Wat Thong Thammachat before ducking beneath Phra Pokklao Bridge, which forms a double span with the river's first crossing, the obelisked Memorial Bridge (built in 1932). Beyond it spreads the Kudi Jeen community, with **Santa Cruz Church** (p71) and its filigree jetty flanked by the triple *chedis* of **Wat Prayoon** (p72) and outsized **Wat Kalayanamit** (p71). It flanks the mouth of Khlong Bangkok Yai with the north-bank Vichai Prasit Fortress, which defends King Taksin's palace, **Ratchawang Derm** (p70).

Meanwhile, on the east bank, a rebuilt miniature of the old post office precedes the statue of King Rama I at Memorial Bridge. More *godowns* follow, this time of the flower market **Pak Khlong Talad**

ITINERARIES

(p69), named after the mouth of Khlong Lord, the former moat of Rattanakosin Island. The pert classical edifice of Ratchinee Girls School was rebuilt after a recent fire. Beside it the lantern-towered Wang Chakrabongse is the palace where Prince Chakrabongse's descendant runs the publisher River Books in a compound that also houses **Chakrabongse Villas** hotel (p167). The spires of **Wat Pho** (p61) peek above gabled shophouses at Tha Tien, where *wai roon* (trendies) head to **Boh** bar (p62) on the pier at dusk.

Boh allows a fine sunset silhouette of Wat Arun's five crockery-covered *prang* on the Thonburi bank. Beside the *wat*, VIPs view royal barge processions from the Royal Navy Pavilion. Further up, you pass **Wat Rakhang**, the Studio 9 restaurant of **Patravadi Theatre** (p73), **Supatra River House** restaurant (p72), Prannok Market and **Siriraj Hospital** (p71) before reaching Bangkok Noi railway station at the mouth of Khlong Bangkok Noi.

But if you're facing that way, you'll miss the main attraction: the **Grand Palace** (p53). To broaden palace views and create a riverside promenade along Rattanakosin Island, officials controversially plan to demolish much of the venerable Tha Phra Chan communities, as well as parts of **Thammasat University** (p60) and the **National Theatre** (p62), which is visible as a boxy bump above the trees.

From under the Bangkok foot of Phra Pinklao Bridge, a stilted walkway from the **Bangkok Tourist Bureau HQ** (p187) passes mansions on Thanon Phra Arthit on its way to **Santichaiprakarn Park** (p83), which contains Phra Sumane Fort and central Bangkok's last *lamphu*

mangrove trees. The classical edifice being restored across the river belongs to Intara School.

North of Khlong Banglamphu in Dusit lie numerous mansions, including the art nouveau **Wang Bangkhunprom** (p78). Looming above, **Rama VIII Bridge** brandishes fussy gilded trimmings on a harp-like 2.1-kilometre long (1.3-mile) span suspended from one 300-metre (984-foot) high inverted-Y pillar; it stands in a park beside the Bangyikhan Distillery for Thailand's favourite tipple, Mekhong whisky.

On the Dusit bank, **Thewet Flower Market** (p80) marks the mouth of Khlong Phadeung Krung Kasem, ahead of the Royal Barge Dock, which houses vessels of the flotilla not displayed in the Royal Barge Museum. Behind it perches **Kaloang Home Kitchen** seafood restaurant (p79). Beyond the green-shuttered royal pier Tha Vasukri, and the wooden *vihaan* of Wat Ratchathiwat, **St Francis Xavier Church** (p78) is the focus of a Vietnamese community.

Most of the day and night cruises turn back at the box-girder Sang Hee (Krung Thon) Bridge, which provides the illuminated backdrop for **River Bar Café** (p79). Thereafter, amid traditional riverine communities of wooden houses you encounter the Singha brewery, Rama VI Bridge (carrying the southern railway), the curious-looking Wat Khien, and Rama V Bridge, before disembarking at Nonthaburi terminus.

Suburbia extends a good 33 kilometres (20 miles) upriver to this province famous for its fruit, though flood damage and heedless building scar its semi-rustic charm. Fronting the sublime wooden fretwork of Nonthaburi Provincial Office, an esplanade (and impromptu skate park) links

Floating market vendors

the expressboat terminal pier with **Rim Fang** restaurant (235/2 Thanon Pracharat, 0 2525 1742, open noon-10pm daily).

Most visitors take tours or hired longtail boats from the northern end of Nonthaburi pier to **Koh Kred** (p150) or make a two-hour loop via Khlong Om back to Khlong Bangkok Noi, ending usually at Tha Chang. The picturesque Om canal meets the river just north of **Wat Chaloem Prakiat**, a landscaped, Chinese-style temple dedicated by Rama III to his mother. Beside it is the culturally themed Chaloem Kanchanaphisek Park. You can feed the huge river carp here.

Massive roads now bisect these canals, bringing encroachments upon the riverine ambience. New mansions dot stretches of planked homes on stilts that back on to road-free plantations. Most houses have a quaint covered pier with benches, where families hang out, eat, drink, bathe, board their canoe to get cash from the floating bank, or hail vendor skiffs to buy provisions or food like the iconic *kwetiao reua* (literally 'boat noodles' in a beefy herbal broth).

In a poignant sign of the times, abandoned stilt houses tilt into carpets of water hyacinths, a weed that clogs waterways, but can be woven into furniture. Thailand's historic water culture is becoming valued as a post-modern lifestyle, but slower than it is being undermined by 'modernity'.

When boating, go in cooler hours, to avoid heat and glare, but still take sunscreen, shades and a hat. Early morning is busier with vendor boats, late afternoon has great light and waterside activity, with the irrepressible spectacle of gleeful boys jumping off bridges.

Democracy Monument p65

Rites and Rights

Ratchadamnoen Avenue is Thailand's political theatre, the national stage for pageantry and protest, absolute monarchy and constitutional rule, democracy and crackdown. A walk along its four kilometre length is a lesson in history and a way to understand the country's current travails. It's also a study in architecture, from traditional to neo-Thai, classical to modernist. And it shows how King Rama V (1868-1910) adopted Western urban design.

The 'Royal Processional Way' begins at the **Grand Palace** (p53), symbolic heart of Phra Nakorn, and ends in Dusit, a palace district that came to host institutions of state. It zig-zags through three sections: Ratchadamnoen Nai (Inner) runs by royal field **Sanam Luang** (p59), then Ratchadamnoen Klang (Middle) veers east to the old city wall, whereupon Ratchadamnoen Nok (Outer) again bears north to Royal Plaza.

Sanam Luang originated as a royal funerary ground. Royalty is still cremated here, the body placed in a temporary temple-like tower symbolizing mythic Mount Meru, abode of the Hindu gods. Over time this grassy oval was used as a park, a kite-flying field every March, a marketplace, a festive venue and a worship site for Buddha images, as at **Songkran** (p34).

It also became a protest rallying point, especially in the anti-dictatorship 'incidents' of 14 October 1973, 6 October 1976 and 10 May 1992. Neighbouring **Thammasat University** (p60) erected monuments to their bloody suppression, most notoriously the 1976 massacre of students by militias here and in Sanam Luang. Since 2006, Sanam Luang has hosted yellow shirt-wearing opponents of deposed Prime Minister Thaksin Shinawatra and his red shirt-wearing supporters. It is the Thai Hyde Park corner.

Ananta Samakhom Throne Hall p75

Ratchadamnoen Klang Avenue cuts a swathe through the dense old town, emulating the Champs-Elysée, which King Rama V had seen in Paris. The streamlined, art deco buildings that line it date from the 1940s and the dictator Phibul. In a roundabout blocking the processional route, Phibul erected the **Democracy Monument** (p65) to the 1932 constitutional revolution that ended absolute monarchy. It bears proletarian bas-reliefs and became another demo site, witnessing the massacres of 1973 and 1992.

Just before it, on the corner of Thanon Tanao, stands the *chedi*-shaped **14 October 1973 Memorial** (p64). A monument to the 1992 'incident' is due to rise at the start of Ratchadamnoen Klang, where the Department of Public Relations was burnt down.

State offices like the National Lottery and Teachers Printing Organisation fill some of the buildings. Politicians and influential families frequent restaurants like **Sky High** (p68). Facing Democracy Monument, **Rim Khob Fah** (78/1

Thanon Ratchadamnoen Klang, 0 2622 3510, 10am-7pm daily) is a shop specialising in books about Bangkok, run by the Muang Boran foundation. Beside it, **Café Democ** (p69) has launched the career of many Thai DJs.

Lights and displays smarten this road during celebrations like the **King's Birthday** (Dec 5, p38), **Queen's Birthday** (Aug 12, p36) and royal anniversaries such as the centenary of King Rama V's death (23 October 2010). As the buildings have deteriorated, planners have begun zoning it for food, shopping, culture and tourist uses. As with many such schemes, residents oppose it, sensing a ruse to evict them.

Two decades ago, the public fretted over demolishing the cherished Chalerm Thai cinema, to open a view to the Loha Prasat of **Wat Ratchanadda** (p67). In its place, a park was made containing the **King Rama III Statue** and the **Mahachesadaobdin Royal Pavilion** for state and civic receptions. Another contest rumbles over **Mahakan Fort** next door. A moat-side park is proposed to replace the ancient community behind the remains of the wall.

The road veers north as it crosses the former city moat at Saphan Phanfa, a terminus for **Canal Expressboats** (p41). Flanking the bridge are the **Queen's Gallery** (p67), a major art space, and **King Prajadhipok Museum** (p66), located in the pepperpot-towered former Public Works Department. It relates the life and reign (1925-35) of King Rama VII, the 'Father of Thai Democracy', who granted the first constitution in the wake of the 1932 coup, then abdicated to England.

Ratchadamnoen Nok broadens into three carriageways, shaded by trees, but with no shops or eating places. During royal celebrations, auspiciously decorated arches span the central route. On the right, **Ratchadamnoen Boxing Stadium** (p78) holds thrice-weekly bills of major *muay thai* bouts. The neo-classical Army Headquarters stands across the road. It is home to the **Royal Thai Army Museum** (113 Thanon Ratchadamnoen Nok, 0 2297 8121-2, www.rta.mi.th, 8.30am-2.30pm by written group appointment only, free), which displays the weapons, flags, uniforms, insignia and the armoury of Chulachomklao Royal Military Academy.

On the corner of Khlong Phadung Krung Kasem, the **UN ESCAP** (United Nations Economic & Social Commission for Asia & the Pacific, 0 2288 1234, www.unescap.org, open by appointment) is housed under a graceful curved cascade of roofs that blends Thai motifs with modern aesthetics. It overlooks the pretty double span of Makkhawan Bridge, which for months in 2008 was blockaded by tyres, fortifications and militia. The barricade protected the occupation of adjacent Government House by yellow shirted opponents

of a government aligned with the self-exiled Thaksin Shinawatra.

Ratchadamnoen Nok culminates at **Royal Plaza** (p74). At this parade ground HM the King reviews the military, resplendent in their dress uniforms and helmet plumes, every 2 Dec in **Trooping the Colours** (p38). Facing down the avenue, the equestrian **Rama V Statue** (p76) receives offerings from well-wishers every Tuesday, his day of birth. Thousands also pay their respects on **Chulalongkorn Day** (p37), 23 October, a public holiday to honour his death.

A **People's Party Plaque** in the plaza commemorates the declaration of democracy on 24 June 1932. The first legislature took place in the Avenue's focal point, the domed Italianate **Ananta Samakhom Throne Hall** (p75). From its balcony, HM the King delivers a speech to thousands of public devotees on his birthday. On his Diamond Jubilee in 2006, Ratchadamnoen Nok was a sea of yellow clothes, the colour of his Monday birthday.

Behind it, past **Dusit Zoo** (p75), spreads the National Assembly. A statue of King Prajadhipok fronts this 1970 essay in ultra-modernist concrete. On another fateful date, 7 October 2008, yellow shirts blockaded parliament from being addressed by a Thaksin-nominated cabinet. An armed confrontation with riot police resulted in injuries on both sides and two protestor deaths. The yellow-shirt occupation of Suvarnabhumi Airport followed soon afterwards.

It remains to be seen whether Thais will work out their differences inside or outside parliament. In 2009, the red shirts delivered a petition to the Grand Palace. It has thus become a maxim that Thai politics repeats in cycles, largely played out along Ratchadamnoen Avenue.

ITINERARIES

Crafting Design

Bangkok's emerging reputation as a design city is starting to overtake its notoriety for copyists. As in food, art, movies and music, Thai creatives have made Bangkok one big showroom for distinctive fashion and furnishings. For a developing country, this has been an exceptional transformation.

The speed of modernisation had threatened many traditions, yet the economic crash of 1997 led young innovators to apply indigenous crafts to new uses. In two half-day programmes, you can visit some of the city's surviving but vulnerable artisans, and trace how designers have leveraged that lineage into a neo-Thai style. Here's how to combine sightseeing, shopping, and supporting a good cause.

In a time of globalised mechanisation, Bangkok designs typically involve handmade skill and sustainable local materials, produced by the designers' own small firms. This artisan mentality

contrasts with the star-designer hype that's rife elsewhere. It reflects the rural roots of crafts still found in Bangkok's 'craft villages' and the social values honouring masters, respecting the sacred – and just plain having fun.

Bangkok's most widely practised craft has a sacred use: garland-making. Stallholders citywide thread jasmine buds, crown-flowers and folded rose petals to form fragrant loops and *leis*. You see garlands in every craft workshop, presented with a *wai* (prayer-like greeting) to past masters and guiding deities of their art. The prime source is **Pak Khlong Talad** flower market (p69), where garland-makers work through the nighttime cool hours creating auspicious abstract patterns from deconstructed plants. Start early and breakfast at its high-quality food stalls.

Save room for something sweet, since traditional Thai desserts are the next craft on show, a short stroll

Baan Khrua Thai Silk p50

up Thanon Triphet at **Old Siam Plaza** (p91). Under the atrium, costumed vendors fold banana leaves into origami-esque packaging for coconut and palm sugar-based *khanom*. They strain delicate strands of sweetened egg into *foy thong*, a dish shared with wedding vows, and sculpt miniature replica fruits from bean paste. The cooks even gold-leaf some of their delicious objet d'art, which, like garlands, embody Buddhist impermanence.

Other Thai crafts last for centuries. Temple murals illustrate how Thai painting has evolved and record Bangkok's social history. There are few new works, but National Artist Chakraphan Posyakrit, a master painter and puppeteer, is applying his romantic brushwork to the walls of **Wat Tri Thosathep** (p79). You can see his mural-in-progress on weekdays only. Get there via the contiguous roads of

Thanons Triphet, Tithong and Dinso (passing the Giant Swing and Democracy Monument) to Thanon Prachathipatai. Return the same route to the Giant Swing.

And if you're going there, why not by *tuk-tuk*? Bangkok's pop icon is not just a noisy, novelty ride, but a classic piece of Thai folk design. Compare it to Indian or Indonesian versions of the Japanese motor-rickshaw and reflect how friendly and elegant the Thais make such a short and clumsy vehicle.

That same knack for beauty and graceful contour infuses the block east of the Giant Swing, flanking **Thanon Bamrung Meuang**. The shophouses here sell Buddha images newly sculpted in bronze. Casing has moved elsewhere, but you can still see metalworkers file down the spurs through which the molten alloy filled the wax form, then polish, gild and lacquer the statue

ITINERARIES

till it gleams. These then get wrapped in monk's robes or orange plastic and shipped on pick-up trucks to their destination altar.

To see an entire metalworking process, just along Bamrung Meuang and over Khlong Ong Ang visit Baan Baat, the **Monk's Bowl Village**. On the corner of Thanon Boriphat, one of the last bowl-crafting families demonstrates the Ayutthaya-era method of fusing a monk's begging bowl (*baat*), from eight pieces of metal – symbolising Buddhism's Eightfold Path. They solder and beat the metal into shape, before lacquering the finished vessel, which emits a sonorous note when struck. Here you can get information about making *baat*, which are now bought more as a collector's item than as a receptacle for food on monks' morning alms rounds. This and other family workshops are hidden down narrow Soi Ban Baat behind the diagonally opposite corner. Signs lead you through Dickensian lanes that resonate with the clanging of mallets, more so during the cooler hours. Compare quality before buying as some now use cheap, inauthentic techniques.

Walking north up **Thanon Boriphat** you inhale aromas of teak as you pass carpentry shophouses. Here again, a city enclave focuses on one trade. Doors form most of the output, but there are some fretworked panels. Carving and cabinet-making has migrated to Soi Prachanarumit (Pracharat Soi 24) in the northern suburb of Bang Sue, which hosts the Thanon Sai Mai Woodwork Festival (last weekend in January).

Thanon Boriphat crosses Khlong Mahanak along a bridge with bas-reliefs illustrating public grief at the passing of King Rama V. From the canal boat terminus on the facing bank, head east to the next craft destination, silk weaving, for which

Panta p50

you alight at Tha Ratchathewi by Saphan Hua Hang bridge. If the boat is too cramped or daunting, hop in a taxi or *tuk-tuk* and head for **Jim Thompson's House** (p112) in Kasemsan Soi 2.

From Tha Ratchathewi, a canalside path leads you on to Thompson's iconic compound of teak stilt houses. The American is legendary, partly for disappearing, partly for turning the jeopardised Thai silk craft into a thriving luxury industry of global renown. He also pioneered the idea of converting wooden houses for modern living, setting a trend that ultimately enabled the Thai design renaissance.

A mission to maintain tradition for future relevance underpins the James HW Thompson Foundation, which preserves his house as a museum, holds world-class exhibitions in its art centre, runs a library, and hosts major symposia

ITINERARIES

on regional textiles. Of course its shop sells the current silk range (p102), while the restaurant, **Thompson**, is perfect for lunch. Eat on the lotus pond terrace or amid an interior by the celebrated Thai designer Ou Baholyodhin, who created the chairs used in the Hong Kong handover ceremony.

Thompson first encountered Thai silk in the Muslim Cham community across the canal in Baan Khrua, where weavers still work in the same way. Walk along the canal path to Kasemsan Soi 3, cross the canal bridge and turn left. After a few dozen metres a sign points right down an alley. The soft clatter of wooden looms reverberates between the houses. The first workshop is more recent; the second one, **Baan Khrua Thai Silk** (837 Baan Krua Soi 9, 08 1243 9089, 7am-6pm daily), is run by a family that worked with Thompson, who the hospitable English-speaking owner Niphon Manuthat recalls. They supply top quality silk to shops, but you can buy direct – and, frankly, you should.

Infused with these cultural insights, backtrack down Kasemsan Soi 3, and walk left for five minutes along Thanon Rama I to **Bangkok Art & Culture Centre** (BACC, see box p112). Inside, much of the contemporary Thai art riffs creatively off Siamese forms, crafts, materials or concepts.

Across the SkyWalk, **Siam Discovery** is a fount of neo-Thai design: **Panta** (p116) specialises in furniture using natural materials in novel, stylised ways. **Mae Fah Luang** (p114) updates tribal weaving techniques in sumptuous rugs, clothes and accessories. On the same floor, **Anyroom** (0 2658 0481, www.anyroom.com) sells hand-hewn mortars and Thai seed-inspired sculptural flower vessels by Sakul Intakul, Southeast Asia's leading floral designer. His installations at

the **Conrad** (p176) and **Sukhothai** hotels (p174) draw on the tradition of Siamese floral offerings.

Walking from Siam Discover through **Siam Centre** (a hub of Thai fashion; see box p115), **Siam Paragon** (p116) devotes its fourth floor to Thai design. **Paragon Passage** stocks high-quality crafts; some traditional, others showing how neo-Thai design can work in modern homes, yet still retain a handmade quality at affordable prices. Meanwhile, **Triphum** (p116) does reproductions and 'inspired-bys' of sacred crafts, including Buddha images and mural paintings of exquisite finesse.

Sakul and other creatives are also represented one BTS stop east at **Gaysorn** (p121) in the Design + Object store (D&O, 3rd floor, 0 2645 1327). Gaysorn has more neo-Thai wares in **Thann Native** (p122) and **Ayodhya** (p120), the pioneers of turning the water hyacinth weed into furnishings.

Water hyacinth weave exemplifies the new textiles that Thais have contributed to the prestigious **Material ConneXion** library, which has a branch in Emporium at **Thailand Creative & Design Centre** (TCDC, closed Mon, see p133) your final stop, via BTS at Phrom Phong. One of the world's top design centres, TCDC showcases local designers and inspires them to draw from Thailand's rich craft heritage, staging exhibitions from food design to diagamatical tattoo graphics. TCDC's logo is emblematic of that idea: the banana leaf wrap of a dessert, like those made at Old Siam Plaza, with a diagram of how to fold this clever everyday craft. The message is clear: Thais are keeping their crafts alive by interpreting the past with an open mind and using sustainable materials, for a nourishing, flourishing result.

Bangkok by Area

Phra Nakorn & Thonburi

BANGKOK BY AREA

Set within the remnants of walls that held the capital for the first of its two centuries, **Phra Nakorn** ('Holy City') retains a vibrant streetlife and contains most of Bangkok's must-see landmarks. Across the Chao Phraya River it faces the preceding capital, **Thonburi**. There, traces remain of the short reign of King Taksin, who united Siam after the earlier capital, Ayutthaya, was destroyed. You need at least a couple of days to cover the sights of these diverse twin towns.

The core of Phra Nakorn is **Ko Rattanakosin**, a conch-shaped island bounded by the river and the first of three concentric canals girdling the city as it expanded eastwards. Around **City Hall** spread communities with bygone trades, storied little restaurants and the spiritual centres of Buddhism and Hinduism. The markets on the

southern side merge seamlessly into **Chinatown**. Flanking City Hall's other side, the ceremonial axis Thanon Ratchadamnoen Klang leads east and then carries on north to **Dusit**. Across that road lies Banglamphu and its bohemian quarters of backpackers and arty Thais. Although royalty has moved to Dusit, Phra Nakorn still hosts frequent pageantry, such as the **Royal Ploughing Ceremony** (p36).

Bangkok is one of few world cities where the old centre retains its original communities. However, an outdated masterplan aims to evict many of them and turn Phra Nakorn into a historical themepark in the name of tourism. Protests at plans to bulldoze irreplaceable shophouse neighbourhoods north and south of the Grand Palace into a sterile riverside promenade seem to have prompted slight changes.

Grand Palace & Wat Phra Kaew

Thus far only half of historic **Tha Tien** has been demolished, and the market is supposed to be restored into a sanitised 'living community'. While the masterplan does save the area from overbearingly tall new constructions, residents and architects must continually fight to preserve pockets of authenticity like Tha Tien, Tha Phra Chan and Mahakan Fort.

The old town is unusually suited to pedestrians and is sprouting characterful hotels. Until the MRT Subway extends to Phra Nakorn and Thonburi, the quickest way to reach it from Downtown remains by water, by river Expressboat or canal boat to Golden Mount.

Entry to sights listed in this chapter is free and 24-hour unless otherwise noted.

Rattanakosin Island

When King Rama I moved Siam's capital to the more defensible east-bank settlement of Bangkok in 1782, he modelled this artificial island on the auspicious layout of lost Ayutthaya. At its centre stand the **Grand Palace** and its astonishing

temple, **Wat Phra Kaew**, home of the Emerald Buddha.

The royal field in front, Sanam Luang, gets used for anything from royal ceremonies to public recreation and is ringed by institutions of state, religion and culture. To the east stands the city pillar, **Lak Muang**. Behind the Grand Palace spreads Bangkok's oldest and largest temple, **Wat Pho**, and its ethereal Reclining Buddha. Beyond the former moat, **Khlong Lord**, lies the commercial and residential part of Phra Nakorn around the City Hall.

Along the riverside, old shophouses between Tha Chang and Tha Prachan burgeon with cultural regalia, traditional massage, herbal preparations and the **Amulet Market** (see box p63). Many of the shops and cafés here cater to students from the Silpakorn University art school and progressive Thammasat University, lending the area a down-to-earth charm.

Sights & museums

Grand Palace & Wat Phra Kaew

Thanon Na Phra Lan (0 2222 8181). Tha Chang. **Open** 8.30am-4pm daily. **Admission** (incl access to Dusit Park & either Ananta Samakhom Throne Hall or Sanam Chan Palace in Nakhon Pathom) B350; free reductions. No credit cards. **Map** p54 B4 ❶

Bangkok's paramount must-see sight is this architectural and spiritual treasure, which is twice as dazzling if you see it on a sunny day. Ignore the gem touts claiming 'it's shut', and immerse yourself in the palace's palpable dignity (while observing the ban on sandals, shorts and bare shoulders). Nearly 2km (1.5 miles) of walls with lotus-shaped crenellations enclose what was once a self-contained city of throne halls, royal chambers, servants' quarters, ministries and a prison. Begun in 1782, it

Phra Nakorn & Thonburi

A B C

1

0   700 m

700 yds

© Copyright Time Out Group 2010

Rama VIII Park

Thewet Flower Market

Wat Siri Aiya Sawan

RAMA VIII BR

Wang Bangkhompom

Tha Saphan Rama VIII

DUSIT

Klong Yikh

Wat Daowadung Sa Ram

THONBURI

Chao Praya River

Wat Sam Phraya

THANON SAMSEN

SOI 5

Wat Dusitaram

River Walk Way

Phra Sumen Fort

SAMSEN

Wang Amatarot

Ancient Boat House

Santichai Prakan Park

Phra Arthit

Wat Sangwet

BANGLAMPHU & DUSIT pp74-83

THANON

Royal Barges Museum

Tha Wat Phra Pinklao

46

PHRA PIN KLAO BRIDGE

TH PHRA ATHIT

Wat Chana Songkhram

THANON CHAO FA

THANON CHAKRABONGSE

Banglamphu Market

Wat Bowon Niwet

THANON

TANAO

Thonburi Station

Bangkok Tourist Bureau HQ

TANAO

Tha Bangkok Noi

National Theatre

19

National Gallery

THANON RATCHADAMNOEN

Democra Monume

Siriraj Hospital & Museums

48

National Museum

5

Mae Toranee Shrine

Royal Hotel

35

October 14 Monument

Tha Wang Lang (Siriraj)

Thammasat University

34

42

PHRA NAKOR

Prannok Market

54

Maharat Market

9

Sanam Luang

TH RATCHA DAMNOEN NAI

City Hall

THANON PRANNOK

MAHARAT

PRA CHAN

Amulet Alley

16

Wat Mahathat

10 18

22

Devastan

Patravadi Theatre

52

57

Silapakorn University

15

8

Lak Muang

41

Dev Mani Temple

SOI BAN CHANG LO

Tha Wat Rakhang

43

TH NA PHRA LAN

Wat Phra Kaeo (Temple of the Emerald Buddha)

TH PHRAENG NARA

33

Sao Ching Cha (Giant Swing)

Wat Suthat

Wat Rakhang Kositaram

Tha Chang

1

Ministry of Defence

THANON NAKHON

Wat Ratchapradit

Dev Mani Temple

THANON ARUN AMARIN

Naval Quartermaster Dpartment

THANON MAHARAT

Royal Grand Palace

Saranrom Palace

Saranrom Park

THANON ATSADANG

THANON RACHINI

Wat Ratchabophit

Sala Chalem Krung

Wat Phraya Tham

THANON THAI WANG

THANON SANAM CHAI

Ban Mo Market

37

THANON BAN MO

Siri Guru Singh Sabha

Khlong Mon

Tha Tien

14

Wat Pho

Territory Defence Dept

THANON TRI PHET

Old Siam Plaza

Wat Khrua Wan

Tha Tien Market

20

Museum Siam

11

Phra Ratcha Wang Police Station

Pahurat Market

Tha Wat Arun

Chakrabongse Villas

38

Wat Ratchburaha

Wat Mai Phiren

Wat Arun (Temple of Dawn)

44

Tha Ratchmee

Flower Market

King Rama I Monument

THANON WANG DOEM

Wang Derm Palace

Wat Kalayanamit

River Walk Way

Tha Saphan Phut

Chakraw Police Station

SOI PHO SAM TON

Bangkok Yai Police Station

50

Santa Cruz Church

MEMORIAL BRIDGE

PHRA POK KLAO BRIDGE

Wat Hong Rattanaram

47

Santa Cruz Convent

THANON ITSARAPHAP

THANON THETSABAN SAI

54   Time Out Shortlist | Bangkok

Wat Ratchasitharam

Praydonwong

was modified by each Chakri king. Since King Rama IX moved to Dusit, it gets only ceremonial use, but remains the kingdom's holiest landmark. Allow at least two hours, perhaps hiring an audio guide (B100 with a passport/credit card deposit) or a guide (B300).

Wat Phra Kaew

From the lawned reception area, you reach the royal audience halls via the palace temple, Wat Phra Sri Rattana Sasadaram. Better known as Wat Phra Kaew, this is the temple of the Emerald Buddha, the palladium of Thai independence. Greeted by a statue of Buddha's physician, Shivaka Kumar Baccha, you are swamped by a kaleidoscope of forms and colours. Modelled on royal chapels in Sukhothai and Ayutthaya, and embellished to an astonishing degree, it omits monastic living quarters, since there are no resident monks.

Upon a raised terrace, the circular, Sri Lankan-style stupa, Phra Si Rattana Chedi, tiled in gold, enshrines a piece of the Buddha's breastbone. Beside it stand the Phra Mondop (library of palm-leaf scriptures), a columned cube of green and blue glass mosaic under a tiered spire, and the cruciform, *prang*-roofed Royal Pantheon, where on Chakri Day (p34) the king honours statues of his forebears. Also on the terrace, multi-coloured guardians support a pair of small gold *chedi*, amid gilded cast creatures from the mythical Himaphan Forest such as the *apsarasingha* (lion-woman) and *kinnorn* (bird-man).

To the north, Ho Phra Nak (the royal mausoleum) and Hor Phra Monthien Tham (a library) flank porcelain-clad Vihaan Yod. Before them spreads a sandstone model of Angkor Wat temple in Cambodia, a vassal state when King Rama IV commissioned this carving.

Eight porcelain-covered pastel *prang* (representing Buddhism's eightfold path) loom down the eastern flank. Two stand within a notch in the cloister, its walls adorned with 178 mural panels. Painted in Thai-Western style and recently restored, they relate the entire

Ramakien epic. In the south-east corner, the shrine of the Gandharara Buddha in rain-summoning posture features in the Royal Ploughing Ceremony (p36).

Emerald Buddha

Six pairs of towering stone *yaksha* (demons) guard the mosaic-covered *bot*, which is ringed by 112 *garuda* man-eagles holding *naga* snakes. From a public altar you enter the *bot*'s murralled interior on your knees, facing the lofty gilded altar of the Emerald Buddha. Carved from jadeite, it stands 66cm (26in) tall and is dressed by the king or Crown Prince in different gold robes for each season: cool, hot or rainy. Of mysterious origin, this prized late Lanna style image appeared in Chiang Rai in 1434 and arrived here via Lampang, Chiang Mai, Vientiane in Laos and Wat Arun in Thonburi.

Grand Palace Halls

The palace precinct, dotted with globular *mai dut* topiary and Chinese statuary, makes for a curious medley of Thai and European design. The belle époque Borom Phiman Mansion was built in 1903 for the future King Rama VI. Now a state guesthouse, it has hosted Queen Elizabeth II and Bill Clinton. Its Sivalai Gardens contain the Phra Buddha Ratana Sathan (Rama IV Chapel). Next, the Phra Maha Montien Buildings include Amarin Winitchai Hall, where the king, upon his boat-like throne, received guests like the 19th-century ambassador Sir John Bowring.

The centrepiece, Chakri Maha Prasat Hall, was built (1876-82) in Renaissance style by the Englishman, John Chinitz. He had planned for a dome, but Chao Phraya Srisuriyawongse, the former regent, convinced King Rama V to add a Thai roof. This influential fusion was dubbed 'a *farang* in a Thai hat'. Beneath its chamber for state banquets is a public Weapons Museum; the top floor houses the ashes of Chakri kings.

To its west sits Aphonphimok Pavilion. Rama IV built it for changing gowns en route via palanquin to the exquisitely proportioned Dusit Throne Hall. It holds the throne of Rama I and hosts coronations and lyings-in-state. Some interiors open on National Children's Day (p34), but not the consorts' inner chambers behind, which now house a finishing school for girls. A restored building will contain the new Queen's Textile Museum.

Khlong Lord

Flanked by Thanon Rachinee & Thanon Atsadang. **Map** p54 C3 **②**

This tree-shaded former moat is lined with timber lamp-posts shaped like old city wall posts and offers a tranquil stroll. The western bank, Thanon Ratchinee, starts at an 1872 drinking fountain depicting Mae Phra Thorani, the goddess who wrung water from her hair to wash away demons trying to corrupt the Buddha. Heading south, you pass the Civil Court, a modernist landmark threatened with demolition, and the Italianate Ministry of Defence. Charoensri 34 Bridge is named for the 34th birthday of the fourth Chakri King, and displays the Thai numeral for four. Garlands hang from a Pig Memorial (1913) to King Rama VI's mother, who was born in the Year of the Pig. Donations for this bronze also paid for Saphan Pee Goon ('pig year bridge'). Beyond Wat Ratchapradit (p62) comes Saphan Hok, a 1982 reconstructed blend of four, old footbridges. By night, gays cruise this side of Saranrom Park (p59), a leafy rest stop with fruit and drink vendors. At Ratchawong Police Station cross the canal.

From Pak Khlong Talad flower market (p69), Thanon Atsadang skirts up the east bank. There stucco crumbling, fifth-reign shophouses flank Baan Mor Market (p68). After Wat Ratchabophit (p61) you circle around the outside of the Euro-classical Ministry of the Interior, the restaurant-filled Sam Phraeng community and the army surplus stores of Lang Krasuang Market – it is behind the Defence Ministry, after all. Finally, opposite Mae Thoranee stands the 1940s deco Royal Hotel.

The real Siam

Museum Siam

The Thai history that is fed to tourists through museums and scripted guides is an exoticised, expurgated version of a distinctly more complex past. History in Thailand has been filtered by a national narrative that's often more concerned with legitimising power and promoting harmony than with scholarship or resolving awkward contradictions.

That's why the **Museum Siam** (p58) makes a refreshing – even a radical – change. It doesn't mythologise 'Big Man' heroes or mould facts to the nation-building ideology. It presents in plain speaking, 'edutaining' displays the hidden histories – social, economic, ethnic, cultural – of the Siamese peoples.

The biggest revelations concern the minority groups that together comprise the majority of what became touted in the early 20th century as a homogenous Thai race, as sung in the national anthem. Museum of Siam questions the very basis of 'Thainess' with signs like: 'Were the cavemen Thai?'

It is the first of several planned 'Discovery Museums' aimed at opening Thai minds to critical thinking. Through interactive displays – thin on artefacts, but high on dioramas – we encounter farmers, soldiers, Lao prisoners of war, Muslim settlers, Mon communities, Indian traders and, the most crucial of the various under-recognised groups, Chinese migrants.

Other sections explore the origins and mapping of this land, modernisation, Buddhism, street culture and foreign influences. The museum illustrates the coming of democracy by inviting visitors to read the news or to suggest policy or examine scenarios that some guardians of official Thainess would dread. Tellingly, it throngs with voluntary young visitors, unlike the old style museums.

This groundbreaking approach extends through other branches of the Office of Knowledge Management and Development, begun by Thaksin Shinawatra, such as **TK Park** (at Central World, p121), **TCDC** (p134) and future Discovery Museums that are planned on ethnicity, ecology and science. The Museum of Siam was built in the old commerce ministry and other branches in converted landmarks will eventually comprise a kind of Siamese Smithsonian.

BANGKOK BY AREA

National Museum

Lak Muang

Thanon Sanam Chai (0 2222 9876).
Tha Chang. **Open** 6.30am-6.30pm
daily. **Map** p54 B3 ❸

Thais believe the guardian spirits of a
Thai town reside at its foundation pillar. Bangkok's birth thus dates from the
auspicious time on 22 April 1782 when
Rama I installed this bud-tipped wooden pillar, now housed in a Khmer-
revival cruciform tower. Some claim it's
a Shiva *lingam* or a link to the southern
Chinese practice of installing a phallus
at a town crossroads. All city distances
are measured from this pillar standing
274cm (108in) above ground, 201cm
(79in) below. Shellacked and gilded, it
is accompanied by another, taller pillar
installed by King Rama IV to improve
Bangkok's horoscope. Statues of the
spirits of the city and country stand in
a pavilion to the east. Those granted
wishes by these spirits pay *lakhon chatri* dancers to perform here.

Museum Siam

Thanon Sanam Chai (0 2357 3999).
Tha Ratchinee. **Open** 10am-6pm Tue-
Sun. **Admission** B100 Thais; B300
foreigners; B150 each per foreigner
group (5 or more); free-B50 reductions.
No credit cards. **Map** p54 B4 ❹
See box p57.

National Museum

4 Thanon Na Phra That (0 2224
1333/www.thailandmuseum.com).
Tha Chang/Tha Prachan. **Open** 9am-
4pm Wed-Sun (last entry 3.30pm).
Admission B30 Thais; B200
foreigners. No credit cards.
Map p54 B2 ❺

Siam's first public museum, and South-
east Asia's largest, originated in 1874
as King Rama IV's collection of regalia
within the Grand Palace. Opening
branches countrywide, it became a
refuge for antiquities from smugglers.
Although the displays and labelling
lacks context or flair, it still provides a
grounding in Thai artistic and cultural
history, and its guidebook fills in many
of the blanks. The National Museum
Volunteers provide tours (9.30am-noon
Wed, Thur) in English, French,
Japanese and (Thur only) German.

Disabled access has improved. Thai-language tours take place Wednesday to Sunday (10am, 1.30pm).

Front Palace buildings

It occupies part of the former Wang Na ('front palace') of the 'deputy king', a rank held by Rama IV's brother Phra Pinklao. Front, left and right are small royal pavilions, including Baan Daeng, an Ayutthayan house with Rattanakosin furnishings and a rare early indoor toilet. Most unmissable is the Buddhaisawan Chapel. Its serene murals focus attention on the revered Phra Buddha Sihing, an image seven centuries old.

Gallery of Thai History

The central audience hall contains rooms of such varied treasures as a life-size model elephant in battle armour, *khon* masks, and the Viceregal Puppets, restored by artist Chakraphan Posyakrit. Controversy surrounds the Ramkhamhaeng Stone, claimed to be the earliest inscription of tonal Thai lettering. The front Throne Hall holds temporary shows.

Classic statuary

Shaded courtyards allow you to recharge before tackling the north and south wings. These hold a badly lit, ill-placed bombardment of religious iconography, running chronologically from Rooms S1-9, spanning the Dvaravati and Lopburi periods, and continuing (Rooms N1-10) with Sukhothai, Ayutthaya, Lanna and Bangkok styles.

But persevere: masterpieces await. Languishing on bare plinths around the rear stairs are the country's most important statuary: a Sukhothai walking Buddha and arrestingly stylised Hindu bronzes, with a Dvaravati figure and a striking Ayutthayan Buddha head hidden under the steps.

Funeral carriage hall

The gilded funerary chariots from the first Chakri reign receive the best display. Their sheer scale and the glass-inlaid teak carving takes your breath away. Moving them takes 300 men – a feat last done in 2008 for King Bhumibol's sister.

Sanam Luang

Thanon Ratchadamnoen Nai.
Tha Chang. **Open** 24hrs daily.
Map p54 B3 ❻

Fringed by tamarind trees, this large oval lawn is one of the city's few truly open spaces. Here elaborate pyres are constructed to resemble sacred Mount Meru for royal cremations, which explains its other name, the *pramane* ground. Annual ceremonies include the bathing of the Phra Buddha Sihing statue at Songkran (p62), the Royal Ploughing Ceremony (p36), and the King's and Queen's Birthday celebrations (p38, p36). In decades past, Bangkok's elite came here for horse racing, bird hunting and golf. Until 1982, it hosted the Weekend Market, which is now at Chatuchak; p144. Sanam Luang's current uses include folk entertainments, festivals, recreations such as kite flying (February-April), and demonstrations.

Saranrom Park

Thanon Charoen Krung, at Thanon Rachini (0 2221 0195). Tha Tien.
Open 5am-9pm daily. **Map**
p54 C4 ❼

This former garden of Saranrom Palace, which is currently being rebuilt, has been open to the public since the 1960s and, like all Thai parks, is liveliest around dawn and dusk, with loud music from mass aerobics. Aside from ponds, a cherub fountain, a Chinese pagoda, and scale models of regional houses, a memorial marks King Rama V's wife Queen Sunanda, who drowned in 1880.

Silpakorn University & Gallery

31 Thanon Na Phra Lan (0 2623 6115 21/www.su.ac.th/0 2221 3841/ www.art-centre.su.ac.th). Tha Chang.
Open 8.30am-4.30pm Mon-Fri. *Art centre* 9am-7pm Mon-Fri; 9am-4pm Sat. Closed hols. **Map** p54 B3 ❽

Thailand's oldest and most venerable fine art university, Silpakorn contains

Wat Pho

a small museum and a courtyard sculpture dedicated to its founder (Silpa Bhirasri, aka Corrado Feroci, an Italian who was commissioned in the 1920s to sculpt such landmarks as the Rama I statue and the Democracy Monument). Hosting exhibitions by students, masters and foreign artists-in-residence, the serene Silpakorn Art Centre Gallery was part of Tha Phra Palace. The faculties of architecture, decorative arts, and painting, sculpture and graphic arts all have galleries.

Thammasat University
2 Thanon Phra Chan (0 2221 6111/www.tu.ac.th). Tha Chang/Tha Prachan. **Open** 8.30am-4.30pm Mon-Fri. **Map** p54 B3 ❸
The country's second most prestigious university (after Chulalongkorn) dates from 1932. A statue of its founder, statesman Pridi Bhanomyong, sits in front of its drill bit-shaped tower, near a Chinese stone lion bedecked with offerings. Free-thinking Thammasat students were the leading demonstrators (and victims) of the 14 October 1973 and 6 October 1976 incidents, recorded on two memorials inside the gate on Thanon Deuan Tula (October Road). However, in 2002, all but postgraduate students moved to the Rangsit campus, thus somewhat muting the activist spirit of this political crucible.

Wat Mahathat
3/5 Thanon Maharat (0 2222 6011). Tha Chang. **Open** 7am-6pm daily. **Map** p54 B3 ❿
Less handsome than its neighbours, this large monastery is nonetheless important and more of a 'working' *wat*. All Thai capitals have ritually required a royal temple of a holy relic (*maha that*), though the public cannot see its interior. It's also the first of Thailand's two Buddhist universities, founded in the 18th century. Later, Rama V donated a library. Its International Buddhist Meditation Centre runs meditation classes in English, Dhamma talks and retreats. From Sanam Luang, you enter through the neo-Khmer Thawornwatthu Building, designed by Prince Naris as a royal funerary hall.

60 Time Out Shortlist | **Bangkok**

ing nirvana. With pillars of the *vihaan* built around it obscuring a full view, photographer's focus on the head and feet; the soles depict 108 auspicious signs in mother-of-pearl inlay (an early Rattanakosin speciality). The mystical number 108 recurs in the quantity of bowls along the wall. A coin dropped in each brings luck and longevity.

Stupa collection
Wat Pho houses 99 *chedi* (stupas), nine being a lucky number to Thais. Signifying the first four Chakri reigns, the colour-themed Phra Maha Chedi show classic Rattanakosin style, with square-bell shape, indented corners and floral ceramic cladding. Two hold the remains of kings Rama II and III, while another enables slim sightseers to climb inside to a unique viewpoint.

Massage and herbalism
King Rama III also made this Siam's 'first university'. Wall inscriptions give lessons in astrology, history, literature and, famously, massage pressure points. It remains a repository of traditional medicine, meditation and *nuad paen boran* (ancient massage). Statuary show yogis in healthful poses, while *salas* offer massage for the weary. Wat Pho Massage School is nearby (p64).

Wat Pho
2 Thanon Sanam Chai (0 2226 0335). Tha Tien. **Open** 8am-6pm daily.
Admission B50. No credit cards.
Map p54 B4 ⑪

This vast, mellow temple rewards wandering, despite some touristy aspects. Its popular name derives from the 16th-century Wat Photharam, which was rebuilt as Wat Phra Chetuphon, in Rama I's grand Rattanakosin scheme. He adorned it with Buddha images retrieved by his brother from Ayutthaya and Sukhothai, including a major Ayutthayan image in the *bot*. (Rama IV interred Rama I's ashes in its base.) Large pairs of stone guards with Western features protect the inner sanctuary. The *kuti* (monks' quarters) lie south of Thanon Chetuphon, where the main gate is less tout-ridden than the Reclining Buddha gate.

Reclining Buddha
In one of several restorations, Rama III added the awesome Reclining Buddha in 1832. Made from brick and gilded plaster, it measures 46m (151ft) by 15m (49ft) and shows the posture of enter-

Wat Ratchabophit
2 Thanon Fuang Nakhon (0 2221 1888). **Open** *Temple* 5am-8pm daily. *Bot* 9-9.30am, 5.30-6pm daily; 8.45am-3.30pm religious hols.
Map p54 C4 ⑫

With a fruit market at the side and schoolchildren playing in its grounds, this seldom-visited but fabulously ornate temple is most lively in late afternoon. Begun in 1869, it encloses the main *chedi* with a unique circular cloister encased in pastel Chinese porcelain, from which other buildings protrude. The small, inner chapel feels European, with Gothic columns and mother-of-pearl doors. The doors bear toy-like carvings of soldiers. In 2008, the King's sister's ashes were interred in the mausoleum for King Rama V's family.

Wat Ratchapradit

2 Thanon Saranrom (0 2223 8215).
Open *Temple* 9.30am-6pm daily. *Bot*
9.30-10am, 5.30-6pm daily; 9am-6pm
religious hols. **Map** p54 C4 ⑬
Less grandiose than its neighbours,
this pretty, little, grey marble temple
has an inviting, contemplative atmosphere. Another East-West hybrid, it
was built in 1864 on a coffee plantation
bought for the Thammayut Nikai sect
by Rama IV (who is depicted observing a lunar eclipse in the murals depicting festivals). His ashes rest under a
replica of the Phra Buddha Sihing in a
vihaan flanked by two *prang*.

Eating & drinking

Boh

*At Tha Tien (Expressboat Pier), 230
Thanon Maharat (0 2622 3081). Tha
Tien.* **Open** 6pm-2am daily. **B**. No
credit cards. **Thai**. **Map** p54 B4 ⑭
Like Boh's drinks list of local whisky
and mixers, its outdoor seating (set on
the actual timbered pier) is hardly
classy. But the views are free and the
sunsets worth staying late for. Popular
with arty youth.

Na Phra Lan

*18 Thanon Na Phra Lan, Phra Nakorn
(0 2221 2312). Tha Chang.* **Open**
10am-10.30pm daily. **B**. No credit cards.
Thai. **Map** p54 B3 ⑮
Old Bangkok is young at heart, with
local students munching here in an
upstairs room that looks more art studio than eatery. Chill here on ice-cream,
beer and air-con, or dig into the pan-
Asian smattering of dishes and
Western comfort foods, from Japanese
dumplings to croissants with a side of
curry, plus a few Thai riffs on spaghetti to fuel your tour.

Shopping

Amulet Market

Trok Wat Mahathat, Thanon Maharat.
Open 9am-6pm daily. **Map** p54 B3 ⑯

Spilling out of a riverside lane, stalls
sell an array of amulets, medals and
Buddhist imagery. Bargaining is a
must, and there are old-school food
stalls aplenty. Find more amulets at
Wat Ratchanadda (p67), and
Chatuchak Weekend Market (p144).
See box p63.

Mor Parinya Ya Thai

*9 Thanon Maharat, Phra Nakorn
(0 2222 1555). Tha Chang.* **Open**
8am-7pm daily. No credit cards.
Map p54 B3 ⑰
Mor Parinya is an old apothecary that
offers Thai and Chinese herb preparations, plus Thai, herbal, acupressure
and reflexology massages. The recipes
for aphrodisiac, herb and alcohol *ya
dong* are real knee-tremblers.

Arts & leisure

International Buddhist Meditation Centre (IBMC)

*Room 106, Vipassana Section,
Mahachulalongkornrajvidyalaya
University, 3 Thanon Maharat, Phra
Nakorn (0 2623 6326/www.mcu.ac.th/
IBMC /www.vipassanadhura.com).*
Open 1-8.30pm Mon-Sat. **Map**
p54 B3 ⑱
Classes in English (6.30am-9pm) include
meals and meditation (7-10am, 1-4pm,
6-8pm daily) and dharma talks (second
and fourth Saturday of the month, 3-
5pm). You can also stay in its crowded
dorms. IBMC country retreats run over
weekends or five to seven days.

National Theatre

*Thanon Rachinee, beside National
Museum, Phra Nakorn (0 2224 1342/0
2222 1092/www.finearts.go.th). Tha
Chang.* **Open** *Shows* 2-5pm 1st or 2nd
Sun of mth; call for details. *Phiphat*
7-9pm 2nd Fri of mth. **Tickets** B60-
B100. No credit cards. **Map** p54 B2 ⑲
Planners want to build a replacement
at the Thailand Cultural Centre for this
neglected venue, which has no company, no café, no shop, and almost no

Spell bound

Amulet Market

Angelina Jolie famously sports a Thai tattoo, and it's not just any image. The cabalistic diagram etched onto skin by monks derives from auspicious yantra designs that also come on cloth or taxi ceilings. Its powers – luck, protection, prosperity, healing, love – are activated by a mantra (spell). Angelina's tattoo is an amulet.

Thai amulets appear everywhere and in myriad forms, tied around necks or waists, on dashboards, wrapped in boxers' armbands, taken to Iraq by soldiers, or displayed for sale at centres like Tha Phrachan's **Amulet Market** (p62), **Wat Ratchanadda** (p67) and **Chatuchak Weekend Market** (p144).

Talismans come in many classes, from medicinal herb roots and natural oddities to yantra embossed on rolled foil (takrut) tiny enough to embed under the skin. Traders recruit fetish objects to bring custom, like miniature fish traps, the beckoning woman (nang kwak), the golden boy (gumarn thong) or palad khik – phallic charms like those displayed at **Nai Lert Shrine** (p118). Lockets contain tablets of wood, clay or

metal depicting Buddha, famous monks, Hindu gods or great kings. Some can cost millions of baht. Others get devalued, as with the craze for Jatukham Ramathep medallions amid the recent political turmoil.

The Buddhist canon rejects faith in rituals and the supernatural, yet animism infuses Thais. Believers claim that bad behaviour (and sometimes female underwear) may negate the spell.

Like the white sacred thread binding wrists (sai sin), amulets bind Thais to the land or spirit world, whether to their khwan (soul), deities or ghosts. The unreborn spirits of the dead (phii) haunt places like big trees, old houses, antique furniture, developments built on cemeteries and road accident sites. Ghost stories dominate movies, comics and soaps, most famously Nang Nak.

Most Thai properties have a miniature temple or stilt-house on a pedestal where they entice the spirit of the land with offerings, food and toy dancers. Just in case. Those with bad karma, or who don't treat the spirits well, might just need that yantra and mantra.

publicity or explanation for its rare shows of traditional dance and music, then demolish its neo-Thai edifice. Sad.

Wat Pho Massage School

392/25-28 Penphat Soi 1, Thanon Maharat (0 2221 3686/www.watpo massage.com). Tha Tian. **Open** 8.30am-6pm daily. No credit cards. **Map** p54 B4 ⑳

Thailand's most famous massage and reflexology school moved across the road into a Tha Tien Market soi flanked by herbalist shops. Massages in open-air *salas* inside the *wat*'s Sanamchai gate are in public view. Murals illustrating the Bangkok massage technique and statues of athletic *ruessi dutton* yogis were awarded 'UNESCO Memory of the World' protection.

City Hall & around

The pleasantly walkable streets around the City Hall and the **Sao Ching Cha** (Giant Swing) reveal vibrant community life. You can see crafts around **Monk's Bowl Village** (p49), tour Buddha image shops and climb the verdant **Golden Mount** for a panorama of the old town and the modern skyline to the east.

Many cherished old restaurants serve bygone styles of Thai cuisine in quaintly shuttered shophouses around **Thanon Dinso**, **Thanon Tanao** and **Samphraeng**, which is a neighbourhood of three parallel 'Phraeng' streets. Thanon Phraeng Phuthon has been turned into a garden square, famed for **Chote Chitr** restaurant and a shop selling ice-cream topped with an unlikely mixture of corn, nuts and red beans. Thanon Phraeng Nara contains a wooden section from the palace of Prince Narathip (who was Rama IV's son) that is now a lawyer's office. Thanon Phraeng Sanphasat preserves a palace gate at its eastern end. Government workers

hereabouts relish the rarer dishes like pig's brain noodles (said to improve the intellect).

To general dismay and protests, planners want to depopulate this city's characterful former heart. The residents of the ancient village around Mahakan Fort, which was part of the old city wall, face eviction. The fort's cannons were disarmed in 2002, amid concern they might be fired in a terrorist plot. Redevelopment is already starting with gradual themed 'restoration', in the name of tourism, of the sleek 1939 buildings that flank Thanon Ratchadamnoen Klang. This middle stretch of the royal processional route (p44) linking the Grand Palace and King Rama V's residences at Dusit is lit by lamps in the shape of mythical *kinnaree/kinnara* (half-bird, half-woman/man). Elaborate decorations bathe the road in fairylights for royal birthdays.

The avenue also features several political landmarks: the **14 October Monument**, **Democracy Monument** and **King Prajadhipok Museum**. By the **Queen's Gallery** at Phanfa Bridge, Ratchadamnoen Avenue veers north towards Dusit.

Sights & museums

14 October Monument

14/16 Thanon Ratchadamnoen Klang, at Thanon Tanao (0 2622 1013-5/www.14tula.com). **Open** 8am-9pm daily. **Map** p54 C3 ㉑

A granite spire bears the names of 73 people killed by the military during the 1973 overthrow of the dictatorship, though an accurate toll still awaits investigation. The surrounding gallery displays inform later generations. Survivors and relatives maintaining the site are keen to talk about their experiences. It also hosts other rights protests.

Monuments to the massacre of 6 October 1976 and other democratic

Golden Mount & Wat Saket p66

struggles occupy a sculpture garden at Thammasat University, just inside the Thanon Na Phra That gate.

Chao Poh Seua Shrine

468 Thanon Tanao (0 2224 2110).
Open 6am-5.30pm daily. **Map** p54 C3 ㉒

This characterful Chinese shrine to a tiger god image is guarded by two further golden tigers, with vendors selling tiger-appeasing offerings such as pork, rice and eggs – and the inevitable lottery tickets. Couples place sugar tigers here in the hope of pregnancy. The shrine stages Chinese opera during the Vegetarian Festival (p37).

Democracy Monument

Thanon Ratchadamnoen Klang.
Map p54 C3 ㉓

Designed by Italian sculptor Corrado Feroci (founder of Silpakorn University; p59), this memorial to the 1932 end of absolutism pointedly sits in a traffic circle interrupting the royal processional avenue. The date infuses the design.

Around a sculpted constitution upon a three-metre (ten-foot) tall tray (June was then the third Thai month) are 75 cannons (for year 2475BE) and four vertical wings (24 metres high for 24 June) symbolising soldiers, police, officials and civilians. Instead of royal or Buddhist imagery, bas-reliefs depict armed revolution, the People's Party and labourers, all in the muscular, 'heroic worker' style typical of mid 20th-century monuments worldwide.

Devasathan & the Giant Swing

268 Thanon Dinso (0 2222 6951).
Open *Bot* 10am-4pm Thur, Sun. *Swing* 24hrs daily. **Map** p54 C3 ㉔

Standing in City Hall square, the Giant Swing (Sao Ching Cha) was originally erected in 1784 as part of the adjacent Devasathan, a Brahmin compound of shrines to Shiva, Ganesha and Vishnu. The Bramin priests based here still officiate at royal and other ceremonies (although no longer at the Brahmin New Year rite). Symbolising an exploit of the god Shiva, four brave men would swing from this lofty red frame to bite pouches of coins. However, due to fatal casualties the ritual stopped in the 1930s. The poles were erected in 1919 by the Louis T Leonowens Company in honour of their namesake, the son of Anna Leonowens (the contentious governess of *The King and I*). In 2006, the rickety timbers were replaced by what you see today.

Golden Mount & Wat Saket

344 Chakkraphatdiphong (0 2223 4561). Tha Saphan Phan Fah. **Open** *Temple* 8am-5.30pm daily. *Golden Mount* 7.30am-5.30pm daily.
Admission free. No credit cards.
Map p55 D3 25

Assembled from canal diggings, the Golden Mount (Phu Khao Thong) was intended by Rama III to be clad as a giant *chedi*. Proving unstable, the rubble was instead reinforced with trees and plants to prevent erosion. Shrines dot the two spiral paths to the summit, where a gilded *chedi* contains Buddha relics from India and Nepal. Its breezy, bell-chiming concrete terrace offers a wonderful 360° panorama of both old and modern Bangkok. Phu Khao Thong belongs to Wat Saket, which spreads eastward with handsome *kuti* (monks' quarters), fine murals and a peaceful atmosphere. This *wat* was where the bodies of people who had died in epidemics were once brought for cremation. Crowds throng through its famous 10-day fair around Loy Krathong (p38).

King Prajadhipok Museum

2 Thanon Lanluang (0 2280 3413-4). Tha Saphan Phan Fah. **Open** 9am-4pm Tue-Sun. **Admission** free. No credit cards. **Map** p55 D3 26

The graceful former Public Works Building displays memorabilia of King Rama VII's reign (1925-35). Coverage of his youth, Eton schooling, marriage to Queen Rambai Barni, unanticipated crowning, constitutional challenges, abdication and last years in England

Pak Khlong Talad p69

provide great insights into early 20th-century Siamese society and the delicate issue of constitutional democracy replacing absolutism.

Krung Thep Signboard

City Hall Square, Thanon Dinso. **Map** p54 C3 27

The Bangkok Metropolitan Authority (BMA) occupies the austere modernist City Hall facing the Giant Swing. In the piazza stands a bus-length sign bearing the city's full Thai title, at 64 syllables the world's longest place name. Take a wide-angle camera. It translates as: 'Great city of angels, the supreme repository of the divine jewels, the supreme unconquerable land of the immortal divinity endowed with the nine noble gems, the delightful capital city abounding in royal palaces, which resemble paradises for the reincarnated deities, granted by Indra for Vishnu to create.' Or for short: Krung Thep, 'City of Angels'.

Monk's Bowl Village

71 Soi Ban Baat (0 2621 2635). Tha Saphan Phan Fah. **Open** 8am-5pm daily. **Admission** free. No credit cards. **Map** p55 D3 28

Buried in lanes within the block where the timber merchant street Thanon Boriphat meets Thanon Bumrung Muang, Descendants of Ayutthayan refugees maintain one of Bangkok's last craft trades. They use a Khmer method of beating out alms bowls from eight strips of metal, representing spokes of the Dharma wheel. Among the five family workshops, the community leader at 71 Soi Ban Baat ensures quality control. Despite the fact that they are a symbol of non-attachment the bowls are prized by collectors, particularly when decorated and lacquered.

Queen's Gallery

101 Thanon Ratchadamnoen Klang (0 2281 5360-1/www.queengallery.org). Tha Saphan Phan Fah. **Open** 10am-7pm Mon, Tue, Thur-Sun. **Admission** B20; free reductions. No credit cards. **Map** p55 D3 ㉙
Dedicated to Queen Sirikit, this major multi-floor space offers world-class exhibitions by leading Thai and foreign artists. Selections by top-line alumni from owner Bangkok Bank's prestigious art prize are often on show. The café's gift shop has a rare stock of monographs and retrospective tomes, although catalogues soon sell out.

Rommaninat Park & Corrections Museum

Thanon Maha Chai (0 2226 1704). **Open** *Park* 5am-9pm daily. *Museum* 9am-4pm Mon-Fri. **Admission** free. **Map** p55 D4 ㉚
In former prison buildings on the site of this park a small penal museum displays instruments of punishment. Amid the gardens' ponds, fountains and a large bronze of a conch shell, locals exercise in the cool hours, including at an alfresco gym.

Wat Ratchanadda

2 Maha Chai Road (0 2224 8807). Tha Saphan Phan Fah. **Open** *Temple* 9am-5pm daily. *Bot* 8-9am, 4-5pm daily; 8.30-10am religious hols. **Map** p55 D3 ㉛

The only version of this step-pyramidal tower style still standing, the Loha Prasat ('Metal Palace') is modelled on a Sri Lankan metal temple from the third century BC, based on an Indian original of 2,500 years ago. Built by Rama III in 1846, it has 37 spires, one for each virtue needed to attain enlightenment. A labyrinth of passages leads to meditation cells (closed to visitors), with a spiral staircase to rooftop views. In order to reveal the Prasat, the art deco Chalerm Thai Theatre was controversially demolished in the early 1990s to create a park containing a statue of Rama III and the Mahachesdabodin Royal Pavilion for official receptions. Behind the *wat*, a market sells amulets.

Wat Suthat

146 Thanon Bamrung Muang (0 2224 9845). **Open** 8.30am-9pm daily. **Admission** B20. No credit cards. **Map** p54 C3 ㉜
Looming behind the Giant Swing, Bangkok's tallest *vihaan* houses the awe-inducing 8m (26ft) Phra Sri Sakyamuni Buddha. One of the largest surviving Sukhothai-era bronzes, it was brought south by boat. Its base contains the ashes of King Rama VIII. Begun by Rama I in 1807, the temple took three reigns to complete, though its mesmerising murals are decaying. Rama II himself started the carving of its original teak doors (now in the National Museum). Numerous Chinese stone statues (found in several Rattanakosin temples) served as both tributes to the king and as valuable ballast for Chinese junks collecting rice.

Eating & drinking

Chote Chitr

146 Thanon Praeng Phuthon (0 2221 4082). **Open** 10.30am-9pm Mon-Sat. **B**. No credit cards. **Thai**. **Map** p54 C3 ㉝
No Bangkok restaurant has garnered so much praise from the cognoscenti, yet managed to retain its unique character. It's as close as you'll get to honest home

Chote Chitr p67

cooking in a restaurant setting. In this open-air, six-table shophouse, three ageing sisters create artfully seasoned dishes like their sublimely smoky grilled aubergine salad, a complex red curry that blankets succulent tiger prawns, and an excellent *mee krob*, crunchy noodles topped with a sauce that balances sour and sweet like a circus act.

Phranakorn Bar

58/2 Soi Damnoen Klang Tai (0 2622 0282). **Open** 6pm-1am daily. **B**. No credit cards. **Thai**. Map p54 C3 ㉞
Young creatives and Khao San escapees gather on the chilled-out roof terrace for spicy Thai food and views of the floodlit Golden Mount and antics outside the soi's gay bars. Others linger near the third-floor pool table listening to indie, house or '80s retro, browse art displayed by the photographer-owner on the second floor, or drink whisky to live music at ground level. Supremely relaxed, with a holiday feel.

Sky High

14 Thanon Ratchadamnoen Klang (0 2224 1947). Phra Nakorn. **Open** 8am-2am daily. **BB**. **Thai**. Map p54 C2 ㉟

Sky High's hushed tones could be coming from politicians, journalists, poets or gossiping friends. This is a seriously Thai place, with lasting popularity and spot-on cooking of Thai-Chinese staples. The steamed Chinese carp fish head is memorable.

Thip Samai

313 Thanon Mahachai, behind Golden Mount (0 2221 6280 ext 0). Tha Saphan Phan Fah. **Open** 5pm-3am daily. **B**. No credit cards. **Thai**. Map p55 D3 ㊱
Pad Thai is the dish that all visitors know before getting their visa. Nicknamed Pad Thai Pratu Pi ('Ghost's Gate Noodles'), Thip Samai is a legend for serving nothing but, in a neon-lit setting. Try out the egg-wrapped version and the nutty-sweet coconut juice.

Shopping

Baan Mor

Thanon Baan Mor & Thanon Atsadang. **Open** 9am-6pm daily. Map p54 C4 ㊲
This spare-parts paradise harbours just about anything for TV, PC and audio – plus vintage LPs and army surplus.

Pak Khlong Talad

Thanon Chakphet, from Memorial Bridge to Khlong Lord. **Open** 24hrs daily. **Map** p54 C5 ㊳

To grasp the Thai love of flowers properly, visit this remnant of Bangkok's original fresh market. It is most spectacular from 10pm until dawn, when night owls descend after bars close. The scent of jasmine fills the air, orchids in forms rarely seen by most non-Asians are stacked taller than people and vendors string devotional offerings with Fabergé delicacy.

Talad Saphan Phut

Thanon Triphet. **Open** 8pm-midnight Tue-Sun. **Map** p54 C5 ㊴

Officials have tried to contain and control this plastic-covered night market, targetting it as an unwanted hotbed of potentially dangerous youth culture. Evicted from a prettified Khlong Lord over a decade ago, it is now strung like costume jewellery around Memorial Bridge. Have fun spotting the Thai designers on the prowl, amid absurdly cheap vintage clothing, T-shirts, handbags, hats and fake perfume. Street food is sold on the periphery.

Nightlife

Café Democ

78 Thanon Ratchadamnoen (0 2622 2571). **Open** 11.30am-1am Tue-Sun. No credit cards. **Thai.** **Map** p54 C3 ㊵

Named after the Democracy Monument it faces, this jazzy chillout café (by day) turns into a clubbers' bar by 10pm, when a lineup of leading Thai DJs keep the tech house, breakbeats and drum 'n' bass fresh and the dancefloor dirty.

Lollipop

Mahannop Soi 1 (08 6339 1390/ www.myspace.com/lullabar). **Open** 5pm-1am Tue-Sun. **Band** 10.30pm-midnight Tue-Thur; 9.30pm-midnight Fri-Sat; (no band on Sun). No credit cards. **Thai.** **Map** p54 C3 ㊶

Drums occupy a quarter of the room in this tiny venue, formerly called Lullabar, at a charmingly weathered wooden house down an old town lane. Sup from the limited menu of beer, spirits and drinking snacks to the rumble of emergent Brit Pop-style rock, punk and indie bands like Desktop Error.

Saké Coffee Pub

Soi Damnoen Klang Tai, Thanon Ratchadamnoen (0 2225 6000). **Open** 8pm-1am daily. No credit cards. **Map** p54 C3 ㊷

Here, less affluent gays fuelled by Thai whisky and hormones bop to a bewildering succession of Thai and Western hits and hoot at the saucy cabaret.

Thonburi

Despite its size and significance as the previous capital, Fang Thon ('Thonburi side') gets dismissed as the 'other' bank, in much the same way as South London, Brooklyn or Sydney's North Shore. Several sights lie between **Khlong Bangkok Noi** and **Khlong San**, the area facing Bangrak, yet even Thonburi's prime tourist fetcher, **Wat Arun**, is usually visited on canal tours starting at piers on Ratanakosin. The *khlongs* (canals) of Thonburi are less pristine than those of Nonthaburi, but feature the **Royal Barge Museum** and residual canalscapes of wooden stilt houses, ancient *wats* (temples), pierside stores and boat vendors selling to residents lounging on their flower-decked verandas.

Fang Thon has two strollable areas that require intervening transport like boat or Thonburi's own-style *tuk-tuk*. Between Khlongs Bangkok Noi and Bangkok Yai, you can wend from **Siriraj Hospital**, which houses several odd museums, through the food-oriented Prannok Market, down the lane to **Patravadi Theatre** and/or the riverfront

Supatra River House restaurant, which are each run by daughters of the Expressboat founder. It's a ten-minute hike along Thanon Arun-Amarin to the temple of the dawn **Wat Arun** and **Wang Derm**, the original palace of King Taksin.

Downstream of Khlong Bangkok Yai, lies the vibrant, 200-year-old Kudi Jeen community. A proposed museum in a wooden mansion should focus the increase in local tourism to this historic neighbourhood. From lofty **Wat Kalayanamit** a river walkway leads round via the ancient Chinese shrine Kiang An Keng and through a maze of wooden houses in the Sino-Portuguese community around **Santa Cruz Church**. The powerful Persian-descended Bunnag clan owns much of this area. They built **Wat Prayoon** and nearby **Wat Pichayat** (Somdet Chaophraya Soi 2), which houses a Sukhothai-era Buddha image from Phitsanulok. Just beyond Saphan Phut (Memorial Bridge) lies the **Princess Mother Memorial Park**.

Sights & museums

Canal tours

Tha Chang or Tha Tien, Phra Nakorn; Tha Saphan Taksin or River City, Bangrak. **Tours** approx 8am-4pm daily. **Hire** by negotiation. No credit cards. **Map** p54 B3 ㊸

One-hour tours show little canal life as they include Wat Arun (p71) and the Royal Barge Museum (right). So take two or more hours (start from B500/hr) to loop through Khlongs Bangkok Noi and Yai, tracing these former meanders of the river before its shorter course was cut. Other stops may include Wat Suwannaram (p72) and its metalworking community at Bang Bu; fish feeding at Wat Sisudaram; Taling Chan Floating Market (p73), set in a fairly rural stretch; and possibly quieter side canals. Much of the central *khlongs* are

hemmed in by flood barriers. Concrete paths and humpback bridges allow for some localised walks.

Phra Ratcha Wang Derm

Royal Thai Navy Headquarters, 2 Thanon Arun Amarin (0 2475 4117/ www.wangdermpalace.com). **Open** 8am-4pm Mon-Fri by written appointment 14 days ahead with passport/visa copy. **Admission** B60; B20 children. No credit cards. **Map** p54 B5 ㊹

Meaning 'original palace', King Taksin's compound of Chinese-influenced buildings once included Wat Arun. Rama V gave the palace to the Thai navy, and its restoration as a museum won a UNESCO award. A shrine features a sword-wielding statue of King Taksin in a century-old *sala* that fuses Thai and Western forms. Canons in Wichaiprasit Fort still guard Khlong Bangkok Yai. Take note of the advance notice and sober dress code.

Princess Mother Memorial Park

Somdet Chaophraya Soi 3, Kudi Jeen (0 2437 7799). **Open** 6am-6pm daily. *Museum* 9am-4pm daily. **Admission** free. **Map** p54 C5 ㊺

The king's late mother, Somdet Phra Srinagarinda Boromarajajonani, beloved as 'Somdet Ya', was born a commoner to goldsmiths and practised nursing. This 1993 memorial amid mature trees recreates her home, a museum documents Thonburi and royal family history, and a gallery holds exhibitions.

Royal Barge Museum

80/1 Rimkhlong Bangkok Noi, Thanon Arun Amarin (0 2424 0004). **Open** 9am-5pm daily. **Admission** B30 Thais, B100 foreigners; camera permit B100; video permit B200. No credit cards. **Map** p54 A2 ㊻

It's an unforgettable sight when fifty slim, elegant and ornate boats carry the royal family from Vasukri Pier to Wat Arun, for a *kathin* ceremony; the most recent marked King Bhumibol's 72nd birthday in 2008. You can view eight of the barges in this canalside hangar, with bilingual displays of regalia, dioramas and barge lore. Seen on the TAT logo, the 45.15m (148ft) long, 3.17m (10.5ft) wide king's barge, Suphannahongse ('Golden Swan') was carved from a single log and seats 50 costumed, chanting oarsmen. A seven-headed *naga* figureheads the 54-oar, Rama IV-era Anantanakaraj, while the newest, Narai Song Suban, with Vishnu riding Garuda at its prow, was built in 1996. The museum is easiest to reach by boat or canal tour, given the badly signed trudge from the road via alleys.

Santa Cruz Church

Soi Kudi Jeen, Thanon Thesaban 1, Kudi Jeen (0 2472 0153-4). Ferry from Tha Ratchini to Tha Kudi Jeen. **Open** daily by written appointment for group visits. **Admission** free. **Map** p54 B5 ㊼

Descendants still remain of the Portuguese Catholics who built this church and convent, known as 'Wat Kudee Jeen'. Often rebuilt since King Taksin donated the land, the current pastel edifice topped by an octagonal dome dates from 1916. A ferry from Tha Rachini serves the church's pier. Some shops nearby still bake *Khanom Farang Kudi Jeen*, sponge cakes of apple and *jujube* made to the recipes of Portuguese mercenaries who defended Ayutthaya from Burma.

Siriraj Hospital Museums

Thanon Phrannok (0 2419 7000 ext 6363). Tha Sirirat. **Open** *Museums* 9am-4pm Mon-Sat. **Admission** B20 Thais; B40 foreigners; free students in uniform. **Map** p54 A2 ㊽

The world's fourth largest hospital, which treats royalty, has six small academic museums. They aren't for the squeamish. The Si Ouey Forensic Medicine Museum (department of forensic medicine, 2nd floor, 0 2419 7000 ext 6547) contains skulls, pickled organs, stillborn babies, crime scene photographs and the body of the notorious murderer Si Ouey. The Congdon Anatomical Museum (anatomy department, 3rd floor, 0 2419 7035) displays human organs and bones from embryo to maturity, including Siamese twins. Two floors down, the Sood Sangvichien Prehistoric Museum & Laboratory (0 2419 7029) looks at evolution.

The Ellis Pathological Museum (department of pathology, 2nd floor; 0 2419 6504) explains diseases, while the Parasitology Museum (parasitology department, 2nd floor, 0 2419 6468) shows preserved worms with their adopted organs. The Ouay Ketusingh Museum of History of Thai Medicine (department of pharmacology, 1st floor, 0 2411 5026) examines indigenous healing techniques.

Wat Arun

34 Thanon Arun Amarin (0 2891 1149/www.watarun.org). Ferry from Tha Tien. **Open** 7.30am-5.30pm daily. **Admission** B20 Thais; B50 foreigners. No credit cards. **Map** p54 B5 ㊾

Seen on the TAT logo and B10 coin, this five-spired landmark has been known as the 'Temple of Dawn' ever since the soon-to-be King Taksin landed by the then Wat Magog at sunrise in October 1767. Renamed Wat Jaeng when it was part of Taksin's palace, Wang Derm (above), it became Wat Arun under Rama II, before being remodelled by Rama IV. The sundry Chinese-style structures pale before the iconic, 81m-high (266ft) Khmer-style *prang* (spire), with four 'corncob' *prang* at the corners, all inlaid with polychromatic ceramic shards. Briefly home to the Emerald Buddha, Wat Arun features a pair of *yaksa* (giant) statues, ceramic gables and 120 Buddha images. Don't rush it on a canal tour, go separately on the B3 ferry from Tha Tien.

Wat Kalayanamit

371 Soi Wat Kalaya, Thanon Tetsaban Sai 1, Kudi Jeen (0 2466

4643). Ferry from Tha Ratchini to Tha Kudi Jeen. **Open** 7am-5pm daily. **Admission** free. **Map** p54 B5 ⑩
Founded in 1825 by a Chinese nobleman, the temple needs Thailand's tallest *vihaan* to house its largest indoor sitting Buddha (15 metres/49 feet high). It also boasts Thailand's highest *chofa* (roof finial) and biggest bell.

Wat Prayoon

Thanon Tetsaban Sai 1, Kudi Jeen (0 2465 5592/www.watprayoon.org). Ferry from Tha Ratchini to Tha Kudi Jeen. **Open** 6am-9pm daily. *Viharn* 8am-8pm daily. Museum 9am-9pm daily. **Admission** free. **Map** p54 C5 ⑪
Fenced in with English-made cast iron, this family temple of the powerful Persian-descended Bunnag clan features Bangkok's first Sri Lankan-style *chedi*. Across the road its verdant Khao Mor (artificial mountain) features Bunnag gravestones.

Wat Rakhang

Soi Wat Rakhang (0 2418 1079). Tha Rakhang/Tha Sirirat. **Open** daily 6am-6pm. **Admission** free. **Map** p54 A3 ⑫
This delightful riverside temple was restored by King Taksin and is famed for its red *hor trai*, a teak scripture hall where Rama I stayed before his reign (his ashes are interred here). King Taksin replaced the melodious *rakhang* (bell) now in Wat Phra Kaew with the five bells hung in the belfry beside a perfectly proportioned *prang*.

Wat Suwannaram

33 Charan Sanit Wong Soi 32 (0 2433 8045). **Open** 8am-5pm daily. **Admission** free. **Map** p54 A2 ⑬
Art students flock to the wat's Ayutthaya-era *bot* (ask a monk to open it) to sketch the Rama III-era murals by Thai artist Thongyu (primarily *jataka* tales of the Buddha's life). Chinese artist Kong Pae used slim brushes and shadows to accentuate motion. Look out for apocalyptic images of Buddha subduing Mara, and some racy erotic poses.

Eating & drinking

Ruam Tai

375/4 Thanon Phrannok (0 2411 0842). Tha Sirirat. **Open** 8am-8pm daily. **B**. No credit cards. **Southern Thai**. **Map** p54 A3 ⑭
Khun Achara has served her sour and spicy curries, which are prepared each morning and displayed in trays, here since 1980. This is Southern Thai cooking, the world's spiciest. Expect to sweat as you spoon thin curries of bamboo and mackerel with tamarind and fresh tumeric (*gaeng som*), or a curry of sathor beans, shrimp and tender pork, (*pet sathor*) over rice. The best antidote are the sides of cucumber and greens – it's no coincidence that refills come free.

Supatra River House

266 Soi Wat Rakhang, Thanon Arun Amarin (0 2411 0305/0874/www. supatrariverhouse.net). Own ferry from Tha Maharat/ferry from Tha Chang to Tha Wat Rakhang. **Open** 11am-2pm, 5.30-10.30pm daily. **BBB**. **Thai**. **Map** p54 A3 ⑮

Patravadi Theatre & Studio 9

River views of the Grand Palace and Wat Arun make reservations wise at this gorgeous Thai restaurant in an old teak house, where classic recipes get slightly de-spiced for *farang*. Weekend dances are held at a tree-shaded stage.

Taling Chan Floating Market

Khlong Chak Phra, near Taling Chan District Office (0 2424 5448/0 2424 1732). **Open** 10am-6pm Sat, Sun. **No credit cards. Thai. Map** p54 A2 🗸
Some canal tours stop at this rather modern floating market in semi-rural environs, but Thais come here to lunch on the superlative seafood cooked on moored canoes. Other stalls on land offer serendipitous browsing.

Arts & leisure

Patravadi Theatre & Studio 9

69/1 Soi Wat Rakang, Thanon Arun Amarin (0 2412 7287-8/www. patravaditheatre.com). Tha Sirirat or ferry from Tha Chang to Tha Wat Rakhang. **Open** 9am-5pm daily.

Tickets *Theatre* B400-B1,000; *Studio 9* free to diners. **B. Thai.** No credit cards. **Map** p54 A3 🗸
Thailand's Broadway diva Patravadi Mejudhon – actor, teacher, dancer, producer, director and writer – turned her compound into the open-air Patravadi Theatre in 1992. Now with a tent-like roof, café and gallery, this space for independent theatre and dance offers shows and classes open to visitors, while the new Studio 9 has regular live music or performance during dinner beside windows overhanging the river.

Thai House

32/4 Moo 8, Bangmuang, Bangyai (0 2903 9611/www.thaihouse.co.th). **Open** by appointment. **Map** p54 A2 🗸
Amid scenic waterways, this teak stilt compound runs day or residential cooking courses in classic Thai dishes (8.30am-3.30pm Mon-Sat min 2 people). Choose from one-day (B3,800), two-day (B8,950 shared room) or three-day (B16,650 shared). It's remote, yet not far from the expressway and a rare chance to stay in a traditional house.

Wat Tri Thosathep p79

Banglamphu & Dusit

A lush break from Bangkok's congestion, Dusit was Siam's first attempt at European-style urban planning and shows how Thai design meshed with the West. King Rama V built it as a spacious retreat outside the city walls. And despite the later urban sprawl, its greenery remains in the grounds of palaces, **Dusit Zoo** (p75), the **Royal Turf Club** (p78) and state institutions. Modelled on the Champs-Elysées (which was seen by Rama V in Paris), Thanon Ratchadamnoen – the Royal Processional Avenue – zigzags from the Grand Palace to **Royal Plaza**. This route and **Chitrlada Palace** (p75) are decorated for the **King's** and **Queen's Birthdays** (p38 and p36).

Between Ratchadamnoen and the river, the streetlife is more diverse. **Banglamphu** is the hub of Thai indie culture and infamous for the backpacker ghetto around **Thanon Khao San**. This guesthouse scene has spread into riverside lanes off Thanon Samsen.

Royal Plaza & around

Every 2 December, vividly uniformed forces parade around Royal Plaza in **Trooping the Colours** (p38). Around it, the headquarters of monarchy, military and government occupy classical edifices designed by Italians a century ago. Nearby Government House and the Prime Minister's official residence Baan Phitsanulok, both on Thanon Phitsanulok, are confections in Venetian Gothic.

From the plaza, an equestrian statue of **King Chulalongkorn** (p76) faces down Thanon Ratchadamnoen Nok. Behind him stand the marble domed **Ananta Samakhom Throne Hall** (p75) and the teak villas of Dusit Park like **Wang Vimanmek** (p75).

This ceremonial area is devoid of food, so eat at **Samsen** (p79) or **Nang Leong Market** (p77).

Sights & museums

Chitrlada Palace

Thanon Ratchawithi (0 2283 9145/ booking 0 2282 8200). **Open** by written appointment only (7 days ahead, with passport/visa copy) 8.30am-4.30pm daily. **Map** p77 D2 ❶

This haven where King Rama VI wrote plays and books is the residence of Rama IX. Access is restricted to tours of the Royal Projects (which are sustainable development schemes). Project and Support Foundation products are sold in Chitrlada Shops here and at the Grand Palace (p53), Dusit Park (below), the Oriental Hotel (p173), the airport at Suvarnabuhmi and at Or Tor Kor Market (p144). Around the date of the royal birthdays (p36, p38) the moat is beautifully illuminated.

Dusit Park

16 Thanon Ratchawithi (0 2628 6300-9 ext 5119-5121). **Open** 9.30am-4pm daily. Closed 5, 10 Dec. **Admission** Thais B75; B20 reductions; foreigners B100; free with Grand Palace ticket. No credit cards. **Map** p76 C1 ❷

This canal-laced royal estate explains court life through museums in fretworked 'tropical European' style mansions, most famously Wang Vimarnmek. Start at the continuous audio-visual display in the Slide Multivision Hall.

The Ancient Cloth Museum illustrates the diversity and meanings of Thai textile patterns, and shows scenes from Rama V's trips to Europe. King Bhumibol Photographic Museums I and II show pictures by Rama IX, while images of his youth appear in Suan Hong Royal Ceremonies Photography Museum. Another fretwork fantasia, Suan Si Reudu Hall, has been reconstructed and displays gifts to Rama IX. Other mansions contain carriages, clocks, various ritual paraphernalia and

treasures from the prehistoric World Heritage Site of Baan Chiang in Isaan. The Chang Ton National Museum displays artefacts of the sacred white elephants housed in a former stable.

Wang Vimarnmek

Completed in 1901, the world's largest golden teak building, Vimanmek ('abode of the angels in the clouds'), was home to Rama V for five years. The free, compulsory guided tour (every 15 minutes, 9.45am-3.15pm daily) includes his apartment, featuring a typewriter, crystal chamber pot and a wooden wheelchair. Downstairs, the Throne Hall connects via sublime panelled corridors with antique-filled rooms. In the lakeside *sala*, dance and martial arts are performed at 10.30am and 2pm (free).

Abhisek Dusit Throne Hall

This gem of wooden tracery displays the Support Museum of exquisite court crafts preserved by the Queen's Support Foundation at Bang Sai.

Ananta Samakhom Throne Hall

Though clad in marble, this was the first Thai building constructed (1908-16) on

Dusit Park, Wang Vimarnmek

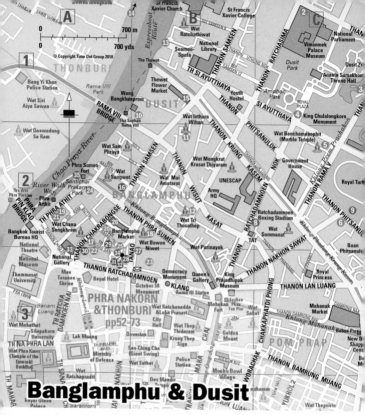

ferro-concrete pilings, a technique Rama V saw in Europe. Its awesome cruciform interior – heavily gilded, with mosaic scenes of Chakri reigns I-IV lining the dome – convened the first Thai parliament, and still hosts state occasions. Behind it lies the modern Parliament (Thanon Uthong Nai, open to the public only on Children's Day, p34) in democratically horizontal concrete, with a Brutalist-yet-breezy Brasilia aesthetic.

Dusit Zoo

71 Thanon Rama V (0 2281 2000/www.zoothailand.org). **Open** 8am-6pm Mon-Thur; 9am-9pm Fri-Sun.

Admission Thais B50; B10 reductions. foreigners B100; B50 reductions. No credit cards. **Map** p76 C1 ❸

This state zoological park in Rama V's former botanical garden is one of Asia's best, but but it does keep rare fauna in rather grim enclosures. Elephant rides and theme park attractions cater to the dressed-up Thai families who also pedalo on the lake and relish its garden restaurants.

King Chulalongkorn Statue

Royal Plaza. **Open** 24hrs daily. *Ceremonies* Tue eve, Thur eve; 23 Oct annually. **Map** p76 C1 ❹

Wat Benchamabophit

69 Thanon Rama V (0 2282 7413). **Open** 9am-5pm daily. **Admission** Thais free; foreigners B20. No credit cards. **Map** p76 C2 ❻

Clad in Italian Carrara marble, the 'marble temple' is a well-proportioned meld of East and West by Italian Hercules Manfredi. It was commissioned in 1899 by Rama V, who was a monk in the original Ayutthaya-era temple, and one room contains his ashes. The *bot* has stained-glass windows of Thai mythology and a replica of Thailand's much-venerated Buddha image: the haloed Phra Phutta Chinirat of Pitsanuloke. Lining the cloister, 53 Buddha images cover every era, style, *mudra* (gesture) and provenance. Monks collect alms every morning by standing out front instead of walking.

Eating & drinking

Nang Leong Market

Thanon Nakhon Sawat, near Thanon Phitsanuloke. **Open** 8am-3pm daily; some restaurants till 8pm. B. **Thai. Map** p76 C2 ❻

Built in 1899, this food market was renovated in 2006 for safety and sanitation, but much charm remains. In the trading hall stands a Chinese shrine, around the edge shops sell various coconut-based *khanom* (sweets). The surrounding warren of shophouses painted in cheerful peach serve classic one-dish meals (see box p79) and old-style coffee. It's best for weekday lunch. Bangkok's oldest wooden cinema languishes at the back.

Shopping

Bo Bae Market

Soi Rong Muang, Thanon Krung Kasem, near Yotse Bridge (0 2628 1888/1999). **Open** 8am-5pm daily. **Map** p77 D3 ❼

This funky canalside *talad* specialises in wholesale clothes, from assembly-line to catwalk-worthy. Bo Bae Tower

Devotees of King Chulalongkorn the Great (Rama V) gather on the anniversary of his death for rites at the six-metre (20-foot) equestrian statue he had cast in bronze during a 1907 visit to France. During his progressive reign (1868-1910) he learned about his subjects' concerns by disguising himself as a commoner. His portrait is widely venerated in homes and businesses, as well as on amulets, banknotes and busts used as talismans. Offerings made here on Tuesday and Thursday evenings, asking for luck, tend to include two of King Chula's favourite things: cognac and cigars.

BANGKOK BY AREA

(488 Thanon Damrongrak) has separate floors for men, women, children and babies. The outdoor area sells outdoor kit and army surplus.

Arts & leisure

Ratchadamnoen Stadium
1 Thanon Ratchadamnoen Nok (ringside reservations 0 2281 4205).
Open 6.30-11pm Mon, Wed, Thur; 5-8pm, 8.30pm-midnight Sun. **Tickets** Thais B250/500/2,000; foreigners B1,000/1,500/2,000. No credit cards. **Map** p76 C2 ❽
This art deco stadium stages *muay Thai* boxing, with stirring live music. Each bill progresses from juniors to prizefights. Ringside seats are best; the stands are animated with betting. It has an equipment shop and, out front, a legendary chicken vendor.

Royal Turf Club
183 Thanon Phitsanulok (0 2628 1810-5). **Races** noon-6pm every fortnight. **Admission** B50-B300. No credit cards. **Map** p76 C2 ❾
Grandstands view biweekly horse races and four annual derbies. Founded by King Rama VI after his father introduced horse racing after his 1897 European tour, it also tests and registers Thai thoroughbreds.

Samsen

Along Dusit's riverbank, Thanon Samsen connects a string of old communities, harbouring restaurants, guesthouses and wooden homes. These focus on places of worship, like **Wat Indrawihan** (right), the picturesque Vietnamese enclave around the dainty Mediterranean-looking St Francis Xavier Church (94 Samsen Soi 13, 0 2243 0060-2), or the temple lane leading to **Kaloang** seafood restaurant (p79).

Take a breather in **Thewet** flower market (p80) or in the park

Ratchadamnoen Stadium

across the river at the foot of the dramatic, harplike **Rama VIII Bridge**, which offers fine views of **Wang Bangkhunprom** (below).

Sights & museums

Wang Bangkhunprom & Bank of Thailand Museum
273 Thanon Samsen (0 2283 5286/ 6723/www.bot.or.th). Tha Wisutkasat.
Open by written appointment only (7 days ahead with passport/visa copy) 9am-4pm Mon-Fri. **Admission** free. **Map** p76 B1 ❿
The palace of Prince Baripatra until the end of absolutism in 1932, this baroque-cum-art nouveau edifice contains the Bank of Thailand's museum. It charts six centuries of Thai monetary evolution from glass beads to notes, via *pot duang* (bullet coins). Women in trousers not admitted.

Wat Indrawihan
144 Thanon Visut Kasat (0 2281 1406). Tha Wisutkasat. **Open** 7am-10pm daily. **Admission** free. **Map** p76 B2 ⓫

Down a shophouse alley, 'Wat In' is notable only for its standing Buddha. Eschewing normal proportions, this figure is a lofty 32m (105ft) tall – you can climb to its head for a so-so panorama – but unfeasibly thin and anchored by outsize feet. The adjacent *vihaan* (chapel) poignantly features jars of human ashes in its terrace walls.

Wat Tri Thosathep

Thanon Prachatipathai (0 2282 4453). Tha Wisutkasat. **Open** 6am-9pm daily. *Murals* 9am-4pm Mon-Sat. **Admission** free. **Map** p76 B2 ⑫
At this relatively recent temple, national artist Chakraphan Posyakrit continues to paint one of the most ambitious murals of our times. See p48.

Eating & drinking

Kaloang Home Kitchen

2 Thanon Sri Ayutthaya, at the end of the soi beside the National Library (0 2281 9228/0 2282 7581). **Open** 10am-10pm daily. **BB**. **Thai seafood**. **Map** p76 B1 ⑬
A rough-and-tumble fish house on stilts is typically found at the coast. Planking, Formica, wind-beaten chairs – every cliché is in place. But the food transcends the riverside setting; sure-handed spicing and faultless freshness informs each sizeable dish. Take your time wandering down the teak-and-temple-lined soi from Thanon Samsen.

River Bar Café

405/1 Soi Chao Phraya Siam, Thanon Ratchawithi (0 2879 1748-9). Tha Saphan Krung Thon (Sang Hee). **Open** 4pm-1.30am daily. **BB**. **Thai seafood**. **Map** p76 A1 ⑭
Facing Dusit from across Sang Hee Bridge, this glazed hall with timber terraces serves sea-fresh fish in style. The delicious preparations (steamed, deep-fried, spicy salads, flamed prawns) are pleasingly unfussy. It can get loud inside from the band, and it makes a boisterous party setting.

Kerbside gourmets

The sidewalk is Bangkok's de facto dining room – a place where people from all walks dine on stews, stir-fries, soups, salads and sweets. Due to stiff competition and demanding diners, Thai streetfood is sanitary and dependably good. But the sublime is rare, and the best vendors attract culinary pilgrims from across town.

Much vendor cuisine has Chinese ancestry – from Hainan chicken rice (*khao man kai*) to duck noodles. So Chinatown, with its sensory blur of vendors at Thanon Yaowarat and Soi Texas (p88) makes a great place to graze. But first get some context at **Talad Nang Leong** (p77), a pretty clean market serving classics from sweet kanom to savoury pork shank rice (*khao ka moo*), along with Ngua Doong Nang Leong's steaming beef offal soup and other oddities. Try **Talad Or Tor Kor** (p144) for upscale regional specialities, or **Sukhumvit Soi 38** (p140). Other one-dish destinations include **Kai Thord Soi Polo** (Isaan-style fried chicken, p107); **Khrua Aroi Aroi** (curry over fresh rice noodles, p94); **Mid Night Kai Ton** (Hainan chicken rice, p124); **Pet Tun Jao Tha** (duck and goose, p87); **Roti Mataba** (stuffed flatbread and curries, p82); and **Thip Samai** (*pad Thai*, p68).

Street eating is a voyage of discovery. If something looks good just try it – there are countless more streetfood shrines hiding in plain sight.

Shopping

Thewet Market

Thanon Krung Kasem, west of Thanon Samsen. Tha Thewet. **Open** 9am-6pm daily. **Map** p76 B1 ⑮

A more neighbourly and less exhaustive plant market than Pak Khlong Talad (p69) or Chatuchak Weekend Market (p144), Thewet makes a pleasant stroll. Liveliest by day and picturesque at dusk, when its river pier restaurant In Love starts to fill.

Nightlife

Ad Here The 13th

13 Thanon Samsen, opposite Soi 2 (08 9769 4613). **Open** 6pm-midnight daily. *Bands* 4pm-midnight daily. No credit cards. **Map** p76 A2 ⑯

Cosy regulars' pub where newcomers can jam the blues nightly (except Mondays acoustic and jazz sets). A lively local rather than destination venue.

Banglamphu

Thanon Khao San (right) may be famous as a backpacker village, but this old neighbourhood has clung to its roots. Descendants of palace dancers and artisans still live here, shop at the labyrinthine Banglamphu Market (between Thanons Rambuttri and Phra Sumen, open 9am-6pm daily) and worship in mosques, Wat Chana Songkhram (Thanon Chakkraphong) or the prestigious **Wat Bowoniwet** (right).

Thanon Phra Arthit midwifed the new indie generation through arty venues and cultural events at the riverside **Santichaiprakarn Park** (p83). From the Bangkok Tourist Bureau under Phra Pinklao Bridge to the park, a walkway in the river accesses restaurants and offers views of mansions, including the UNICEF offices in a home of a consort to Rama IV; a house of the

late prime minister, novelist and cultural pundit, Kukrit Pramoj; and the UN-FAO building, Baan Maliwan, where Pridi Bhanomyong lived as regent for Rama VIII and directed the anti-fascist wartime Seri Thai Movement.

Something of a slog to reach by road, Banglamphu is best accessed by river Expressboat to Tha Phra Arthit or by canal boat to Tha Saphan Phan Fah.

Sights & museums

Thanon Khao San

www.khaosanroad.com. Tha Phra Arthit. **Map** p76 A2 ⑰

Alex Garland's 1997 novel *The Beach* opens in a Khao San flophouse, immortalising the world's most infamous haunt for budget travellers. Now Khao San ('street of uncooked rice') has gentrified, with 'flashpackers' wheeling backpacks to boutique digs and hip Thais relishing a parallel nightlife scene.

The first guesthouses opened in 1982 to soak up the human flotsam from the city's bicentennial celebrations. A few wooden shophouses remain, along with converted mansions like the Starbucks in Sunset Street. For transients, the road is one long bucket shop, for air, bus and ferry tickets, not to mention fake ID. It also flogs clothes, beachwear and sandals – and services to 'buy anything', fill iPods or braid hair. The second-hand bookshops have great, serious selections. Meanwhile, costumed Akha tribesfolk pester everyone to buy silverware.

Wat Bowoniwet

248 Thanon Phra Sumen (0 2281 6411). **Open** *Temple* 8.30am-5pm daily. *Bot* 8.30am-5pm Sat, Sun, religious hols. **Admission** free. **Map** p76 B2 ⑱

Home to the city's second Buddhist university and the Supreme Patriarch (leader) of Thai Buddhism, this *wat* becomes a major focus on Buddhist

Thanon Khao San

holidays. Founded in 1826, it melds Thai and Chinese designs. Kings Rama IV and Rama IX were both ordained here, the former becoming its abbot before his reign.

Eating & drinking

Bar Bali

58 Thanon Phra Arthit, Banglamphu (0 2629 0318). **Open** 5pm-midnight daily. **B**. No credit cards.

Bar/Restaurant. Map p76 A2 ⑲
Typical of the arty single-room bars on riverside Phra Arthit, softly lit Bali consists of four walls of pictures, as well as the requisite food and cocktails.

Chabad

96 Soi Rambuttri, Thanon Chakkraphong (0 2629 2770-1/www.chabadthailand.com). **Open** 10am-10pm Mon-Thur, Sun; 10am-3pm Fri. **B**. **Israeli**. Map p76 A2 ⑳
Banglamphu boasts a few Israeli cafés and a good falafel stall opposite Gulliver's bar, but Rabbi Nechemya Wilhelm's Chabad offers comfortable, upmarket surroundings without it

costing much extra for the usual chips and dips and occasional North African specials, such as Moroccan-style fish.

Hemlock

56 Thanon Phra Arthit (0 2282 7507). **Open** 4pm-midnight Mon-Fri; 5pm-midnight Sat. **BB** No credit cards.
Bar/Restaurant. Map p76 A2 ㉑
A pioneer of this hip bar/restaurant strip, Hemlock maintains a near-Mediterranean breeziness (white-washed walls and a rock-strewn interior). Exhibitions and performances upstairs add to the diversity of the wines, teas and Thai food.

Hippie de Bar

46 Thanon Khao San (0 2629 3508/08 1820 2762). **Open** 3pm-1am daily. *Hippie Hi* 3am-1am daily. **Bar/Restaurant**. Map p76 A3 ㉒
Tucked in an alley of used-book shops, the retro-kitsch Hippie attracts not hippies but young, alternative Thais. Mismatched furniture, quirky wall hangings and psychedelic paraphernalia cram into two floors and funky chairs litter the garden. A lively sound

BANGKOK BY AREA

track veers from oldie to indie. Its nearby branch is Hippie Gallery (Thanon Phra Arthit, open 3pm-1am daily).

Mai Kaidee

111 Thanon Tanao, down soi beside Burger King, then take first left (0 2281 7137/08 9137 3173/www.maykaidee.com). **Open** 9am-11pm daily. B. No credit cards. **Vegetarian**. Map p76 B3 23

Khun May serves veggie versions of Thai and Chinese standards, including great spring rolls. She also gives cooking classes (9am-1pm daily, B1,200 per ten dishes; private B2,000 per ten dishes). Also at 33 Thanon Samsen (0 2281 7699).

Roti Mataba

136 Thanon Phra Arthit, nr Santichaiprakarn Park (0 2282 2119). Tha Phra Arthit. **Open** 9am-10pm Tue-Sun. B. No credit cards. **Indian**. Map p76 A2 24

The women here are expert at patting, flipping, filling and plaiting roti. This flatbread comes stuffed (with chicken, egg, veggies) and drizzled (with sweet milk or honey) or it's put to work dipping and scooping curries.

Suzie Pub

1085-9 Soi Rambuttri (0 2282 4459). **Open** 6pm-2am daily. No credit cards. **Bar**. Map p76 A2 25

Down an alley dubbed Soi Suzie, this US college bar-cum-dance club brought Thai nightlife to Khao San. On weekends travellers and students cram in for the rock standards, while the laid-back weeknights leave elbowroom for pool and pub dinners.

Shopping

Banglamphu Market

Thanon Chakkraphong. **Open** 9am-6pm daily. No credit cards. Map p76 A2 26

This traditional, sprawling *talad* stocks fabrics, satay, crafts, fruits, clothes, uniforms – the range is enormous.

Brick Bar

Chang Torn

95 Thanon Tanao (0 2282 9390). **Open** 9am-7pm Mon-Sat. Map p76 B3 27

In a district full of tailors, veteran Chang Torn's comes lauded by fabric sellers. His small, unassuming version of Savile Row makes suits from B6,000, shirts from B900. Allow ten days.

Nightlife

Brick Bar

1st floor, Buddy Lodge, 265 Thanon Khao San (0 2629 4477/www.brickbarkhaosan.com). **Open** 7.30pm-1.30am daily. *Bands* 8pm-1am daily (3 bands). Map p76 A3 28

Resembling a cavernous Chicago speakeasy adorned with Americana, this cracking music bar hosts each night a trio of bands (ska, jazz, blues) as cool as the beers. A trendy crowd jive around the wooden stools or play pool. Part of the Buddy Lodge (p169) group that dominates Khao San: the Club (p83), and old house conversions at Tom Yum Goong restaurant, Sunset Street and Sidewalk Café.

Club

123 Thanon Khao San (0 2629 1010/www.theclubkhaosan.com).
Open 10pm-2am daily. **Admission** free; concerts from B300. **Map** p76 A2 ㉙

Glow-stick-brandishing backpackers and Thai house music fans flock to this laser-sprayed dancefloor, hoping for Full Moon Party cred. Radiant walls sponsored by drinks brands help light two dark floors dotted with silver sofas.

Gazebo

Rooftop, 44 Thanon Chakrapong (0 2629 0705). Tha Banglamphu.
Open 8pm-late. **BB. Map** p76 A3 ㉚

Persian rugs, plump cushions, shisha pipes and a lack of air-conditioning make this open-air rooftop bar feel like a balmy Moroccan loft. Upscale backpackers, ex-pats and local Thais mingle between the indoor nightclub and outdoor live band areas.

Immortal Bar

1st floor, Bayon Building, 249 Thanon Khao San (no phone). **Open** 6pm-1.30am daily. No credit cards. **Map** p76 A3 ㉛

A totemic space as dilapidated and charming as New York's CBGBs or the Garage in London, Immortal Bar embraces any underground band (send demo) especially of the rock/punk/speed-metal, reggae, hip hop and drum 'n' bass genres. The owner, who plays hard rock here (Tue-Thur), runs the biennial Demonic metal fest.

Lava

Basement, Bayon Building, 249 Thanon Khao San (0 2281 6565).
Open 8pm-1am daily. No credit cards. **Map** p76 A3 ㉜

This basement club changes hands more often than the decor (cement, metallic stools and glass tables). Currently red and true to its name, Lava gets pretty hot, especially when the fug of young locals bobs and paws the air to nightly hip hop.

Arts & leisure

National Gallery

5 Thanon Chao Fa (0 2282 2639). Tha Phra Arthit. **Open** 9am-4pm Wed-Sun. **Admission** B10 Thais; B30 foreigners. No credit cards. **Map** p76 A3 ㉝

Established in 1977 in the neo-classical former Royal Mint, this institution has occasional impressive shows, but its small collection hasn't kept pace with the boom in Thai art. It includes work by Impressionist painter Fua Haripitak, sculptor Misiem Yipintsoi, portraitist Chamrus Khietkong and watercolourist Sawasdi Tantisuk.

Pian

108/15-16 Thanon Khao San (0 2629 0924). **Open** 8am-midnight daily. No credit cards. **Map** p76 A3 ㉞

Rivalry keeps the prices low and the quality high in Banglamphu's cramped open-plan traditional massage parlours, of which Pian is best. Men and women give (and teach; call for rates) reflexology, traditional and herbal massage, as well as (rather public) Swedish oil massages.

Santichaiprakarn Park

Thanon Phra Arthit. Tha Phra Arthit. **Map** p76 A2 ㉟

Flanking the river and Khlong Banglamphu, which was dug by Lao POWs, this park has Braille-marked paths and maps of attractions, such as the district's last *lamphu* trees, for which Banglamphu is named, and the octagonal Phra Sumen Fort, one of only two city wall watchtowers to survive.

On weekend afternoons, the park brims with activity, from fire juggling and breakdancing to jams of classical *phiphat* music. It hosts events like Loy Krathong (p38), and gatherings of the indie subculture of contrarian youth. They hawk self-made books, postcards, music and artwork here at the Indy Festival (p38) and Bangkok Theatre Festival (p38) and in adjacent art bars on Thanon Phra Athit.

BANGKOK BY AREA

Yaowarat

Chinatown

BANGKOK BY AREA

One of the world's oldest, biggest and best-preserved Chinatowns occupies the swathe of riverside between Phra Nakorn and the Old Farang Quarter. It may seem like a quaint enclave, but before Bangkok sprawled, this was the hub of Thai commerce, shopping and pop culture. The neighbourhoods remain maze-like because no one can gather enough land to redevelop, though the planned MRT subway extension may change this living museum. Bangkok may be the capital, but it has never been a quintessentially Thai town. Chinatown embodies how Sino-Thais have shaped this city, both economically and physically, from market to shophouse to mall.

The ancient lanes between the river and **Sampeng** invite strolling. Further inland, the major roads of **Yaowarat** and Charoen Krung clamour day and night with vendors, shophouses and traffic.

Abutting Phra Nakorn, the ethnic focus shifts at **Pahurat**, otherwise known as Little India.

Explorers need a spirit of adventure, a tolerance for heat and crowds, light clothing, comfortable shoes, plenty of fluids and a copy of the invaluably annotated *Nancy Chandler's Map*. Or you could follow two sign-posted walks from a booth dispensing maps at River City (p95). Confusingly, Chinese street names are giving way to Thai ones, so Soi Issaranuphap is officially Charoen Krung Sois 16 and 21, and Sampeng Lane the anonymous Wanit Soi 1.

To 'do' Chinatown, you could focus on temples (Buddhist, Taoist, Chinese and Sikh). Or food (from stalls to fancy restaurants). Or markets, which are Bangkok's oldest and most diverse. Or weird juxtapositions: casket makers near chicken hatcheries; mosquito coils beside cock rings. Or gawk at the eclectic, mouldering architecture, notably along Thanons Charoen Krung, Songwat and Ratchawong. Or just follow your nose (both scents and stenches) down microscopic *trok* (paths) and risk getting lost until a landmark pops up.

The surging confidence in Chinese cultural expression emerges most at festivals. The formerly quiet, family-and-temple-oriented **Chinese New Year** (Jan/Feb, p34) has become a state-sponsored street fest of food and lanterns. **Mid-Autumn Festival** (Sept, p36) commercialises the celebratory mooncakes, while the **Chinese Vegetarian Festival** (Oct, p37) sees yellow pennants citywide, signifying ten days of unspicy veganism, white-clad parades and incense-smoked rites. In these periods many temples host funfairs and vivid, high-pitched *ngiew* (Chinese opera).

Sampeng

Sampeng Lane was once notorious for opium and gambling dens, brothels and pawnshops. Now it teems with nothing more risky than roving snack merchants and overloaded motorbikes. Some time-warp alleys reach down to the river via Thanon Songwat, where many tycoon dynasties began. Between Songwat's unrestored Sino-European shophouses, *godowns* with deceptively modern frontages store rice, spice and gunny sacks and display huge grandfather clocks and heavy mother-of-pearl-inlaid furniture. Where Songwat meets Thanon Ratchawong, a famous vendor peddles *khanom jeeb* (Chinese minced pork dumplings) from a huge antique brass steamer. The other end of Songwat enters Talad Noi, a precinct coated in oil from its trade in engine parts.

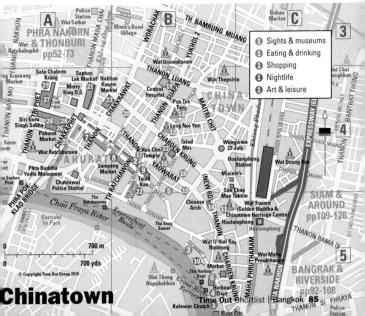

Sino-Thaitown

Chinatown has a new landmark, containing two contrasting museums. At Wat Trimit, the famous solid gold Buddha image has been moved from a drab hall into the soaring spire of a marble *mondop* (artefact tower) that is so glaringly white you need shades to view its neo-traditional detailing.

A museum below explains how it had been cast and then hidden unrecognised within stucco for centuries, probably to keep it from marauding Burmese. Then in 1955, its shell cracked on being dropped from a crane during its move here. Weighing 5.5 tonnes and sitting 3m (10ft) high in 'Calming Mara' pose, the Sukothai-era statue gleams with near-liquid lustre.

Beneath it, the Chinatown Heritage Centre presents an expurgated history of Bangkok's Sino-Thai, the biggest ethnic group since before this trading post became the capital. Entertaining, accessible displays and dioramas untangle Chinatown's cultural, civic, commercial and culinary maze.

Panels show how junk traders gained powerful leverage in Siam. Millions of poor Southern Chinese then immigrated in waves, from the Thonburi era of King Thaksin (himself half-Teochiu) up to the 1940s. When King Rama I (part-Hokkien) relocated his palace to Rattanakosin, the Chinese were shifted south of the Phra Nakorn walls in 1782 to a dirt alley called Sampheng. From that nucleus grew Chinatown's golden age.

Sights & museums

Holy Rosary Church
Thanon Yotha, Talad Noi (0 2266 4849). Tha Sriphraya/Hualumphong MRT. **Open** 6pm daily for service. **Admission** free. **Map** p85 B5 ❶
Beside River City antiques mall (see p95), stands a spired Gothic confection built in 1787 on land given to the Portuguese for helping to fight the Burmese. Its nickname Wat Kalawar comes from the Thai for 'Calvary'.

Pratu Sun Yat Sen
Trok Prasai at Thanon Ratchawong. Tha Ratchawong. **Map** p85 B4 ❷
This nondescript arch marks a dramatic moment, when China's nationalist revolutionary Sun Yat Sen fundraised in Bangkok – and was twice deported. A century later descendants of his supporters erected the gate in 2004 at Trok Sun (Sun Alley), now nicknamed Trok Prasai (Speechgiving Alley).

San Jao Sien Khong
Soi Wanit 2, Talad Noi (no phone). Hualumphong MRT. **Open** 6am-6pm daily. **Admission** free. **Map** p85 B5 ❸
Behind Riverview Guesthouse (see p170), this 200-year-old riverbank shrine comes alive during the Vegetarian Festival (Oct, see p37), when it stages Chinese opera and fairground games amid stalls selling meat-and spice-free dishes to the white-clad devotees of the goddess Kuan Yin.

Siam Commercial Bank
1280 Thanon Yotha, Talad Noi (0 2266 8937). Tha Sriphraya/ Hualumphong MRT. **Open** 8.30am-4.30pm daily. **Map** p85 B5 ❹
An ATM in a stucco sentrybox marks Thailand's first bank building (1904), a classical Italian-built edifice set in riverside gardens behind a humungous tree. It retains original grilled teller counters, with wood-panelled offices upstairs, though the museum has moved to the bank's headquarters.

Sampeng Lane Market

Eating & drinking

Ia Sae Coffee Shop

58-60 Thanon Padsai (0 2622 4080).
Open 4am-8.30pm daily. **B. Coffee.**
Map p85 B4 ❺
A decades-old Chinese café, with old
men and local chefs swapping tales
over sock-strained coffee, washed down
with buns and tea.

Pet Tun Jao Tha

*941-7 Wanit Soi 2 (0 2233 2541). Tha
River City/Hualumphong MRT.* **Open**
8.30am-4pm Mon-Sat. **B.** No credit
cards. **Chinese.** **Map** p85 B5 ❻
This is *the* place to tuck into duck and
goose served straight up with rice noodles and condiments.

Shopping

Chao Krom Pho

*229-231 Thanon Chakkrawat (0 2221
3272). Tha Saphan Phut.* **Open** 8am-
5pm Mon-Sat. No credit cards.
Map p85 A4 ❼

Traditional herbalist dispensing Thai
and Chinese prescriptions from walls of
wooden drawers and sacks strewn
about the floor. If you don't have a pre-
scription, ask for an examination by the
owner Khun Tawan, whose family has
run this apothecary for over a century.

Sampeng Lane Market

Soi Wanit 1. Tha Ratchawong. **Open**
9am-6pm daily. **Map** p85 B4 ❽
Sampeng's oldest market is losing
some charm, but remains an epic alley
crammed with bric-a-brac, costume
accoutrements, honking motorbikes,
smoky quarters and shouting hawkers.
It is best tackled in sections. Out east
you'll   discover   accessories-ville.
Midway is miscellany, with ceramics,
monks' bowls, Chinese lanterns, kids'
shoes and wrapping paper. West of
Thanon Ratchawong is fabric, from
jeans and fatigues to chiffon. At the
Mahachai end are blankets, sarongs,
buttons and laces.

Tang Toh Kang

*345 Wanit Soi 1, at Thanon Mangkorn
(0 2224 2422/www.tang-toh-kang.com).
Tha Ratchawong.* **Open** 9.30am-4pm
Mon-Sat. **Admission** free. *Museum*
group visit by appointment at least 2
days ahead. **Map** p85 B4 ❾
Yaowarat is a world gold trade hub.
Thai bullion is soft and yellow from its
97.5 per cent purity. It's sold not in
ounces, but in baht (not the currency;
one baht weight is 15.2g). Above the
elaborate shop of this most famous
gold merchant, chain-making workshops and a quaint museum are open
by appointment. Other notable gold
shops include Hua Seng Heng (332-334
Thanon Yaowarat, 0 2225 0202) and
Chin Hua Heng (295-297 Thanon
Yaowarat, 0 2224 0077).

Arts & leisure

Dumnam

*282/1 Soi Duang Tawanaka (Trok Jao
Seua Song), Talad Noi (0 2639 5577/*

*www.dumnam.net). Hualumphong
MRT.* **Open** for courses only.
Map p85 B5 ⑩
Bangkok's strangest conversion of a
historic home is this diving school on a
tiny riverside lane. Behind ornate gates,
NAUI instructor Phusak Posayachinda
built a pool in the courtyard of the
Fujian style compound, Baan Jao Seua
Song, under seventh generation owner-
ship. Between dives and decompression
calculations, explore the carved wooden rooms and ancestor altar.

Yaowarat

To locals, Yaowarat *is* Chinatown –
an orientation word for taxi drivers,
synonymous with gold shops and
wonderful, if pricey, food. Thanon
Yaowarat was an attempt at
city planning on the model of
Bangkok's first paved road,
Thanon Charoen Krung, built in
1861 yet still dubbed 'New Road'.
Chinese settlement spread
inexorably beyond Charoen Krung
into Pomprab district, and thence
to Bangrak then everywhere else.
   Geomancers claim Yaowarat
resembles a dragon – a lucky one
of course. At its eye stands the gate
Soom Pratu Chalerm Prakiat,
with Wat Traimit's **Golden
Buddha** atop its head. The spine
undulates west, its belly becoming
one huge night market between dusk
and 9pm, with vendors spreading
into Soi Plaeng Nam and Soi
Phadung Dao (aka **Soi Texas
Suki**, p88). Dragons come from
water, so its tail (lined with
hardware shops) ends at Khlong
Ong Ang near **Talad Saphan Lek**.

Sights & museums

Chinatown Heritage
Centre & Golden Buddha
*Wat Traimit, 661 Thanon Charoen
Krung (0 2225 9775). Hualumphong
MRT.* **Open** 9am-5pm daily.

Leng Noi Yee (Wat Mangkorn)

Admission *Temple* free. *Golden
Buddha* free Thais; B20 foreigners.
No credit cards. **Map** p85 B5 ⑪
See box p86.

Leng Noi Yee
(Wat Mangkorn)
*Thanon Charoen Krung, between
Thanon Mangkorn & Soi Issaranuphap
(0 2222 3975).* **Open** 6am-6pm daily.
Map p85 B4 ⑫
Set behind an imposing multi-tiered
entrance, the 'Dragon Flower Temple'
(aka Wat Mangkorn Kamalawat) is
Chinatown's first and biggest. Several
sermon halls ring a courtyard filled
with statues of Mahayana Buddhist
and Taoist deities. It takes on a livelier
and folksier ambience during festivals.

Poh Teck Tung
*326 Thanon Chao Khamrob (0 2226
4444-8).* **Open** 7am-8pm daily.
Map p85 B4 ⑬
The shrine of a charity foundation that
collects accident victims and conducts
funerals for unclaimed corpses. Dealers
in funerary paraphernalia gather around

the nearby Taoist temple Li Thi Miew (494 Thanon Phlubphlachai, 0 2221 6985). You can see satin banners and paper offerings – fake money, clothes, houses, cars – being made for burning to provide for the souls of the dead.

Soom Pratu Chalerm Prakiat

Odeon Circle, Thanon Yaowarat. Hualumphong MRT. **Open** 24hrs daily. **Map** p85 B5 ⑭

Chinatown's ceremonial arch commemorated King Rama IX's 72nd birthday in 1999, the illustrious sixth cycle of both Thai and Chinese 12-year calendars. It features a calligraphy by Princess Sirindhorn and has become a focus of Chinese New Year blessings.

Eating & drinking

Canton House

530 Thanon Yaowarat (0 2221 3335). **Open** 11am-10pm daily. **B**. **Chinese**. **Map** p85 B4 ⑮

Yaowarat's delightful chaos can overwhelm, so savour the air-conditioning of this clean Chinese restaurant and its simple, cheap dim sum, Cantonese roast meats and cold drinks. It's not the best Chinese show in town, but it does provide a wallet-friendly refuge.

Hua Seng Hong

371-373 Thanon Yaowarat (0 2222 0635). **Open** 8am-1am daily. **BB**. No credit cards. **Chinese**. **Map** p85 B4 ⑯

Obscured by glass cases of sharks' fins, Hua Seng Hong sits in the heart of Yaowarat's early-evening madness. *Ba mee* noodles stir-fried with crab, plates of greens with salted fish, roast duck and oyster omelettes can be procured elsewhere – but they won't be handmade on site and served by no-nonsense yet grinning staff as they are here.

Shangri-La Restaurant

306 Thanon Yaowarat (0 2224 5807/0 2622 7870). **Open** 10am-10pm daily. **BB**. **Chinese**. **Map** p85 B4 ⑰

This institution (with four branches in Bangrak) is the kind of full-throttle Chinese place that belongs in the movies. It's big, always busy with families, has round tables and serves dependable (and fun) dim sum daily, as well as all the sweet and sour this and that in existence.

Soi Texas

Thanon Phadungdao (no phone). **Open** 6.30pm-2am daily. **BB**. No credit cards. **Chinese**. **Map** p85 B4 ⑱

Visit Soi Texas by day and there's not much to see. But by night, customers in this hectic spur off Yaowarat dig into lobster-sized river prawns, mud crabs, sea bass and other specialties. Rut and Lek run the more famous of two seafood operations on facing corners. Just upstream, another exulted institution, Texas Suki, serves all manner of Cantonese and Thai fare in raucous atmosphere, but the real reason to eat here is the *suki* – simmering, tabletop steamboats filled with veg and seafood, destined to be dunked in sauces.

Shopping

Bangkokians know Yaowarat sells certain products in certain streets. Aside from gold (**Thanon Yaowarat**) and specialist markets, one-street wonders include: herbalists (start of **Thanon Rama IV**); stationery (**Thanon Phatsai**); sacks (**Thanon Songsawat**); paper funeral offerings (**Thanon Phlubphlachai**) or ritual paraphernalia (**Thanon Plangnam**) such as masks, swords, tea sets and musical instruments.

Talad Fai Chai

Around Central Hospital on Thanons Luang, Chakrawat, Charoen Krung & Suapa. **Open** 5pm Sat-2am Sun. **Map** p85 B4 ⑲

Every Saturday, night vendors pitch trestles and mats to flog miscellany from amulets to old postcards. It's

BANGKOK BY AREA

Soi Texas p89

called Talad Fai Chai (Flashlight Market) as you often need a torch to sift treasures from all the dreck.

Talad Khlong Thom
Thanon Mahachak, between Thanon Yaowarat & Thanon Charoen Krung.
Open 9am-6pm daily. **Map** p85 B4 ⑳
Foreigners rub chest-to-shoulder with Thais amid engines, wheels and other machinery in an area also rife with electrical repairers and homewares.

Talad Saphan Lek
Thanon Boriphat, around Grande Ville Hotel. **Open** 9am-6pm daily.
Map p85 A4 ㉑
Named after an old iron bridge over Khlong Ong Ang, this meandering alley market dips below street level. Shelves heave with cameras, toy guns, sunglasses and shoes, while shops stock appliances.

Trok Itsaranuphap
Soi Itsaranupharp, Yaowarat Sois 23 & 14, Charoen Krung Sois 16 & 21. **Open** 5am-6pm Mon-Sat.
Map p85 B4 ㉒

Chinatown's narrowest, most diverse thoroughfare begins at Pei-Ing School on Thanon Songwat with toy and game shops. Beyond Sampeng Lane, dried fish predominates. Skirting the 200-year-old Talad Kao (Old Market) meat and fish centre, Trok Itsaranuphap widens and changes name to fruit-filled Yaowarat Soi 23. Across Thanon Yaowarat, as Soi 14, it purveys pickles and spices. The lane becomes Charoen Krung Soi 16 as it passes Talad Mai (New Market), a more popular, century-old meat wholesaler with a famous shrine. Across Thanon Charoen Krung, as Soi 21, it ends flogging funeral wares.

Woeng Nakhon Kasem
Thanon Chakrawat, at Thanon Charoen Krung. **Open** 9am-6pm Mon-Sat. **Map** p85 A4 ㉓
Once dubbed 'Thieves Market', though it's no longer fencing stolen goods, this charming, hectic area hosts all things audio, as well as culinary contraptions. Home cooks, DJs, producers and the curious mingle. At a vendor on Nakhon Kasem Soi 4, create your own dessert from what's in antique copper bowls.

BANGKOK BY AREA

Pahurat

Chinatown is divided into ethnic trading areas, with Little India defined by Thanon Chakkaphet, Thanon Triphet and Thanon Pahurat. On the east side of Chakkaphet huddle travel agents, seedy cafés blasting Punjabi rock, restaurants, dessert sellers and video outlets. Bangkok's main Sikh temple looms amid the textile-focused **Pahurat Market**. On its Thanon Pahruat side, Thai dance costumiers face the **Old Siam Plaza** and its adjacent gun shops.

Sights & museums

Sri Guru Singh Sabha

Thanon Pahurat (0 2221 1011). Tha Saphan Phut. **Open** 6am-5pm daily. **Admission** free. **Map** p85 A4 ㉔
Sikh community life revolves around their principal temple, a four-storey tower topped by gilded onion domes. Vendors skirting the base sell garlands, incense, statues, saris, bangles, bindis and spiced *chai* tea.

Eating & drinking

Royal India

392/1 Thanon Chakraphet (0 2221 6565). Tha Saphan Phut. **Open** 11am-10pm daily. **B**. No credit cards. **Indian**. **Map** p85 A4 ㉕
Pahurat teems with small curry operations, most famously Royal India. Photos of Thai politicians adorn the walls, although as Thais tend to dislike Indian food, they may not have actually sampled the excellent North Indian dishes. Outside its ornately carved door, Indian sweet makers stir huge woks of confectionery.

Shopping

India Emporium

Thanon Chakkaphet at Thanon Pahurat (0 2623 9301-2/www.indian emporiummall.com). Tha Saphan Phut. **Open** 9am-6pm daily. **Map** p85 A4 ㉖
Sweltering sightseers and shoppers craving air-con can breathe in Bangkok's first mall for Indian goods. Replacing the burnt-out ATM Department Store, it holds tailors, accessories, a café, chain restaurants and a top-floor Indian food court.

Old Siam Plaza

12 Thanon Tripetch (0 2226 0156-8). **Open** 9am-7pm daily. **Map** p85 A4 ㉗
Retro-styled, this three-storey air-con bazaar holds traditional jewellers and silk retailers, clothes, household goods and computer repairs. Under the atrium, costumed women use original recipes and equipment to create Thai snacks and desserts like *khanom krok* (coconut milk batter steamed in tiny iron moulds). In a quirky top-floor food court, elders croon from a stage.

Talad Pahurat

Thanon Chakkaphet & Thanon Pahurat. Tha Saphan Phut. **Open** 9am-6pm daily. **Map** p85 A4 ㉘
The heart of Little India, Pahurat is awash with fabrics and textiles, from rainbows of saris to Thai and Chinese silks, synthetics and cottons. Winding alleys are filled with incense sellers, teahouses stocking fine *chai* tea and lassis, plus food markets, collectives of sewing women and a Sikh temple.

Arts & leisure

Sala Chalermkrung

66 Thanon Charoen Krung (0 2224 4499/0 2623 8148-9/www. salachalermkrung.com). **Open** *Khon* 7.30pm Fri, Sat. **Tickets** B1,200-B1,000. No credit cards. **Map** p85 A4 ㉙
Amid art deco and wrought-iron grandeur, condensed *khon* is staged at this early cinema with more narrative clarity and audience explanation than is provided elsewhere. The dancing is fair to good, and the staging spectacular, if a little impersonal.

Bangrak

Bangrak & Riverside

Bangrak is Bangkok's CBD (downtown), wedged between the river and Thanon Rama IV like a harp with strings along Thanons Sathorn, Silom, Surawong and Siphraya. These are all paved along or above *khlongs* (canals), part of a 19th-century city expansion of plantations and compounds of the Sino-Thai new-rich, some of whose mansions survive. The CBD spread from the original port of the Old Farang Quarter, around the **Oriental Hotel**. Now luxury hotels line both banks: the Bangrak riverside and Khlong San, the latter now reached by a BTS Skytrain extension as well as ferries.

Khlong Chong Nonsi, flanked by Thanon Narathiwat Ratchanakharin, divides Bangrak in half. The area north towards **Lumphini Park** is increasingly known by its BTS station name Saladaeng. Bangrak means 'village of love', and Saladaeng plays host to the gay scene and the fleshpots of **Patpong**.

Old Farang Quarter

Farang is Thai for Westerner (probably from *français*), and the left bank of the Chao Phraya between Chinatown to Sathorn was the European settlement. One of many ethnic enclaves ringing the walled old city, it was served by Siam's first paved road, British-built Thanon Charoen Krung (aka New Road). But it wasn't only Christian. Muslim, Hindu, Mon and Chinese communities added to the cosmopolitan colour amid the banks, businesses, shops, households and hotels.

The **Oriental Hotel** retains some of that bygone charm in its Author's Wing. This is a neighbourhood best seen by walking – and by boat to see the frontages. By land, beyond the antiques mall OP Place housed, in a 1905 department store (Charoenkrung Soi 38), Soi 38 has the stately French Embassy, the

BANGKOK BY AREA

wooden homes surrounding Haroon Mosque and the mouldering classical Customs House (a future Aman resort). Past the art deco Central Post Office stand the grand Portuguese Embassy and a bigger antiques mall, **River City**.

'New Road' maintains a human-scale appeal, with antique and craft shops, tailors, restaurants and the animated Bangrak Market. Heritage reminders further inland include **Blue Elephant**, **Silom Village**, **Bangkokian Museum** and the **Neilson Hays Library**. As well as antiques, this area is a hub of contemporary art galleries.

Sights & museums

Assumption Cathedral
23 Charoen Krung Soi 4 (0 2234 8556). Tha Oriental. **Open** 6am-6pm daily. **Admission** free. No credit cards. **Map** p94 B1 **1**
Through an arch facing the Oriental, a tree-lined piazza links a Catholic mission with this red brick cathedral. Built in 1910, it has twin towers and a fine marble altar. At its riverfront stand the classical edifices of the neglected East Asiatic Company (EAC built in 1901), and Chartered Bank, now part of Assumption School.

Bangkokian Museum
273 Charoen Krung Soi 43 (0 2234 6741). Tha Oriental. **Open** 10am-4pm Wed-Sun. **Admission** free. No credit cards. **Map** p94 B4 **2**
A charming residence kept in the decor of the owner's parents, it records mid 20th-century bourgeois Thai lifestyle. An Indian doctor's house in the grounds adds diversity.

Maha Uma Devi
2 Thanon Pan (0 2238 4007). Surasak BTS. **Open** 6am-8pm daily. **Admission** free. **Map** p94 C5 **3**
Founded in the 1860s by resident Tamils, this teeming Hindu temple is

dubbed Wat Khaek ('guest temple'). Thais and Chinese, too, make offerings to Uma Devi (Shiva's consort), and images of Vishnu, Buddha and Ganesh. The multi-hue walls and tower bristle with sculptures. Rites of self-mortification take place here during October's Navaratree Festival (p37), and the temple observes Diwali (October/November).

Neilson Hays Library
195 Thanon Surawong (0 2233 1731/ www.neilsonhayslibrary.com). **Open** 9.30am-5pm Tue-Sun. **Admission** non-members B50. **Map** p94 C4 **4**
This beautiful colonial-ish building from 1922 offers the best English reading in town, plus art shows in the Rotunda. The British Club next door runs its café.

Eating & drinking

For hotel dining, see box p131.

Dome: Sirocco, Mezzaluna, Breeze & Distil
63rd floor, LeBua at State Tower, 1055 Thanon Silom (0 2624 9555). Saphan Taksin BTS. **Open** 6pm-1am daily. **BBBB**. **International**. **Map** p94 B5 **5**
An astonishing 200m-high (656-foot) rooftop restaurant, Sirocco boasts unrestrained Greco-Roman architecture and giddying views over Bangkok and the river (see box p96). Sweep down the large stone staircase past the jazz quartet to the garden terrace tables for some quite good Mediterranean cuisine. Its Sky Bar mixes the stiff drinks needed to look down. Inside, the sumptuous Distil bar boasts an imposing choice of drinks and cigars, with a breezy bed-lined terrace. It shares the Dome with Mezzaluna, a half-moon-shaped fine-dining Italian restaurant with string quartet. A few floors lower, the Breeze serves Pan-Asian seafood on a terrace, accessed via a sci-fi style bridge. Booking is essential. Premium prices.

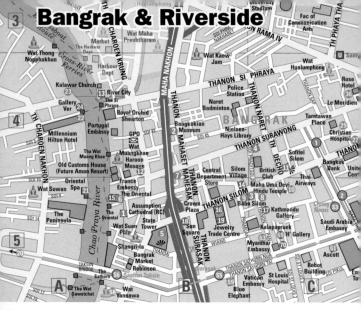

Bangrak & Riverside

China House

*Charoen Krung Soi 38 (0 2236 0400
ext 3378/www.mandarinoriental.com).*
Saphan Taksin BTS. **Open** 6-10pm
Mon-Sat; 11.30am-2.30pm Sun. **BBBB**.
Chinese. Map p94 A5 ⑥
Just by the Oriental door, this quiet,
timeless dining space occupies a
Fabergé-delicate heritage house,
redone in sumptuous 1930s Shanghai
style with red silk, wood screens and
'opium bed' booths. The long menu is
rooted in haunting Cantonese flavours,
with some fun innovations.

Indian Hut

*311/2-5 Thanon Surawong (0 2237
8812). Surawong MRT then taxi.*
Open 11am-11pm daily. **BBB**.
Indian. Map p94 B4 ⑦
Don't be misled by the ill-advised Pizza
Hut-style logo – this top-notch north
Indian offers deep, robust flavours, and
exceptional creamy Kashmiri options.
If you can, eat upstairs, as the decor is
much better on the first floor.

Khrua Aroi Aroi

*Thanon Pan, opposite Wat Khaek
(0 2635 2365).* Surasak BTS. **Open**
7am-6.30pm daily. **B**. No credit cards.
Thai. Map p94 C5 ⑧
Khanom jeen is a quick-fix fave of curries spooned over rice noodles and
eaten with cooling, crunchy herbs and
vegetables. This two-level shop (it
means 'delicious delicious') offers
tastes from jungle curries and chilli
dips to coconuty Muslim varieties and
classic green curry.

Silom Restaurant

*793 Silom Soi 15 (0 2236 4443/4268).
Chong Nonsri BTS.* **Open** 10.30am-
9pm daily. **BB**. No credit cards.
Thai/Chinese. Map p94 B5 ⑨
Hainanese-fusion was an early Asian
fad. Here, pork chops, noodles and the
like bear the imprint of palates colonial,
Thai and Chinese. Protein to satisfy a
big foreigner, with bold, salty overtones
of soy, garlic and spice that lure Sino-
Thais to this timewarp dining hall.

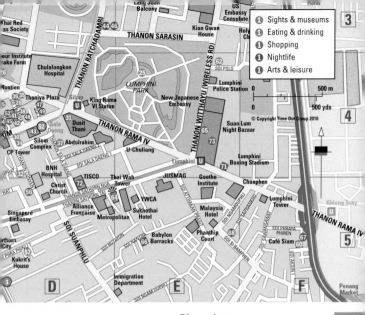

Tamil Nadu

5/1 Silom Soi 11 (0 2235 6336/6325). Chong Nonsri BTS. **Open** 10am-9pm daily. **B**. No credit cards. **Indian**. Map p94 C5 ❿

Bangrak's Hindu population has spawned a plethora of cheap, no-frills cafés. This one is clean, has air-con and offers good south Indian food, in particular the *masala dosa*.

V9

37th floor, Sofitel Silom Hotel, 188 Thanon Silom (0 2238 1991/www. sofitel.com). Chong Nonsi BTS. **Open** 5pm-2am Mon-Sat. **BBBB. Wine Bar/International**. Map p94 C4 ⓫

Given high taxes, this slick wine bar – with fine views – is great value for sampling from the Wine Connection chain (www.wineconnection.co.th) via a 'wine buffet' of three mini-glasses for the price of one. A sommelier also pairs wines to dishes on the global menu. DJs (10pm-1.30am Mon-Sat) play chillout to get diners on to the dance area.

Shopping

OP Garden

Thanon Charoen Krung at Soi 36. Saphan Thaksin BTS. **Open** *Shops vary, but typically* 11am-8pm daily. Map p94 B4 ⓬

A charming old wooden hospital converted into a select lifestyle precinct. Buying ops include chic kitsch by Reflections (see p179) and Himalayan-focused arts, photography and books from Sirindia Gallery (0 2238 6410, www.sirindiagallery.com). In the middle, Mango Tree Signature's restaurant and open-sided bar (0 238 6400) concocts Thai dishes with high end imported ingredients.

River City

River City Complex, 23 Thanon Yotha (0 2237 0077-8/www.rivercity.co.th). Tha Siphraya. **Open** 10am-7pm daily. Map p94 A4 ⓭

A specialist mall with antiquities of museum standard. The auction lots get

Hi in the sky

Sirocco

Bangkokians are all too familiar with the street, where they eat, drink, sweat and sometimes suffer. Thus, it's easy to see why rooftop restaurants have gained such cachet in this cramped, humid soi-scape – they offer escapism, a view and a breeze.

Vertigo (p107), which sits astride the saddle-roofed Banyan Tree hotel on Sathorn, started the trend for open-air dining atop a skyscraper. **Sirocco**, which looms over a slow elbow of the river from the Dome at LeBua (p93), made the idea iconic – the global signal that Bangkok was suddenly chic.

The narrow Vertigo and its casual **Moon Bar** inspire queasiness as you step onto the 61st-floor deck, to which runners stair-race every September in a Vertical Marathon. Dining here is an intimate affair with crisp linens, doting service and a menu of steaks and grilled seafood.

Its strict dress code is surpassed by the highfalutin' LeBua – not even knapsacks allowed. **Sirocco** places greater emphasis on the food, with an upscale Italian menu served against a backdrop of hulking classical pillars, and extraordinary views. The **Sky Bar**, a crowded cusp with glass rails overhanging a 65-storey drop, provides Bangkok's coolest snapshot – if the zealous bouncers let you.

New vistas open up as skyscrapers in-build this concept; both Vertigo and Sirocco were add-ons. Central World has two. **Red Sky** (p120) offers fine dining and a wine bar from a 55th-floor perch, framed by vari-coloured hoops. Slightly cheaper, **Zense**, on the 17th floor of Zen department store, is a something-for-everyone eaterie that serves Japanese, Indian, Italian and Thai fare.

To avoid the hundred-dollar-a-head bills and overly dim lighting many people skip the eating and go to these bars just for sundowner drinks.

Those with lower budgets have less elevated rooftop alternatives, like the **Gazebo** Moroccan bar-restaurants in Banglamphu and Sukhumvit (p83), and **Phranakorn Bar** (p68), where in-the-know hipsters have a private panorama of the Golden Mount.

displayed in the week before gavel time. The Riverside Auction House of River City mall (p95) shows East Asian antiques for a week before auctions (1.30-4pm 1st Sat). Old Maps & Prints (shop 432, 0 2237 0077, www.classicmaps.com) is the city's finest source of historical charts and hand-coloured engravings, mainly of Asia.

Silom Village

286 Thanon Silom, between Sois 22 & 24 (0 2234 4581/www.silomvillage. co.th). Surasak MRT. **Open** 11.30am-11pm daily. **Shows** *Indoors* 8.20-9.30pm daily. *Outdoors* 7.45, 8.45pm daily. **BBB. Map** p94 B5 ⑭

Get lacquer, *lakhon* and lobster simultaneously! Arcades of craft shops adapted from old houses ring a seafood dinner theatre where the camera-happy snap regional dances. Opposite, Baan Silom is a new-resembling-old court of shops and eateries.

Nightlife

Bamboo Bar

Oriental Hotel, 48 Charoen Krung Soi 38 (0 2236 0400). Saphan Taksin BTS. **Open** 11am-1am Mon-Thur, Sun; 11am-2am Fri, Sat. **BBB. Map** p94 A5 ⑮

A snug, low-ceilinged cocktail lounge of 1940s mystique. Despite the long jazz pedigree and fine house band, the US singers have dipped in quality.

Arts & leisure

Asian Institute of Gemological Sciences

33rd floor, Jewellery Trade Centre, 919/1 Thanon Silom (0 2267 4315-9/www.aigsthailand.com). Surasak BTS. **Open** 8am-6pm Mon-Fri. No credit cards. **Map** p94 B5 ⑯

Avoid scams in this world jewel hub; learn to identify genuine gems on short courses, or take degree-level classes in such lapidary topics as crystal structure, geology, design and synthetics.

Kathmandu Photo Gallery

87 Thanon Pan (0 2234 6700). Surasak BTS. **Open** 11am-7pm Tue-Sun. **Map** p94 C5 ⑰

Photographer Manit Srivanichpoom and artist-filmmaker Ing K exhibit artful lenswork upstairs in this retro, mint-green shophouse facing the Hindu temple. They also stock South Asian crafts and books on photography and philosophy.

Nicolie Asian Massage Centre

Sun Square, 1041/5 Thanon Silom (0 2233 6957/www.nicolie-th.com). Surasak BTS. **Open** 12.30am-9pm daily. **Map** p94 B5 ⑱

Resembling an antiques gallery on several floors, Nicolie carefully conducts Thai, shiatsu, Chinese *tui na*, Balinese and Ayurvedic massages.

Silom Galleria

919/1 Thanon Silom (0 2630 0944-50/www.thesilomgalleria.com). Surasak BTS. **Open** 10am-8pm daily. **Map** p94 B5 ⑲

Contemporary Thai art and Chinese antiques draw aesthetes to this vast atrium in the back of the Jewellery Trade Center. You can join exhibition openings at its half-dozen galleries. Thavibu (3rd floor, 0 2266 5454, www.thavibu. com, 10am-7pm Tue-Sat; noon-6pm Sun) promotes artists from the lands in its name (THAIland, VIetnam, BUrma) – plus Laos. Tang (basement, 0 2630 1114 ext 0, www.tangcontemporary.com, 11am-7pm Mon-Sat) spotlights big-ticket Chinese and Thai names. Soulflower (basement, 0 2630 0032, www. gallerysoulflower.com, 11am-7pm Mon-Sat) curates Thai and Indian shows.

Khlong San

Across the Chao Phraya from Bangrak, this district on *Fang Thon* (Thonburi side) has spawned three top hotels. Best reached by ferry, the Marriott Bangkok Resort is like

Kathmandu Photo Gallery p97

staying upcountry, while the luxurious Peninsula soars beside the Oriental Spa. Facing River City, the white saucer-topped Millennium Hilton stands by lively, commuter-jammed Khlong San Market and Yok Yor restaurant. The BTS extension here really only leads to the King Taksin statue.

Some boat tours from Tha Saphan Thaksin may offer glimpses of old canal life along Khlong Daokhanong, Khlong Bangkhuntien and Khlong Lart towards picturesque Wat Sai.

Sights & museums

King Taksin the Great Statue

Wong Wien Yai roundabout. Wong Wien Yai BTS. **Map** p94 A5 ⑳
Cast in 1951 by Silpa Bhirasri (p59), this equestrian statue (a lucky 9m tall by 9m long) marks Thonburi's founder, who re-united Siam after the sack of Ayutthaya in 1767. Brandishing a sword and Stetson-esque hat, he directs a vehicular armada through daunting gridlock from a park within a round-about. Rites are held here on the date of his coronation (28 Dec).

Eating & drinking

For hotel dining, see box p131.

Sala Rim Nam

Opposite Oriental Hotel, 48 Charoen Krung Soi 38 (0 2236 0400). Saphan Taksin BTS then take the Oriental shuttle boat. **Open** 7-10pm daily. **Shows** 8.30-9.45pm daily. **BBBB.** **Thai.** **Map** p94 A5 ㉑
Performers do excerpts of *khon* masked dance at this opulent, *vihaan*-style restaurant serving a reasonable Thai menu. Reach it by ferry from its owner, the Oriental.

Three Sixty

32nd floor, Millennium Hilton Bangkok Hotel, 123 Thanon Charoen Nakorn (0 2442 2000/www.hilton.com). Take the Hilton ferry from Tha Saphan Thaksin or Tha River City. **Open** 5pm-2am daily. **Bar.** **Map** p94 A4 ㉒
Via a dizzying trip in a glazed elevator, you whizz up to this flying saucer-shaped penthouse bar, for a full-circle panorama of both old town and new, while overhanging the river. Otherwise, it's merely plush seating, cocktails and live soft jazz.

Yok Yor Marina & Restaurant

885 Somdet Chao Praya Soi 17 (0 2863 0565-6/www.yokyor.co.th). **Open** *Restaurant* 11am-midnight daily. *Tours* 8am-10pm daily. **BB**.

Thai. **Map** p94 A4 ㉓

This pier seafood restaurant has a dance stage, and runs dinner cruises aboard a double-decker steel boat, live band and a taped guide in Thai and English (B140 plus food).

Arts & leisure

Gallery Ver

2nd floor, 71/31-35 Khlong San Plaza, Thanon Charoen Nakorn (0 2861 0933/ www.verver.info). **Open** 1-7pm Tue-Sat. No credit cards. **Map** p94 A4 ㉔

Named for the Thai slang for 'severe' (from the English 'over'), this breezy riverside gallery is homebase for Rirkrit Tiravanija, a world-renowned relational artist. Pivotal art figures attend openings that are typically curated by Pratchaya Phinthong, and watch indy video screenings.

Saladaeng

An old red pavilion (*saladaeng*) once stood in plantations where this office and social hub now churns night and day. Thanon Silom gets its name from irrigation windmills, hence the turbine sculpture where it crosses Khlong Chong Nonsi. Now the sky's obscured by the BTS, bringing commuters and visitors to get things done and wind down in the only one of Bangkok's official nightlife zones that's located downtown: **Patpong**.

Go-go bars line Patpong Soi 1, while bar-beers tank up lonely boozehounds in Patpong Soi 2 (see box p104). Silom Soi 4 has trendy, non-prostitution bars, the increasing majority being gay as mainstream nightlife disperses

citywide. Other all-gay bar/club sois are Silom Soi 2 and Silom Soi 2/1, while the gay go-go enclaves are Silom Soi 6 and Soi Duangthawee Plaza (aka Soi Twilight) off Thanon Surawong. Massage parlours flood the entire area. Some are overtly sexual, but many on Silom and in Surawong Plaza are legit, offering reflexology and spa treatments by women or men; however, staff at some may discreetly offer 'happy endings'.

Facing **Lumpini Park**, the spired, triangular **Dusit Thani** hotel provides fine dining and **Deverana Spa** (see box p172). Off Silom towards Sathorn, Soi Saladaeng and Soi Convent offer dining options. Connecting to tawdrier Thanon Surawong, **Soi Thaniya** is a 'Little Tokyo' of sushi joints and Japanese-only hostess bars.

Visitors to Saladaeng are often as surprised by passing elephants (their mahouts expecting payment for photos), as they are by the fried insect snacks sold from carts, and deposits from the thousands of Siberian swallows that flock here from October to March. Copping a dropping is, rationalise the Thais, good luck.

Sights & museums

Lumphini Park

192 Thanon Rama IV (0 2252 7006). Ratchadamri BTS/Silom MRT/ Lumphini MRT. **Open** 4.30am-9pm daily. **Map** p95 E4 ㉕

Named after Buddha's birthplace in Nepal, the capital's best green enclave was donated in 1925 by King Rama VI, whose statue dominates the gate opposite Silom. It's most interesting early and late, when paths encircling its pagoda and lakes (pedalos can be hired) host joggers, t'ai chi classes, mass aerobics, outdoor gym workouts, ballroom dancers and acrobatic *takraw* games.

There's a restaurant to the north-west, and even more picnickers than usual attend free Music in the Park concerts (p38). By night, women solicit along the east side, gays on the west.

Snake Farm

Queen Saovabha Memorial Institute, 1871 Thanon Rama IV (0 2252 0161-4/www.redcross.or.th). Saladaeng BTS/Silom MRT. **Open** 9.30am-4pm Mon-Fri; 9.30am-noon Sat, Sun. **Shows** 11am, 2.30pm Mon-Fri; 11am Sat, Sun. Closed 5 Dec. **Admission** B40 Thais; B200 foreigners. No credit cards.
Map p95 D4 ㉖

Run by the Thai Red Cross, the world's second snake farm (1922) does research and treatment on venomous bites. Since the serpents mostly doze, go for the slideshow and demo, where wise-cracking hosts handle lethal snakes and milk their venom. Yes, you can wear a boa (a live one).

Eating & drinking

Aoi

132/10-11 Silom Soi 6 (0 2235 2321-2). Saladaeng BTS/Silom MRT. **Open** 11am-2.30pm, 6-10.30pm daily. **BBB**. **Japanese**. **Map** p94 C4 ㉗

This traditional slate-walled tavern a few blocks south of Thaniya's Little Tokyo is the area's best Japanese restaurant. Prices are slightly higher, but reflect the quality, service and Kyoto-esque interior, all pebbles, lanterns and paper screens.

Barbican

9/4-5 Soi Thaniya (0 2234 3590/www.greatbritishpub.com). Saladaeng BTS/Silom MRT. **Open** 11.30am-1am daily. **BBB**. **English pub**. **Map** p95 D4 ㉘

From the owners of the Bull's Head (p134), this modernist pub goes against the Japanese grain of Soi Thaniya. It draws expats and westernised Thais with regular DJs, lucrative prize games and Premiership screenings upstairs.

Coca Suki

8 Soi Anuman Ratchadhon (0 2236 0107). Saladaeng BTS/Silom MRT. **Open** 11am-2pm, 5-10pm Mon-Sat; 11am-10pm Sun. **BB**. **Sukiyaki**.
Map p94 C4 ㉙

Sociability and *sanuk* converge in *suki*, a favourite Thai variant of Japanese *sukiyaki*, where you order trays of ingredients to cook in a table-top pot.

Coyote

Sivadon Building, 1/2 Thanon Convent (0 2631 2325/www.coyoteoncovent. com). Saladaeng BTS/Silom subway. **Open** 11am-midnight daily. **BBB**. **Mexican**. **Map** p95 D4 ㉚

This fun Mexican restaurant bar boasts the country's largest selection of tequilas and Margaritas. Among the office crowd, ties loosen over two buzzing terracotta floors. Chilled jugs and gargantuan spicy platters fuel the mood.

D'Sens

Dusit Thani Hotel, 946 Thanon Rama IV (0 2236 9999). Saladaeng BTS/ Silom MRT. **Open** 11.30am-2pm, 6.30-10pm Mon-Fri; 6.30-10pm Sat. **BBBB**. **Modern French**.
Map p95 D4 ㉛

The angular 1970 architecture of the Dusit Thani penthouse (p171) makes a distinctive setting for this branch of the three Michelin-starred brothers Jacques and Laurent Pourcel. They tweak the menu with chef Philippe Keller (ex-Sketch, London). Masterful dishes like roasted turbot fillet on a bed of parsley-stuffed pig's trotter with citrus flavoured meat *jus*, and wonderful desserts, justify the prices.

Eat Me!

1/6 Phiphat Soi 2, Thanon Convent (0 2238 0931). Saladaeng BTS/Silom MRT. **Open** 3pm-1am daily. **BBB**. **Australian fusion**. **Map** p95 D4 ㉜

Expanding into roof and garden, but ever full, the city's premier art restaurant attracts a cool clientele and an interesting East-West fusion menu that

Aoi

includes tuna tartare with soba noodles and cabbage salad. People linger for drinks over the well-selected music.

Le Bouchon

37/17 Patpong Soi 2 (0 2234 9109). Saladaeng BTS/Silom MRT. **Open** noon-3pm, 7-11pm Mon-Sat; 7-11pm Sun. **BBB**. **French**. **Map** p95 D4 ⓷⓷

Le Bouchon is perhaps BKK's most authentic French bistro, and the top regular dining spot for local Gauls. The very small bar buzzes with *joie de vivre* as diners wait to be seated at one of only seven tables. Expect simple but good country cooking.

Molly Malone's

1/5-6 Sivadol Building, Soi Convent (0 2266 7160-1/www.irishxchange.com). Saladaeng BTS/Silom subway. **Open** 8.30am-1am daily. **BBB**. **Irish pub**. **Map** p95 D4 ⓷⓸

Yet another name change for this brass and mahogany pub. It acts as a social embassy for expats, with Irish stew and ales aplenty on tap (including Guinness), footie on the TV and the occasional live gig. You might just forget that you're in Thailand – presumably that's the point.

Roadhouse BBQ

942/1-4 Thanon Rama IV, at Surawong (0 2236 8010). Saladaeng BTS/Silom MRT/Samyan MRT. **Open** 10.30am-1am daily. **BBB**. **American**. **Map** p95 D4 ⓷⓹

Roadhouse BBQ is a monster three-storey pub with a distinctly American character, barbecue food and smokery. Check out the excellent buffalo wings from the meaty menu, good-value wines and choice of microbrewed beers. The top-floor games room offers pool and shuffleboard.

Ruen Urai

Rose Hotel, Thanon Surawong (0 2266 8268-72) Saladaeng BTS/Samyan MRT. **Open** 11am-11pm daily. **BBB**. **Thai**. **Map** p95 C4 ⓷⓺

Patpong's sleaze soon dissolves in the lane to Ruen Urai. Suddenly, you'll find an exquisite early-Rattanakosin era teak house, painstakingly restored and decorated with weathered antiques and vivid silk. Ruen Urai traffics in easy sophistication – classic cocktails and a well-curated wine list alongside Thai recipes with subtle updates. It was once home to an herbalist doctor, hence the focus on fragrant Thai herbs.

Ruen Urai p101

Zanotti

Saladaeng Colonnade, 21/2 Soi Saladaeng (0 2636 0002). Saladaeng BTS/Silom MRT. **Open** 11.30am-2pm, 6-11pm daily. **BBBB. Italian.** **Map** p95 D4 ㊲

A frenetic, upmarket must-dine for over a decade. The pace means quality can vary on the excellent, diverse menu, specialising in orange wood charcoaling. Ebullient chef-patron Gian-Maria Zanotti also runs Torino café next door, Vino di Zanotti wine bar opposite (41 Soi Yommarat, 0 2636 0855) and wood-fired Pizza Patio delivery (0 2718 7000).

Shopping

Art's Tailors

62/15-16 Soi Thaniya (0 2234 0874). Saladaeng BTS/Silom MRT. **Open** 9am-4.30pm Mon-Sat. No credit cards. **Map** p95 D4 ㊳

Master tailors hunch over benches to churn out high-quality suits at this decades-old institution – a favourite with powerful politicians and corporate fat cats. Quality comes at a price: two-piece suits start from B40,000. Allow for two fittings over two weeks.

Jim Thompson Thai Silk

9 Thanon Surawong (0 2632 8100-4/www.jimthompson.com). Saladaeng BTS/Silom MRT. **Open** 9am-9pm daily. **Map** p95 D4 ㊴

The Thai silk pioneer has ventured beyond pillowcases, scarves and clubby neckties into high fashion, palatial interior design and experimental silk art projects. Witness its revival of block printing and the lustrous furnishings by trend leaders like Ed Tuttle, Christian Duc and Ou Baholyodhin. Branches are found at Jim Thompson's House Museum (p112) and many malls and five-star hotels.

Patpong & Silom Night Bazaar

Thanon Silom between & Patpong Soi 1. Saladaeng BTS. **Open** 6pm-2am daily. **Map** p95 D4 ㊵

Aside from the string of lurid go-go bars (p99), Patpong Soi 1 also bombards shoppers – who mostly consist of couples, groups and families – with stalls flogging copy watches, fake Levi's or pirate discs of music, movies, games and – via whispers and hand-scrawled signs – 'DVD Sex'. Stalls vending trendier clubwear and decor items spread outward between Silom Sois 8 and Thanon Rama IV.

Tamnan Mingmuang

3rd floor, Thaniya Plaza, Thanon Silom (0 2231 2120). Saladaeng BTS/Silom MRT. **Open** 11am-8pm daily. **Map** p95 D4 ④

Pornroj Angsanakul applies weaving expertise in fresh ways and exhibits astonishingly lifelike figurines. His baskets, boxes and handbags also come in wild grass, water hyacinth and ultra-fine *yan lipao* vine. On the same floor, the Legend branch (0 2231 2170) sells more mainstream souvenirs.

Thaniya Plaza

52 Thanon Thaniya (0 2231 2244/ www.thaniyagroup.com). Saladaeng BTS/Silom MRT. **Open** 10am-10pm daily. **Map** p95 D4 ④

A veritable world of Tiger wannabes with over 30 golf shops, some at discounts, many catering to Japanese.

Viera by Ragazze

2nd floor, Silom Complex, Thanon Silom (0 2231 3190/www.ragazze. co.th). Saladaeng BTS/Silom MRT. **Open** 10.30am-9pm daily. **Map** p95 D4 ④

Employing both leather and lighter materials, this Italian-influenced Thai company's bags, footwear and wallets remain up-to-the-minute stylish.

Nightlife

70s Bar

231/16 Thanon Sarasin (0 2253 4433). Ratchadamri BTS. **Open** 6pm-1am daily. **Map** p95 D3 ④

Dressy young Thai gays now rule this packed retro bar – and many of the other pubs on a long-standing parkside strip that faces redevelopment.

Balcony

86-88 Silom Soi 4, off Thanon Silom (0 2235 5891/www.balconypub.com).

Saladaeng BTS/Silom MRT. **Open** 5.30pm-2am daily. **Thai**. **Map** p95 D4 ④

People-watching terraces spread out from this cheap and cheerful rendezvous, with happy hour prize draws, ultra-familiar staff and chalkboards in the loo for scrawling profundities.

Brown Sugar

231/20 Thanon Sarasin (0 2250 1826). Ratchadamri BTS/Silom MRT. **Open** 5pm-1am daily. *Bands* 8pm-1am Sat-Sun. **BB**. **International**. **Map** p95 D3 ④

An old favourite that retains an earthy, clubby ambience, but is getting shabby. Thai and expat musicians and singers reel out jazz covers with often inspired playing, jams (some Sun) and a bit of blues (Fri, Sat).

DJ Station

Silom Soi 2, Thanon Silom (0 2266 4029/www.dj-station.com). Saladaeng BTS/Silom MRT. **Open** 10pm-2am daily. **Admission** B100 incl 1 drink Sun-Thur; Sun-Thur B200 incl 2 drinks Sun-Thur. No credit cards. **Map** p95 D4 ④

Despite extending via a bridge across Soi 2, all three floors heave with Thais and *farang* of all ages, tastes and agendas; it's more commercial the higher up you go. Opposite, the dance bar branch Disco Disco (DD) is less crowded. In between, sticky-rice queens stick together in The Expresso (0 2632 7223), a dance 'lounge' by the same owner with a waterfall wall, ladyboy staff and a catty 1am drag cabaret.

GOD (Guys on Display)

60/18-21 Silom Soi 2/1 (0 2632 8033). Saladaeng BTS/Silom MRT. **Open** 10pm-late daily. **Shows** midnight-12.30am daily. **Admission** B120 before 1am (incl 1 drink); B240 after 1am (incl 2 drinks). No credit cards. **Map** p95 D4 ④

Post-DJ Station clubbers shift to this three-storey club with coyote dancers and edgier music.

Poles apart

Patpong

The infamous eldest sibling of Bangkok's entertainment districts, **Patpong** (p99) today proffers some of the city's grubbier go-go bars. Visitors run a gauntlet of touts armed with laminated menus down the neon-lit Patpong Soi 1 nightmarket: ping-pong show, shoot-dart show, open-bottle show.

For decades visitors have been ushered – by concierges, guides and sensationalist media – to Bangkok's adult nightlife. Anecdotes, boasts and jokes pump up its 'sexotic' reputation – though the often unerotic reality suffers from premature expectation.

Go-go bars aimed at Westerners have declined through changing tastes. In response, The Strip (Patpong Soi 2) started curtained table-dancing, with S&M the fetish at Bar Bar next door. Dance pubs like the semi open-air Funky Dojo (105 Patpong Soi 2, 08 155 0691) have also sprung up and stay open later.

On Sukhumvit, several 'bar-beer' (open-air hostess bar) areas have been cleared, but they persist on Sois 21-23 (Soi Cowboy, p139), Soi 22 and Soi 3-8 (Nana),

especially in **Nana Entertainment Plaza** (Sukhumvit Soi 4, p127), an escalator-equipped, three-storey 'go-go mall'. Some Nana bars employ *kathoeys* (ladyboys), while others (Casanova, Temptations and Cascade) are *kathoey*-only. The **Soi Cowboy** strip was fairly sedate, but has boomed due to shiny refurbishments.

Citywide, imaginative choreography (Angelwitch, Nana; Long Gun, Soi Cowboy) elevates some go-gos above the pack. Others rely on such gimmicks as mechanical bulls (Carnival, Nana) and glass dancefloors (Baccarac, Soi Cowboy). A few are more pub-like, such as Cathouse (Nana).

Many night workers are entrepreneurial husband-hunters and often aren't young. Rights tend to be more infringed in the Thai- and Asian-oriented sex industry, which is larger but less visible.

Moralistic crackdowns periodically tame the shows, but they resume unabated. Inflated bar bills and doped drinks are rarer now, with prices often fixed. But be alert to touts, scams, your valuables and dubious scenarios.

JJ Park & Club Café
8/3 Silom Soi 2 (0 2235 1227).
Saladaeng BTS/Silom MRT. **Open**
10.30pm-2am daily. **Map** p95 D4 🟠
A show gay bar with loyal customers,
JJ is warm and chatty, with nightly
singers (real and lip-sync) and comics.
Upstairs it connects via nooks to Club
Café, a Moorish chill-out bar with
under-floor water.

Lucifer
3rd floor, 76/1-3 Patpong Soi 1 (0
2266 4567). Saladaeng BTS/Silom
MRT. **Open** 10pm-2am daily.
Admission B150 (incl 1 drink).
Map p94 C4 🟠
Devil-uniformed attendants welcome
you to this hell-themed disco with dia-
bolically loud trance music luring
young tourists and expats. Well laid-
out and unlike the 'Pong's go-go bars,
it shares owners with open-terraced
Muzzik Café opposite.

Patpong
Patpong Sois 1 & 2. Saladaeng BTS.
Open 6pm-2am daily. **Map** p94 C4 🟠
The late Thai-Chinese millionaire Udom
Patpongpanit turned banana groves
into a playground for locals, expats and
aircrews. Patpong went a-go-go in the
late 1960s as US GIs flocked here on
R&R from the Vietnam War. The 'Pong
later blanded out into a Disneyfied
coach party stop, flogging tit and tat to
tourists. Guys gawp through doors at
lacklustre pole-dancing and novelty sex
shows in Patpong Soi 1, while open-air
bar-beers on Patpong Soi 2 take
drinkers to wherever they want to go.

Sphinx & Pharaoh's
Silom Soi 4 (0 2234 7249/www.
sphinxpub.com). Saladaeng BTS/Silom
MRT. **Open** 6pm-2am daily. *Karaoke*
8pm-2am daily. **BB. Thai/**
international. **Map** p95 D4 🟠
This classy, intimate bar-restaurant has
served the gay scene's best food (Thai
and foreign) for two decades. Pharaoh's
upstairs is a cosy karaoke lounge.

Tapas
114/17 Silom Soi 4 (0 2234 4737).
Saladaeng BTS/Silom MRT. **Open**
6.30pm-2am daily. **Admission** B100.
Map p95 D4 🟠
Originating in the 1990s house-music
boom, Tapas keeps hip *farang* and
media Thais trippy with its house-
party vibe, people-watching forecourt
and upstairs members' bar. DJs spin
Latin, deep, funk and house.

Telephone Pub
114/11-13 Silom Soi 4 (0 2234 3279/
www.telephonepub.com). Saladaeng
BTS/Silom MRT. **Open** 5pm-2am
daily. **BB. Thai**. **Map** p95 D4 🟠
Fun and flirty, Bangkok's first Western-
style gay bar-restaurant fills its terrace
with pretties, expats and tourists.
Phones allow cross-room dialling.

Arts & leisure

For Deverana Spa, see box p172.

Arima Onsen
37/10-14 Soi Surawong Plaza, Thanon
Surawong (0 2235 2142-3). Saladaeng
BTS/Silom MRT. **Open** 9am-1am
daily. No credit cards. **Map** p95 D4 🟠
Reflexology, *akasuri* body rubs, Thai
massage and Nipponese-style communal showers, steam room and baths,
plus VIP rooms and hair/nail care. Also
at 62/10-14 Soi Thaniya (0 2234 1777-8).

Ruen Nuad
2nd floor, 42 Thanon Convent (0 2632
2663). Saladaeng BTS. **Open** 10am-
9pm daily. **Map** p95 D5 🟠
This picturesque wooden home (at the
rear of an old house restaurant) provides
Thai, aromatherapy and herbal massages, with classy attention to detail.

Sathorn

This thunderous road was a genteel
millionaire's row until corporate
towers replaced most of the
European-style tropical wooden

mansions. The flame-tree lined canal was narrowed into a concrete chute, divorcing Thanon Sathorn Tai (north) from Thanon Sathorn Tai (south). Heritage gets little protection here. But the splendid Thai-Chinese Chamber of Commerce (built as the Bombay Department Store) was saved as **Blue Elephant** restaurant.

Among modern landmarks stand the robot-like Bank of Asia, designed by Sumet Jumsai, and the precariously narrow Thai Wah II Tower. It has a hole at the 50th floor, where you'll find the **Banyan Tree Bangkok** hotel. By 2012, Bangkok's tallest building, Mahanakorn, will rise by Chong Nonsi BTS, designed in 'eroded' style by Ole Scheeren.

In Sathorn's hinterland sois, cultural sights include **MR Kukrit Pramoj's Heritage Home**. Around Soi Ngam Duphli's grungy guesthouse zone (p175) lurk some bohemian bars.

At Sathorn's river end beside **Wat Yannawa**, the BTS usefully links to the Expressboats at Sathorn Bridge. At the Thanon Rama IV end, a gold-crested tower contains the holistic mall Life Centre. It faces **Suan Lum Night Bazaar** on the leafy embassy avenue of Thanon Witthayu. Once zoned as parkland, this popular asset – along with **Thai Traditional Puppet Theater** and **Lumphini Muay Thai Stadium** – faces eviction for condos, a mall and a rival 'tallest skyscraper'.

Sights & museums

MR Kukrit Pramoj's Heritage Home
19 Soi Phra Phinij, Thanon Sathorn Tai (0 2286 8185). **Open** 10am-5pm Sat, Sun. **Admission** B50; B20 students in uniform. No credit cards. **Map** p95 D5 ㊗

These five Central Plains stilt houses were the seat of the late aristocrat Mom Ratchawong Kukrit Pramoj. A cultural colossus, he is best known for his writing, promotion of *khon* dance, acting as an Asian prime minister in 1963 film *The Ugly American* with Marlon Brando, and being a real prime minister in the turbulent mid-1970s. Set by a pond in a garden of indigenous species, the house contains antiquities, photos and memorabilia.

Wat Yannawa
1648 Thanon Charoen Krung (0 2672 3216/www.watyan.com). Saphan Taksin BTS. **Open** *Temple* 5am-9pm daily. *Bot* 8-9am, 5-6pm daily. **Admission** free. **Map** p94 A5 ㊳ King Rama I first restored this Ayutthaya-era temple, and later King Rama III added a *chedi* platform that is shaped like a Chinese junk, complete with eyes on the prow, four cannons and a shrine in the stern. Amid considerable outrage, the *wat* demolished the historic Soi Wanglee neighbourhood at Charoen Krung Soi 52, where the shophouses were similarly styled to resemble the junks on which Chinese immigrants arrived at the pier that was once located here.

Eating & drinking

Blue Elephant
233 Thanon Sathorn Tai (0 2673 9353-4/www.blueelephant.com). Surasak BTS. **Open** 10.30am-2.30pm, 6.30-10pm daily. **BBB. Thai fusion.** **Map** p94 B5 ㊴ This Belgium-based Thai chain converted the century-old Thai-Chinese Chamber of Commerce building into a nostalgic restaurant with intimate nooks and grand dining rooms. Innovation infuses the menu (think foie gras in tamarind sauce). The well-equipped cooking school upstairs teaches four dishes per day (1 day B2,800, 5 days B10,000, 7 days for professionals B68,000).

Café Siam

4 Soi Si Aksorn, Thanon Chua Ploeng (0 2671 0030-1). **Open** 6-11.30pm daily. **BBB. French/Thai.**
Map p95 F5 ㉚

This 1922 home of an early Thai railway boss has antique and reproduction furnishings for sale, such as the brass pestle-and-mortar ashtrays. The half-French, half-Thai menu does a decent job living up to the luscious setting. A *digestif* upstairs is so beguiling that you'll need to be evicted.

Hu'u

Ascott Sathorn, 187 Thanon Sathorn Tai (0 2676 6868/www.the-ascott.com). Chong Nonsi BTS. **Open** 5.30pm-midnight daily. **BBB. Pacific Rim.**
Map p94 C5 ㉛

A dark, laid-back Singaporean lounge that's ideal for suits to deal, date, dance or dine (with DJs on Fridays and Saturdays). Barmen scale a two-storey glass matrix storing prime wines and spirits (for 150-plus cocktails). Hu'u Epicure on the glazed mezzanine serves holistic Pacific Rim fusions and exhibits photography.

Kai Thord Soi Polo

137/1-2 Soi Polo, Thanon Witthayu (0 2252 2252). **Open** 7am-10pm daily. **B.** No credit cards. **Thai Isaan.**
Map p95 E4 ㉜

There's fried chicken and there's fried chicken from Soi Polo. Its oily, crispy, aromatic, fleshy balance has won devotees. Owner J-Kee, though a southerner, has four decades of Isaan cooking.

Taling Pling

60 Thanon Pan (0 2234 4872). Surasak BTS. **Open** 11am-10pm daily. **BB. Thai.** Map p94 C5 ㉝

This homely, buzzing restaurant combines bright decor with tasty rural cooking. It excels at green curry with roti, spicy sour soup with prawn, and pomelo salad, along with Thai and Western desserts. Fruit from a *taling pling* tree in the garden ends up in the food.

Vertigo Restaurant & Moon Bar

61st floor, Banyan Tree Bangkok Hotel, 21/100 Thanon Sathorn Tai (0 2679 1200/www.banyantreebangkok.com).
Open 5.30pm-1am daily. **BBBB.**
International. Map p95 E5 ㉞

One of the highest open-air bar/restaurants in the world, Vertigo boasts jaw-dropping views, so booking is essential, despite premium pricing. Its Moon Bar appears to hover at one raised end, lending the roof the feel of a Baron Munchausen flying galleon. As you sip cocktails, loungey tunes waft in the considerable breeze. If it rains, there's shelter in three other restaurants. See box p96.

Shopping

Suan Lum Night Bazaar

Thanon Witthayu, at Thanon Rama IV (0 2252 4776/www.thainightbazaar. com). Lumphini subway. **Open** 4pm-midnight daily. **BB.** Map p95 E4 ㉟

This covered maze holds several thousand stalls of souvenirs and decor items, plus beer gardens, restaurants and events in Bangkok Hall. A cool, convenient, relaxed alternative to Chatuchak Weekend Market (p144). Slated for eviction, it may still cling on.

Nightlife

For Met Bar, see the Metropolitan (p173).

Babylon & Babylon Barracks

34 Soi Nantha, Sathorn Soi 1 (0 2679 7984-5/www.babylonbangkok.com). Lumphini MRT. **Open** noon-midnight daily. **Admission** B230 Mon-Fri; B260 Sat, Sun. **B. International.**
Map p95 E5 ㊱

Perhaps the world's most opulent gay sauna, with a gym, pool, garden bars, restaurants (jazz on Sundays), cabaret, monthly foam parties and Babylon Barracks hotel (rooms B1,700-B9,500).

Rain Dogs

16 Soi Phraya Phiren, off Soi Suwan Sawat (08 1720 6989). Khlong Toei MRT. **Open** 7pm-1am daily. **Admission** free. No credit cards. **Map** p95 F5 ⑰

Lurking beside an expressway down a dark lane off a dark soi off Thanon Rama IV, this ramshackle hideaway rewards those who want to mix with the arty and photo-journalist expats who sup, chat and bop here. However, it's only worth coming here when there are events on like concerts, exhibitions, films or parties, so call first.

Wong's Place

27/3 Soi Sri Bumphen (no phone) Lumpini MRT. **Open** midnight-late daily. **Admission** free. No credit cards. **Map** p95 E5 ⑱

A dimly-lit shophouse door hides this dusty late-night institution. Friendly expat regulars, as diverse as the bar's memorabilia, help themselves to beers from the fridge. The TV replays vintage rock and pop music from a wall of VHS cassettes behind the bar.

Arts & leisure

H Gallery

201 Sathorn Soi 12 (08 1310 4428/ www.hgallerybkk.com). **Open** 10am-6pm Mon, Wed-Sat; by appointment Tue. **Map** p94 C5 ⑲

American art dealer H Earnest Lee fostered new markets for emerging Thai artists at this converted wooden house, other hip venues and in New York. Look out for work by Thaweesak 'Lolay' Srithongdee (perverse pop), Top Changtrakul (cartoonesque mindscapes), Jakkai Siributr (fabric art), and pieces by the minimalist abstract master Somboon Hormthienthong.

Health Land

Thanon Sathorn Nua at Soi 12 (0 2637 8883/www.healthlandspa.com). Surasak BTS. **Open** 9am-11pm daily. **Map** p94 C5 ⑳

A busy, great-value centre of no-nonsense Thai massage. This extended old mansion also provides reflexology, aromatherapy, tourmaline sauna, facials, herbal compresses, a Vichy shower, a juice bar and Ayurveda (at a bargain B300/hr). It has a branch at 96/1 Sukhumvit Soi 63 (0 2392 2233).

Lumphini Stadium

Thanon Rama IV, beside Suan Lum Night Bazaar (0 2251 4303/ringside reservations 08 3137 8938). Lumpini MRT. **Open** 6.30-10.30pm Tue, Fri-Sat. **Tickets** Thais B2,000, B480, B240; foreigners B2,000, B1,500, B1,000. No credit cards. **Map** p95 E4 ㉑

Likely to be relocated, this legendary arena has equipment shops, Spartan ringside seats and flurries of betting in the stands. Bouts of ancient-style *muay boran* break up long bills of bouts that climax in title fights.

Surapon Gallery

1st floor, Tisco Tower, Thanon Sathorn North (0 2638 0033-4). **Open** 11am-6pm Tue-Sat. **Map** p95 D5 ㉒

Selecting exquisite works for this two-storey space, Surapon interperses prominent painters of Thai subjects, such as Surasit Saokhong, with one-offs such as the whimsical ceramicist Vipoo Srivilasa.

Thai Puppet Theater

Suan Lum Night Bazaar, 1875 Thanon Rama IV (0 2252 9683-4/www.thai puppet.com). Lumphini MRT. **Open** 9.30am-9.30pm Mon-Fri; 1-9pm Sat, Sun. **Shows** 8pm daily. **Tickets** B400 Thais; B900 foreigners. **BB**. **Thai**. **Map** p95 E4 ㉓

In well-explained plays at this purpose-built theatre, exquisite toddler-sized *hun lakhon lek* puppets come uncannily (and wittily) to life, moved with sticks by three dancing handlers. Previously known by the nickname of their late master, Joe Louis, this family-run troupe may have to move. It has an average Thai restaurant.

Siam Center p116

Siam & Around

Bangkok has many centres: the sacred root in Phra Nakorn, state institutions in Dusit, the CBD in Bangrak, the bus terminus at Victory Monument. The Siam and Ratchaprasong strip, too, lays valid claim to the 'downtown' title. Not only do the BTS lines cross here; this is the shopping hub, the heart of Thai pop, and the site of Bangkok's adopted talisman, the **Erawan Shrine**. It is the most convenient place to stay, eat, shop and get things done.

The continually mutating skyline and streetscapes epitomise the juxtapositions of modern Thai life: faith versus materialism, tastefulness fending off vulgarity, extravagance skirting destitution. Amid the gleaming malls and mouldering slums you will find traditional houses, antiquities, parks and spiritual retreats. Think of Siam BTS Station as the centre, linking directly to the top malls and the youth culture hub of Siam Square. Greater Siam covers the next stop or so down each of the four radiating lines. You can walk the entire 2km-long 'Ratchprasong Shopping Street' from National Stadium BTS to beyond Chidlom BTS — all without touching the ground, via cooled malls and breezy 'Skybridges'.

The Silom line skirts the area's plushest hotels and Lumpini Park. The line north opened up Phyathai district as a blossoming destination. Further up the BTS beyond Victory Monument, Aree and Chatuchak count as suburbia.

Siam Square

Siam Square is the opposite of a piazza – a warren of shoplets so dense that the owners felt compelled to plug its main open space for teens, Centerpoint, with a new micro mall for techies, **Digital Gateway**. Siam is the epicentre of Thai youth culture: a mash-up of things cute,

cheap, arty, loud, colourful, slogan-clad and clued-into trends from the West, Japan and Korea. It runs its own radio station and magazine, and is full of extra-study schools. After dark, impromptu fashion stalls crowd the BTS steps.

Ground zero for teens is the tumultuous maze of stalls, fast food and karaoke boxes at **MBK** next door. Thai designers who start in Siam Square can graduate to **Siam Centre** boutiques opposite, then if they go 'inter' (get foreign success) perhaps join global brands in the luxury behemoth **Siam Paragon**.

This is Thailand's movie centre, with old theatres in Siam Square facing sumptuous multiplexes in malls. Art has its redoubts, with **Jim Thompson's House Museum** and **Chulalongkorn Art Centre** joined by **Bangkok Art & Culture Centre**. For respite, stroll the parklike grounds of Chulalongkorn University or contemplate the surrounding materialism in the sanctuary of **Wat Pathumwan**.

Sights & museums

Bangkok Art & Culture Centre

939 Thanon Rama I, opposite MBK (0 2214 6630-1/www.bacc.or.th). National Stadium BTS. **Open** 10am-9pm Tue-Sun. **Admission** free. **Map** p110 B4 ❶
See box p112.

Chulalongkorn Art Centre

7th Floor, Centre of Academic Resources, Chulalongkorn University, Thanon Phayathai (0 2218 2964/5/ www.car.chula.ac.th/art). **Open** *Term time* 9am-7pm Mon-Fri; 9am-4pm Sat. *Holidays* 9am-4pm Mon-Fri.
Admission free. **Map** p110 B5 ❷
An important space that has hosted socially relevant shows by Sakharin Krue-on, Michael Shaowanasai, Navin Rawanchaikul, Pinaree Sanpitak and

BACC in earnest

Thai modern art used to say a lot about Thai ideals – spiritual, nationalistic, aesthetic – but not so much about local life. Then, in the mid 1990s, it started getting real. Thai art went contemporary with a capital C, increasingly packed with politics, humour, sexuality, and quotes from popular culture and media.

A smart district to find the art is Siam, the throbbing heart of youth culture. Spiral up the Guggenheim-esque atrium of the **Bangkok Art & Culture Centre** (BACC, p111). The top three of the building's 11 storeys are exhibition halls, where beyond painting and sculpture, you'll see video, conceptual photography, installation and performance – sometimes all at once, in the case of a show by Navin Ravanchaikul. Rotating BACC curators like Luckana Kunavichayanont and Apinan Poshyananda mix up categories even further by showing cutting-edge work alongside traditional Thai, Western academic, modernist and foreign shows.

It's an art centre, not a museum, so there's no permanent collection; some shows even list prices. It previews Biennale-bound exhibits and holds events like the **Bangkok Design Festival** (p37) and **Bangkok Short Film Festival** (p36). True to the BACC's grass-roots mandate, it hosts events by civic groups, prominent figures and schools, plus graduate shows (stalked by collectors and gallerists).

Vasan Sitthiket, plus top foreign names such as Yasumasa Morimura and Nobuyashi Araki.

Jim Thompson's House

6 Kasemsan Soi 2, Thanon Rama I (0 2216 7368/www.jimthompsonhouse. com). National Stadium BTS. **Open** 9am-5pm daily. **Admission** B100; B10-B50 reductions. **BB**. Map p110 B3 ❸

The revival and global fame of Thai silk owes much to Jim Thompson, a US architect who came to Thailand at the end of World War II with the OSS (now the CIA) and settled. He spotted the marketing potential of the declining silk weaving then still practised by the Muslims of Baan Krhua. Influentially, in 1959 he adapted six reassembled teak houses to modern living. Now a museum in lush grounds, it exhibits Thompson's Asian artefacts and looks much like it did when he disappeared in Malaysia's Cameron Highlands in 1967. Conspiracy theories abound.

After the guided tour, relax in the canalside bar/restaurant Thompson, browse the silk shop and view the Jim Thompson Center for the Arts. It holds world-class exhibitions on regional textiles and culture. Nearby, the William Warren Library, named after Jim's friend and biographer, also hosts talks.

Siam Ocean World

Siam Paragon, Thanon Rama I (0 2687 2000/0 2610 6603/www.siam oceanworld.co.th). Siam BTS. **Open** 10am-8pm daily. *X-venture every 30mins 10.30am-8.30pm daily.* **Admission** *Siam Ocean World* B350 Thais; B850 foreigners; B250-B650 reductions. *X-venture* B250. *Both* B750 Thais; B950 foreigners; B400-B500 reductions. Map p110 C4 ❹

The largest aquarium in South-east Asia holds over 400 species and 30,000 fish with good interactive displays. Zones include a simulated reef, an 'Amazon Rainforest' and an acrylic tunnel through the main tank where you can boat, dive with sharks or get mar-

Jim Thompson's House

ried underwater. Best at feeding times. Beside it experience multi-sensory simulator films at Sanyo 4-D X-venture.

Wat Pathumwanaram

969 Thanon Rama I (0 2254 2545). Siam BTS. **Open** 8.30am-6pm daily. **Admission** free. **Map** p110 C4 **⑤**
Fronted by a terrapin pond, this tranquil *wat*, undergoing restoration, houses superlative murals and the ashes of Prince Mahidol, father of Kings Rama XIII and IX. In 1996 the ashes and elaborate crematorium of the king's mother were brought here.

Eating & drinking

Somtam Nua

392/14 Siam Square Soi 5 (0 2251 4880). Siam BTS. **Open** 10.45am-9.30pm daily. **B**. **Thai Isaan**. **Map** p110 C4 **⑥**
Siam Square's not a very interesting place to eat, but the queues outside this Isaan kitchen at lunch testify to its spirited renditions of the papaya salad (even a vegan version), fried chicken hiding beneath fried garlic, fermented Isaan-style sausage, and salads that sing.

Shopping

Baking Soda

3rd floor, Siam Center, Thanon Rama I (0 2251 4995). Siam BTS. **Open** 11am-8.30pm daily. **Map** p110 B4 **⑦**
Creating bold, sexy and diverse styles for the impossibly slim (male and female), Soda embellishes core items such as jeans and Ts with innovative sequinned, printed and see-through fabrics. Branch in Emporium (p138).

Books Kinokuniya

3rd floor, Siam Paragon, Thanon Rama I (0 2610 9500/www.kinokuniya. com). Siam BTS. **Open** 10am-10pm daily. **Map** p110 C4 **⑧**
This Japanese chain has the biggest, best and best-organised stock of books in English, plus great ranges of magazines, maps, art, poetry and children's literature. Staff are courteous and informed.

Digital Gateway

Btwn Siam Square Sois 3 & 4 (0 2658 4637-8/www.mydigitalgateway.com). Siam BTS. **Open** 10am-10pm daily, 3rd floor midnight. **Map** p110 B4 **⑨**

A new five-floor parabola-roofed mall squeezed between shophouses. It caters to the digitised lifestyle, with gadgets and cameras, PCs and toys, plus a Mac iStudio, event spaces, eating places and a roof terrace.

Dinakara

1st floor, Siam Paragon, Thanon Rama I (0 2129 4399). Siam BTS. **Open** 10am-6.30pm daily. **Map** p110 C4 ⑩
Bold statements in precious stones and metals ensure that Yukala Iamla-or's distinctively Asian creations earn devotion among artistic types.

Doi Tung

4th floor, Siam Discovery, Thanon Rama I (0 2658 0424/www.doitung. org). Siam BTS. **Open** 10am-9pm daily. **Map** p110 B4 ⑪
The worthy Mae Fah Luang Foundation has wowed catwalks by updating weaving traditions into a stylishly cosmopolitan form. Innovative hand-loomed cottons and linens provide the key materials. Rugs too beautiful to step on adorn the walls. Doi Tung also grows coffee and runs quality cafés.

Do Re Me

Siam Square Soi 11 (0 2251 4351). Siam BTS. **Open** 2pm-10pm daily. No credit cards. **Map** p110 B4 ⑫
This treasured little music shop discounts new releases on labels major and minor. The absence of any organisation tests the owner's incredible memory to its limits.

Headquarter

3rd floor, Siam Center, Thanon Rama I (0 2658 1048). Siam BTS. **Open** 10am-9pm daily. **Map** p110 C4 ⑬
Inspirational wear for both sexes from a trio of Thai designers, with an emphasis on details, unusual cuts and wit.

Issue

266/10 Siam Square Soi 3 (0 2658 4416). Siam BTS. **Open** noon-9pm daily. **Map** p110 B4 ⑭

Designer Roj Singhakul incorporates ethnic hieroglyphs, primitive forms and religious symbols into his creations. Casual tops and Issue-branded T-shirts are the mainstays among this casual clubwear for individualists.

It's Happened to be a Closet

266/3 Siam Square Soi 3 (0 2985 9345/www.itshappenedtobeacloset.word press.com). Siam BTS. **Open** 11am-9pm Tue-Sun. **BBB. International.** **Map** p110 B4 ⑮
Like an *Alice in Wonderland* outfitters, this magic box conceals retro-boho clothing in colour-coded racks amid an overflow of artful accessories, old books and decorative flourishes. Its good but pricey café has spawned a chain and the shop a branch: The Nero (32 Thanon Khao San, 0 2629 5271-2).

Jaspal

2nd floor, Siam Center, Thanon Rama I (0 2251 5918/www.jaspal.com). Siam BTS. **Open** 10am-9pm daily. **Map** p110 B4 ⑯
Local fashion giant Jaspal takes its cue mainly from Europe, hiring Kate Moss and other supermodels for its adverts. The menswear can be a tad overdesigned, but you can't argue with the quality. The decor spin-off purveys sumptuous bedding.

Loft

3rd floor, Siam Discovery, Thanon Rama I (0 2658 0328-30). Siam BTS. **Open** 10am-9pm daily. **Map** p110 B4 ⑰
There's something for every budget at this Japanese shop jumbled with novelties to gadgets to designery objets. Myriad wrappings and cards make it a one-stop gift solution.

Mah Boon Krong (MBK)

444 Thanon Phayathai (0 2620 9000/www.mbk-center.com). National Stadium BTS. **Open** 10am-10pm daily. **Map** p110 B4 ⑱

Square to be hip

Siam Square has for decades been a laboratory for Thai fashion. The sartorially inventive teens promenading here take their cue from Japan but delight in Thai whimsy. Young designers start in tiny shoplets threading between the sois, or at **Chatuchak Weekend Market** (p144). Some open boutiques in **Siam Center** opposite (p116), with **Theatre** (p117) and **Baking Soda** (p113) among the most fondly enduring. Although global chains have muscled in, indie labels still cater to the trendiest of tastes.

Those that 'go inter' (gain international success) graduate to **Gaysorn** (p121) or **Siam Paragon** (p116). The labels Greyhound, Senada, Sretsis and Issue were showcased at Milan's annual White Milano fair in 2004, and the Institut Français de la Mode and the French Textile Machinery Manufacturers' Association help to train young Thai couturiers, as does the branch of Accademia Italiana at H1 in Soi Thonglor.

Few have proven to be as savvy at design, marketing and logistics as the pioneering **Fly Now** (p121),

which has twice opened London Fashion Week. Its designer Chamnan Phakdeesuk traditionally ends **Bangkok International Fashion Week** (p34).

Held each March at Siam Paragon, BIFW inherited the mantle of Bangkok Fashion City, a B1.8 billion project by Thaksin Shinawatra's former government to create the 'Milan of Asia'. Thailand's 1.2 million garment workers need brand identity fast to prevent obliteration by cheaper Chinese rivals. While Thais show irrepressible creativity they are hampered by poor business acumen and censorious officials who have tried to dictate a dress code for catwalks.

Still, you can't stop Thais putting on a show, especially if it involves beautiful people parading around in costumes. Long predating BIFW, **Elle Fashion Week** (p34) helps emergent designers and is now held twice a year at Central World. Limited tickets are available to the public for the two fashion weeks, but it takes chutzpah or connections for fashionistas to gatecrash the parties.

Don't even try to make sense of this frenzied, overcrowded mall linked to the Pathumwan Princess hotel (p177). More than 1,000 shops and stalls flog gold, footwear, sausages, furniture, suitcases, youth fashion, cameras, portraits and, famously, mobile phones. On top sit a food court, SF cinema (p123) and bowling rink.

Ong's Tea

4th floor, Siam Discovery, Thanon Rama I (0 2658 0445). Siam BTS. **Open** 10am-9pm daily. Map p110 B4 ⑲
Sample the leaves, mostly from China, Japan and Taiwan, amid tea ceremony calligraphy, pots and *chai*-sipping music. There's also a branch on the ground floor of Siam Paragon, Pathumwan (0 2610 7516).

Panta

4th floor, Siam Discovery, Thanon Rama I (0 2658 0415). Siam BTS. **Open** 10am-9pm daily. Map p110 B4 ⑳
A showroom of top Thai furniture designers, including Ayodhya, Yothaka, Ango World and Planet 2001, focusing on seductively experimental furniture made from natural materials. Has a branch in Siam Paragon (4th floor, 0 2129 4430).

Propaganda

4th floor, Siam Discovery, Thanon Rama I (0 2658 0430/www.propaganda online.com). Siam BTS. **Open** 10am-9pm daily. Map p110 B4 ㉑
A cross between Philippe Starck and Damien Hirst, Chaiyuth Plypetch has won awards for his playful innovations since 1994. Museum-standard pieces like the Match Lamp and Shark-Fin Bottle Opener have garnered international rave reviews, while the Mr P range finds cute new functions for the male accessory. Also in Emporium (p138, 4th floor, 0 2664 8574).

Roominteriorproducts

4th floor, Siam Discovery, Thanon Rama I (0 2658 0411). Siam BTS.

Open 11am-8pm Mon-Thur; 11am-9pm Fri-Sun. **Map** p110 B4 ㉒
Got a penchant for plastic stuff? This Australian designer duo sell a rainbow of kitschy props for your poptastic home, such as folding chairs and beanbags in funky patterns. Also stocks Lomo cameras.

Triphum

4th floor, Siam Paragon, Thanon Rama I (0 2610 9458). Siam BTS. **Open** 10am-7.30pm daily. Map p110 C4 ㉓
Reproduction mural paintings on tapestries and planks (plus frames and Siamese knick-knacks). All are reasonably priced, considering they're as meticulously crafted as a temple restoration. The original outlet is in Gaysorn (3rd floor, 0 2656 1795).

Siam Center & Siam Discovery

989 Thanon Rama I (0 2658 1000 Siam Centre ext 500, Siam Discovery ext 400/0 2687 5000/www.siam center.co.th, www.siamdiscovery.co.th). Siam BTS. **Open** 10am-9pm daily. **Map** p110 B4 ㉔
Long a showcase of Thai fashion (see box p115), Siam Center had a 'Shubuya' J-Pop makeover, stocking youth brand boutiques, sportswear, first-apartment decor, a live radio station (94.0 EFM), Cheeze modelling studio, and plenty of eats. It's like a precocious teen between imperious Siam Paragon (below) and yuppie sibling Siam Discovery, which focuses on mid-range global brands and Thai designer furnishings, including anyroom, Panta (left) and Roominteriorproducts (left).

Siam Paragon

Thanon Rama I (0 2610 9000/www. siamparagon.co.th). Siam BTS. **Open** 10am-10pm daily. **Map** p110 C4 ㉕
Behind a six-storey atrium lobby of vertical gardens, this bombastic, town-sized mall likens itself to a multi-faceted gem. Enclosing the cavernous Paragon department store, swish shops flaunt

Propaganda

jewellery, decor, digital gadgets, A-list labels and supercar showrooms. Yet it's busiest in Zara, Books Kinokuniya (p113) and the basement's restaurants and speciality food hall. It also holds True Urban Park tech lounge, a 16-screen cinema (p117), Blu-O bowling alley (below), a family 'edutainment' Explorium, a conference hall and Siam Ocean World aquarium (p112). A five-star hotel is rising on the site's remnant canalside gardens.

Theatre
3rd floor, Siam Center, Pathumwan (0 2251 3599). Siam BTS. **Open** 10am-9pm daily. **Map** p110 B4 ㉖
Award-winning designer Taned Boonprasarn combines hardy fabrics with lace and chiffon. His glamorous gowns and mix-and-matches with accompanying frilly details evoke a neo-romanticism.

Arts & leisure

Blu-O Rhythm & Bowl
5th floor Siam Paragon (0 2129 4625/ www.blu-o.com). Siam BTS. **Open** 11am-midnight Mon-Thur; 11am-1am Fri-Sun. **Prices** B100/game before 5pm; B120 after 5pm. *Karaoke* B250-B350/hr. **Map** p110 C4 ㉗
Most malls offer ten-pin bowling beside their cinema. Thais have particular *sanuk* (fun) at disco-ish day-glo rinks like Blu-O.

Lido, Siam & Scala
Thanon Rama I, facing Siam Center (0 2252 6498/www.apexsiam-square.com). Siam BTS. **Tickets** B100. No credit cards. **Map** p110 B4 ㉘
Apex runs three special cinemas in a row. Lido Multiplex shows progressive World film, but lacks good seating or soundproofing. Or relish the rare big-screen impact at the tatty Siam (Thanon Rama I, 0 2251 1735) or the stunning art deco Scala (Siam Square Soi 1, 0 2251 2861).

Paragon Cineplex & IMAX
5th floor, Siam Paragon, Thanon Rama I (0 2515 5555/www.paragon cineplex.com). Siam BTS. **Tickets** B140-B600. **Map** p110 C4 ㉙
The 600-seat Krungsri IMAX theatre (3-D or DMR effects) and 1,140-seat, balconied Siam Pavalai theatre headline at the country's most luxurious cinema, hosting festivals and premières. The 34-seat Enigma private cinema has a lounge bar and suits parties.

Royal Bangkok Sports Club (RBSC)
1 Thanon Henri Dunant (0 2255 1420-9/www.rbsc.org). Siam BTS. **Open** *Races* noon-6pm Sun every fortnight. **Admission** B50-B500. No credit cards. **Map** p110 C5 ㉚
This century-old member's club, whose patrons either own or run the country, lets in anyone else for boisterous horse racing on alternate weeks to the Royal Turf Club (p78).

Thann Sanctuary
5th floor, Siam Discovery, Thanon Rama I (0 2658 0550/www.thann.

Erawan Shrine

info/www.harrn.com). *Siam BTS.*
Open 10am-9pm daily. **Map**
p110 B4 ③

This chain of chic micro-spas reflect the body-product brand styles of Thann (contemporary Asian) and Harrn (herbal apothecary). As well as facials and body cleansers, the massages include Ayurvedic, Swedish, Thai aromatic and a concentrated Black & White Onyx Stone Massage.

Ratchaprasong & Ploenchit

Ratchaprasong intersection – where Thanon Ratchdamri meets Thanons Rama I and Ploenchit – is the crossroads of modern Bangkok. Thais and visiting Asians worship shrines to Hindu gods guarding each direction, most famously the **Erawan Shrine**. Malls stand on three corners: the upmarket **Erawan**, exclusive **Gaysorn**, and vast **Central World**, where the forecourt holds events like Elle Fashion Week, exhibitions, beer gardens (November-January) and the New Year countdown under the glow of South-east Asia's largest LCD screen.

East along Thanon Ploenchit the best department store, **Central Chidlom**, faces the restaurant-packed Soi Lang Suan. Before Ploenchit becomes Thanon Sukhumvit it crosses the leafy Thanon Witthayu (aka Wireless Road), which is lined with embassies and hotels.

Sights & museums

Chao Mae Tubtim Shrine
Soi Nai Lert, service entrance of Nai Lert Park Hotel. Chidlom BTS. **Open** 24hrs daily. **Admission** free. **Map** p111 D4 ㉜

Thais worship for fertility or prosperity at this canalside shrine to the female deity Chao Mae Tubtim. They offer *palad khik* (animist phallic totems) in every shape, size and material, from Shiva lingams to realistic shafts swathed in sacred scarves. Some even have legs (to make luck mobile).

Erawan Shrine

At Erawan mall, Thanon Ratchadamri (0 2252 8754). Chidlom BTS. **Open** 6am-10.30pm daily. **Admission** free. **Map** p111 D4 ❸❸

Thais seamlessly fuse modernity with spirit beliefs. This ability is encapsulated at the frenetic, smoky Hindu shrine to Brahma, erected in 1956 to appease displaced spirits who were blamed for mishaps in building the old Erawan Hotel. Pilgrims with granted wishes return to make offerings; many pay for costumed dancers to perform. In 2006, a crazed (or well-paid) man smashed the statue and received instant karma: bystanders beat him to death. Thousands scrambled to see the restored image reinstalled.

Erawan is the elephant mount of Indra, whose green statue outside neighbouring Amarin Plaza joins a circuit of Hindu shrines at Ratchaprasong. The InterContinental Hotel erected a bronze Vishnu upon his man-bird mount Garuda. Vishnu's wife Lakshmi promotes prosperity atop Gaysorn Plaza (p121), and at Central World (p121) devotees worship Ganesha and Trimurthi. Trimurthi combines Brahma, Vishnu and Shiva, but the young revere him as the 'god of love', making red offerings, especially on Thursdays.

Eating & drinking

Bacchus Wine Bar

20/6-7 Soi Ruam Rudi (0 2650 8986/www.bacchus.tv). Ploenchit BTS. **Open** 5.30pm-1am daily. **BBB**. **Wine bar**. **Map** p111 E5 ❸❹

Ruam Rudi Village venues either stay forever or last a wink. This four-floor, Japanese-run wine bar has endured: cellar (sommelier-selected), cuisine (Franco-Italian), cocktails (herbal and classic), humidor (Cubans) and decor (rusticated stone, water, wood). It makes for intimate lounging, whether at the bar, armchairs or 'floating' bed (both floor and ceiling are see-through). DJs can slip patrons into dance mode.

Biscotti

1st floor, Four Seasons Hotel, 155 Thanon Ratchadamri (0 2254 9999). Ratchadamri BTS. **Open** 11.30-2.30pm, 6-10.30pm daily. **BBBB**. **Italian**. **Map** p110 C5 ❸❺

Politicians, stars and tycoons choose this animated, Tony Chi-designed restaurant. And they're easily spotted in the huge room of terracotta and white, dominated by an open kitchen. Jammed at lunch and dinner with devotees of its Italian food by chef Danilo, it has a long table for solo diners.

Café LeNôtre

Ground floor, Natural Ville Executive Residences, 61 Soi Lang Suan (0 2250 7050-1). Chidlom BTS. **Open** 6am-11pm daily. *Bakery* 6am-10pm daily. **BBB**. **French**. **Map** p111 D5 ❸❻

This chic outlet of a Parisian chain exudes Gallic savoir-faire. A short menu has decent appetisers, salads and mains, such as tomato Bayaldi, named after Imam Bayaldi, who fainted at its richness. Fab desserts: think chocolate mousse around green tea crème brûlée.

Curries & More

63/3 Soi Ruam Rudee, at Soi 3 (02 253 5405-7/www.baan-khanitha.com). Ploenchit BTS. **Open** 11am-2pm, 6-11pm daily. **BBB**. **Thai**. **Map** p111 E5 ❸❼

It's really Curries & Everything, so varied is the menu. Besides Thai staples are rare curries and good Western dishes. Many can be adapted for vegans. Fine cakes and crêpes follow. Well-trained waiters whisk around this converted house with art-laden rooms on two floors, and a water-cooled, all-weather patio. It's a branch of the more traditionally Thai restaurant Baan Khanitha (67-69 Thanon Sathorn Tai, 0 2675 4200-1, and 36/1 Sukhumvit Soi 23, 0 2258 4181).

Diplomat Bar

Conrad Bangkok Hotel, All Seasons Place, 87 Thanon Witthayu (0 2690 9999/www.conradbangkok.com).

BANGKOK BY AREA

Ploenchit BTS. **Open** 10am-1am Mon-Thur, Sun; 10am-2am Fri, Sat. *Bands* 6.30pm-12.15am Mon-Thur, Sun; 9.30pm-1am Fri, Sat. **BBB. Bar.** Map p111 E5 ㊳

A premier live jazz lounge. Floral installations by Sakul Intakul offset dark wood and backlit silk in this lofty den for deal-making and rendezvous. The drinks list is extensive, and graceful service accompanies the smooth tones of the chanteuses.

Gianni

51/5 Soi Tonson (0 2252 1619). Chidlom BTS. **Open** 11-2.30pm, 6-10.30pm daily. **BBBB. Italian.** Map p111 D4 ㊴

A Bangkok institution, run by 'celebrity' chef Gianni Favro. The airy interior sets a cheery tone for Venetian cuisine and specials. You leave talking about the food – like rabbit ravioli and risotto of artichoke and lobster – not the price.

Khrua Nai Baan

94 Soi Lang Suan (0 2252 0069). Chidlom BTS. **Open** 9am-midnight daily. **BB. Seafood.** Map p111 D5 ㊵

This simple white wooden house on bopping Lang Suan is a nightly dinner party of sorts, being full of regulars. The cooking focuses on seafood from the tanks out front. Whether you opt for Chinese veggies or steamed squid in lemon sauce, it's hard to go wrong.

Red Sky

55th floor, Centara Grand Hotel, 99/999 Thanon Rama I (0 2210 1234/www.centarahotelsresorts.com/cgc w/restaurant.asp). Chidlom BTS. **Open** 6-11pm daily. **BBBB. International.** Map p110 C4 ㊶

Central's fine dining jewel aims high with extravagant ingredients, exceptional open-air views, gastronomic cocktails and a broad wine list, but dim lighting hides what's on your plate. The brief menu focuses on imported ingredients at premium prices: Maine lobster, French foie gras. There was no shortage of technique in a dish of slow-braised pork belly topped with foie gras in a rich red wine reduction.

Thang Long

82/5 Soi Lang Suan (0 2251 3504/4491). Chidlom BTS. **Open** 11am-2pm, 5-11pm daily. **BBB. Vietnamese.** Map p111 D5 ㊷

There's a clean, minimalist cool feel to this Vietnamese eaterie – with boxy rattan chairs, loungey music and strategic placing of plants – which makes it a busy hangout for arty types.

Zense

17th floor, Zen, Thanon Rama I (0 2100 9898/www.zensebangkok.com). Chidlom BTS. **Open** 5.30pm-midnight daily. **BBB. International.** Map p110 C4 ㊸

The best value (well, relatively) rooftop open-air restaurant also has the youngest vibe. Views apart, the windiness, low light and decor of 'ponds and irregular stairs' create challenges. Like an upmarket version of the posh food court Food Loft in Zen store below, famous restaurants share the hip menu: Gianni (Italian, left), White Café (Thai), Kikusui (Japanese) and Red (Indian), which succeeds at making curry pasta, and most expensively To Die For (fusion; p141).

Shopping

Ayodhya

3rd floor, Gaysorn, 999 Thanon Ploenchit (0 2656 1089). Chidlom BTS. **Open** 10am-8pm daily. Map p111 D4 ㊹

A pioneer of updating trad Thai products to today's aesthetics, Ayodhya's chain turns out understated, useful items such as seats made from tree vines and home-made soaps scented with local flowers.

Central Chidlom

1027 Thanon Ploenchit (0 2793 7777/ www.central.co.th). Chidlom BTS. **Open** 10am-10pm daily. Map p111 D4 ㊺

Central's seven-storey flagship has the best selection and layout in town. It excels in cosmetics, international and local fashion, leatherware, decor, children's and sporting goods. Micro-stores include Muji, Jim Thompson Thai Silk (p102), Oriental Shop and Tops food hall. Food Loft combines restaurant outlets in a superb gourmet food court.

Central World

4/1-2 Thanon Ratchadamri (0 2255 9500/www.centralworld.co.th). Chidlom BTS. **Open** 10am-9pm daily. **Map** p110 C4 ㊻

South-east Asia's biggest retailer has expanded the dim hulk of the old World Trade Centre into a gleaming, sunlit complex that's easier to navigate, more diverse and friendlier than Paragon. Aside from new-to-Bangkok shops, it harbours three department stores: unchanged Isetan for Nipponophiles; an enlarged Zen (0 2100 9999, www.zen.co.th), which introduces rarer brands to hip young professionals; and a Central, disguised as separate vast SuperSports, PowerBuy and B2S (books, music, stationery) stores. Up top are SF World cinema (p123), a bowling alley, TK Park kids' centre, and countless restaurants.

Fashion Society

2nd floor, Gaysorn, 999 Thanon Ploenchit (0 2656 1358/www.gaysornbkk.com). Chidlom BTS. **Open** 10am-8pm daily. **Map** p111 D4 ㊼

This one-stop clearing house of play and work clothes for men and women mixes leading Thai labels and up-and-coming names, such as Muse, Muungdoo and Sarit. Metal racks and raw decor produce a factory feel. Staff are friendly, not fawning.

Fly Now

2nd floor, Gaysorn, 999 Thanon Ploenchit (0 2656 1359). Chidlom BTS. **Open** 10am-8pm daily. **Map** p111 D4 ㊽

Established over a decade ago, Fly Now entered jet-set realms through principal designer Chamnam Pakdisuk, whose voguish, feminine tailoring has twice opened London Fashion Week. Branches in Siam Center (2nd floor, 0 2658 1735), Siam Paragon (2nd floor, 0 2610 9410/7883) and Central World (1st floor, 0 2646 1037) have diverse decor.

Gaysorn

999 Thanon Ploenchit (0 2656 1516-9/www.gaysorn.com). Chidlom BTS. **Open** 10am-8pm daily. **Map** p111 D4 ㊾

This swanky corner landmark has posh brands (Louis Vuitton, Prada, Hermès), regional fashion houses and contemporary Thai design outlets.

iStudio by Copperwired

4th floor, Central World, Thanon Ratchadamri (0 2613 1540/www.copperwired.co.th). Chidlom BTS. **Open** 10am-9pm daily. **Map** p110 C4 ㊿

Adept staff demonstrate Apple models at Copperwired's experiential showrooms (also in Siam Paragon, 3rd floor, 0 2610 9315). Competitive pricing and great after-sales service.

Kai Boutique

187/1 Bangkok Cable Building, Thanon Ratchadamri (0 2251 0728-9/www.kaiboutique.com). Ratchadamri BTS. **Open** 9am-7.30pm Mon-Fri. **Map** p110 C5 (51)

Pioneer of *dek bou* (boutique kids), Somchai 'Kai' Kaewtong has begowned local fashionistas for three decades. A breeding ground for new talent, this spacious flagship focuses on wedding and evening wear.

Lamont Contemporary

3rd floor, Gaysorn, 999 Thanon Ploenchit (0 2656 1392/1048/www.lamont-design.com). Chidlom BTS. **Open** 10am-8pm daily. **Map** p111 D4 (52)

Across the concourse from Lamont Antiques' East Asian collectibles you find Lamont's designs of equal élan, which utilise unusual materials, such as shells microsliced in lacquer, carved bone, and stingray leather.

Lotus Arts de Vivre

Four Seasons Hotel, 155 Thanon Ratchadamri (0 2250 0732/www.lotusartsdevivre.com). Saphan Taksin BTS/Pier. **Open** 8.30am-8pm daily. **Map** p110 C5 ⑬

An Asian Fabergé, Lotus's jewellery, decorations and trinkets are as mysteriously oriental as they come. One-off pieces employ exotic materials from oyster shells and stingray leather to fine-grained roots and tyre rubber.

NV Aranyik

3rd floor, Gaysorn, 999 Thanon Ploenchit (0 2656 1081/www.niwataranyik.com). Chidlom BTS. **Open** 10am-7pm daily. **Map** p111 D4 ⑭

Derived from swordmaking traditions, Aranyik's much-imitated spoons, forks and knives – with twisted, textured or dimpled handles – feature on top restaurant tables around the world. Simple, elegant cutlery worth forking out for.

Promenade Décor

In front of Nai Lert Park Hotel, Thanon Witthayu (0 2252 0160). Ploenchit BTS. **Open** 10am-7pm daily. **Map** p111 E4 ⑮

Promenade is a high-end mall of interiors shops. It veers from imports like über-suave Christian Liaigre to the whimsical work of aristo stylist ML Chirathorn Chirapravati and the kitsch expressionism of celebrity artist Kongpat Sakdapitak.

Senada Theory

2nd floor, Gaysorn, 999 Thanon Ploenchit (0 2656 1350). Chidlom BTS. **Open** 10am-8pm daily. **Map** p111 D4 ⑯

Ethnic influences drive this fashion house. Lead designer Chanita Preechawityayakul is renowned for reconstructing Indian embroidery, Chinese silks and even grandma's tablecloths into hip streetwear.

Sretsis

2nd floor, Gaysorn Mall, 999 Thanon Ploenchit (0 2656 1125/

Thann Native

www.sretsis.com). Chidlom BTS/Ratchadamri BTS. **Open** 10am-8pm daily. **Map** p111 D4 ⑰

With a sensational and ultra-feminine 2003 debut collection, former Marc Jacobs intern Pimdao Sukhahuta became the darling of Thailand's fashion frontline. The quirky, retro style, with floaty chiffons and frilly laces, has ensured that this label remains an ever-innovative hit.

Thann Native

3rd floor, Gaysorn, 999 Thanon Ploenchit (0 2656 1399/www.thann.info). Chidlom BTS. **Open** 10am-8pm daily. **Map** p111 D4 ⑱

From many firms adapting Thai herbalism, Harnn & Thann has spun a global chain of high performance, eco-friendly body products. Think rice bran scrubs, lemongrass aromatherapy oil and strings of multi-spice soaps. In products and in-store spas, Harnn evokes an old apothecary, Thann a swish lab chic. Thann Native also sells decor and furnishings by top Thai designers. It also runs Thann Sanctuary spas.

Nightlife

Spasso

1st floor (lower lobby), Grand Hyatt Erawan Hotel, 494 Thanon Ratchadamri (0 2254 1234). Ratchadamri or Chidlom BTS. **Open** noon-2.30pm Mon-Sat; noon-3pm Sun; 6.30pm-2am daily. *Bands* 10pm-2am daily. **BBB. Pizza. Map** p111 D4 ❺❾
The Bangkok hotel club template for getting middlebrow diners to bop to black/white US pop-soul showbands. Plus good pizza.

Arts & leisure

100 Tonson

100 Soi Tonson (0 2684 1527/www. 100tonsongallery.com). Chidlom BTS. **Open** 11am-7pm Thur-Sun. **Map** p111 D5 ❻⓪
Canny curatorship makes this converted modernist house a showcase for many leading local folk such as Thaiwijit, Chatchai Puipia and Sutee Kunavichayanont, expat Thais like Richard Tsao, and even Damien Hirst and Louise Bourgeois.

S Art & Science Medical Spa

Ground floor, Bhakdi Building, 2/2 Thanon Witthayu (0 2253 1010/ www.smedspa.com). Ploenchit BTS. **Open** 10am-10pm Tue-Sun. *Clinic* 10am-8pm Tue-Sun. **Map** p111 E4 ❻❶
Holistic purifications (one hour to three days), colonics and hydrobath massage at this detox centre and clinic. Also massage, facials and body wraps, plus yoga, reiki, Pilates and Ayurveda.

S F World Cinema

7th floor, Central World Plaza, Thanon Ratchadamri (all branches 0 2268 8888/www.sfcinemacity.co.th). Chidlom BTS. **Tickets** B120-B1,000. **Map** p110 C4 ❻❷
Flagship of a 10-screen multiplex chain with clear views and superb seats, including opera and honeymoon chairs. Hosts film festivals and premières.

The entire city is visible from its tallest structure, **Baiyoke II Tower**, which soars out of congested **Pratunam Market**. This is a wholesale cloth hub, where Indian, African and myriad other traders buy in bulk. *Pratunam* means water gate. It abuts at the interchange on filthy Khlong Saen Saeb, where convenient but cramped commuter boats hurtle west to the Golden Mount and east to Minburi in the eastern 'burbs. The new Ratchaprarop Station connects it to mass transit on the Airport Link (AL).

Sights & museums

Baiyoke II Tower

84th floor, 22 Thanon Ratchaprarop, in soi beside Indra Regent Hotel (0 2656 3000). Ratchaprarop AL/Tha Pratunam. **Open** 10am-10.30pm daily. **Admission** B250. **Map** p110 C3 ❻❸
This tower has an 84th-floor observation deck for vertiginous panoramas of the megalopolis and (on a clear day) the sea. There are also telescopic viewfinders, some drab displays and a bland restaurant.

Bangkok Dolls

85 Soi Mor Leng, Thanon Ratchaprarop (0 2245 3008). Ratchaprarop AL. **Open** 8am-5pm Mon-Sat. **Admission** free. **Map** p111 D2 ❻❹
This small doll museum and cottage industry has occupied its modest location since the 1950s. Its bright displays of ornate costumes and traditional scenes have homespun charm. You can watch them being made. Some are for sale (B290-1,300).

Eating & drinking

Mid Night Kai Ton

Thanon Petchaburi Tut Mai (no phone). Ratchaprarop AL/Tha

Pratunam. **Open** 7pm-4am daily. **B**. No credit cards. **Khao man kai**. **Map** p111 D3 ⑥⑤

Legendary late-night food in the form of *khao man kai*, a Hainanese trader dish of steamed chicken, pinguid rice and broth offset by hits of ginger and chilli sauce.

Shopping

Pantip Plaza

604/3 Thanon Petchaburi (0 2251 9008). **Open** 10am-9pm daily. **Map** p110 C3 ⑥⑥

A geek's paradise, Pantip is crammed with vendors hawking everything and anything (new or used) that you can plug into your PC (or Mac). Knowledgeable staff offer servicing, parts and software, with raids barely pausing the pirate trade. Brand items carry warranty, but most shops pride themselves on free follow-up service.

Pratunam Market

Thanon Phetchaburi, at Thanon Ratchaprarop (0 2309 9700-3). Ratchaprarop AL/Tha Pratunam. **Open** *Day market* 10am-9pm daily. *Night market* 6pm-midnight daily. **Map** p111 D3 ⑥⑦

The stalls burrow around the Indra and Bayoke hotels, burgeoning with textiles, lingerie, bags, Ts and street fashion. The seamstresses will stitch anything, while the African and Arab traders are reflected in the food available. Adjacent Pratunam Centre (across Phetchburi) and Platinum Mall (across Ratchaprarop) offer similar in air-con. Nothing to wear for Mardi Gras? Pratunam's best drag costumier, Sequin Queen (www.sequinqueen.com) can hand-sew a custom-made, spangled gown, complete with feathers.

Phyathai

Bangkok development is finally following mass transit logic, and starting to gentrify neighbourhoods

en route. The hotels, condos and nightlife blossoming here will only increase with the new Airport Link (AL) terminating at Phyathai BTS. Bus riders interchange at **Victory Monument**, a bayonet-like obelisk that was erected in 1941 to mark the short-lived occupation of parts of French Laos in World War II. There's great streetfood at Victory Point on the southeast rim of the roundabout, in front of the legendary **Saxophone** pub.

At the south end of Victory Monument BTS, Thanon Rangnam is busily transforming itself from a lane of Isaan restaurants into a cosmopolitan area served by a small park, cafés and at King Power Duty Free, the **Aksra Theatre** and the **Pullman Hotel**.

As for tourist sights, Phyathai boasts no fewer than three palaces, including the new **Queen Savang Vadhana Museum**.

Sights & museums

Phyathai Palace

King Mongkutklao Hospital, 315 Thanon Ratchawithi (0 2354 7732/ www.phyathaipalace.info/Phya_Thai_P alace). Victory Monument BTS. **Open** 9.30am, 1.30pm Sat; by appointment Mon-Fri. **Admission** free. **Map** p110 B1 ⑥⑧

A getaway of King Rama V, this European-style complex became a luxury hotel, then Thailand's first radio station, then a hospital, and now a museum. Amid restored halls, turrets and filigree pavilions, the fading frescoed corridors lend poignancy to the place where King Rama VI experimented with democracy at a miniature town called Dusit Thani, which had its own economy and newspaper. It houses the Army Medical Corps Museum and hosts concerts in the neo-classical grounds. Tours in English require a written request a week ahead (B500 per 10-15 persons).

Aksra Theatre p126

and Princess Chumbhot, this delightful museum exhibits artefacts including Khmer Buddha statues, monks' fans, betel nut sets, shells and prehistoric Baan Chiang pottery. Most exquisite is the pond-side Lacquer Pavilion, an Ayutthaya-era library with gold and black lacquer scenes from Buddha scripture, the *Ramakien* and Thai life. The grounds also contain Marsi Gallery, and the Khon Museum on classical Thai drama.

Eating & drinking

Isaan Rot Det
Thanon Rangnam (0 2245 6854). Victory Monument BTS. **Open** 11am-10pm daily. **B.** No credit cards. **Thai Isaan. Map** p110 C2 ⓐ
While Rangnam gentrifies, a few great Isaan restaurants remain on a street known for them. Isaan Rot Det (loosely, 'Northeast Car Garage') has all the classics – a superb duck *laab*, grilled chicken, garlic-studded sausages, papaya salads – on a menu in English.

Tak Sura
499/2 Ratchawithi Soi 12 (0 2354 9286). Victory Monument BTS. **Open** 5pm-1am daily. **B.** No credit cards. **Thai. Map** p110 C1 ⓑ
There's a blurred, smoky quality to this bar in an old house, decked out in train benches and Chinese tea-house chairs. It's an oasis of charm behind a Victory Monument bus stop. Yuppie-student-artist regulars quaff whisky or beer and chow on chilli-laced *kub klaem* (bar food). Tak Sura repeat the unformulaic formula at Soi Thansarot (334/1 Thanon Phyathai, beside the canal bridge, 0 2215 8879) and 156/1 Thanon Tanao, Phra Nakorn (0 2622 0708).

Wine Pub
2nd floor, Pullman Hotel, Thanon Rangnam (0 2680 9999). Victory Monument BTS. **Open** 6pm-2am daily. **BBB. Wine bar/French. Map** p110 C2 ⓒ

Queen Savang Vadhana Museum
Srapathum Palace, 195 Thanon Phayathai (0 2252 9137/www.queen savang.org). Ratchathewi BTS. **Open** to be announced. **Admission** to be announced. **Map** p110 B4 ⓓ
Between Siam's malls and Khlong Saen Saeb, you can glimpse the lush grounds of Saprathum Palace, home to King Bhumibol's daughter Princess Sirindhorn, previously to his late mother, and originally to his grandmother, Queen Savang Vadhana, a wife of King Rama V. From late 2009 a museum to Queen Savang's long life (1862-1955) opens in the restored ochre Tamnak Yai (Main Mansion).

Suan Pakkard Palace
352 Thanon Si Ayutthaya (0 2245 4934/ www.suanpakkad.com). Phyathai BTS/AL. **Open** 9am-4pm daily. **Admission** B50 Thais; B100 foreigners. No credit cards. **Map** p110 C2 ⓔ
Named 'Cabbage Patch Palace' after the site where these five teak houses were reassembled in 1952 by Prince

Despite a pedestrian name, this is not your everyday hotel outlet, but Bangkok's most evolved wine bar. Buzzing till late, it overflows on Thursday due to a superb dinner deal.

Shopping

King Power Duty Free

Thanon Rangnam (0 2205 8888/ www.kingpower.com). Victory Monument BTS. **Open** 10am-9pm daily. **BB. International.** Map p110 C2 ⓸
Pre-flight, you can buy duty free at this modern domed complex which is home to Aksra Theatre (below), then collect it at Suvarnabhumi Airport. Take your passport and air ticket.

Nightlife

Club Culture

Thanon Sri Ayutthaya (08 1832 2363). Phyathai BTS/AL. **Open** 9.30pm-2am Tue-Sun. No credit cards. Map p110 C2 ⓹
Run by pioneers of hosting international DJs in Bangkok, Club Culture runs dizzying theme nights. It combines a traditional Thai ambience of carved teak and gilded mirrors with a stream of top DJs playing house, techno, drum'n'bass, electro and transient styles of the moment.

Raintree

116/64 Soi Rang Nam, Thanon Phayathai (0 2245 7230). Victory Monument BTS. **Open** 6pm-1am daily. *Band* 8.30pm-1am daily. **BB. Thai.** Map p111 D2 ⓺
Stuffed with country and western motifs, this stalwart live pub and restaurant feels more like a little blues bar with *pleng puer cheewit* sets nightly and fiery food.

Rock Pub

Hollywood Street Centre, 93/26 Thanon Phyathai (0 2251 9980 daytime/08 6977 0621/www.therockpub-bangkok. com). Ratchatewi BTS. **Open** 7pm-2am

daily. *Bands* 9.30-11.30pm, midnight-2am daily. No credit cards. **Map** p110 B3 ⓻
Entering via the mouth of an Angkor version of the talking tree from *The Wizard of Oz*, heavy metal devotees shake their heads to local bands expertly riffing on standards, from Scorpions to Judas Priest.

Saxophone Pub & Restaurant

3/8 Thanon Phayathai, south east side of Victory Monument (0 2246 5472/ www.saxophonepub.com). Victory Monument BTS. **Open** 6pm-1.30am daily. *Shows* 9pm-1.30am Mon-Tue; 7.30pm-1.30am Thur-Sun. **BB. Thai.** Map p110 C1 ⓸
Any night can be fun at this knocked-through, two-storey, log and beam sculpture. Booze, food, pool and music, with regulars laying down roots, rock, reggae, jazz and blues. They play good-to-great and the sound system excels. But Friday belongs to T-Bone's husky rasp and flapping dreads, from ska to samba to the Senegal stomp.

Arts & leisure

Aksra Theater

King Power Complex, 8 Thanon Rangnam (0 2205 8888). Victory Monument BTS. **Open** *Puppets* 7pm Thur, Fri; 1pm, 7pm Sat, Sun. **Tickets** vary; *Puppets* B800. Map p110 C2 ⓹
A sumptuous, well-equipped theatre staging diverse traditional and modern performances, with a permanent troupe of *hun lakorn lek* puppetry.

New Calypso Cabaret

1st floor, Asia Hotel, 296 Thanon Phayathai (reservations 0 2653 3960-2/www.calypsocabaret.com). Ratchathewi BTS. **Shows** 8.15-9.30pm, 9.45-11pm daily. **Tickets** B1,200. Map p110 B3 ⓾
Bangkok's original ladyboy cabaret has intimate, plush table seating, vaguely Vegas routines and fees for photoposing with the stars.

Long Table p136

Sukhumvit

Thanon Sukhumvit is a road so long that it actually reaches all the way to Cambodia. It starts in Bangkok, and its inner end became an affluent residential suburb after World War II. Today, hotels, condos, spas, bars, boutiques, mini-malls, nightclubs and foreign fine dining continue to edge out lower income quarters.

Sukhumvit is not just international; it is multicultural, with ethnic enclaves lending character amid all the chic-chasing. As elsewhere, localities are beginning to gel around BTS stations. Nana has the most cosmopolitan, sometimes grungy, streetlife from Soi 1 to Soi 21 (aka Asoke). The stretch to Phromphong (Soi 39) is more focused dining in the zig-zaging side-sois, while Sukhumvit Soi 55 (Thonglor) and Sukhumvit Soi 63 (Ekamai) have become the high streets of a nouveau-riche scene.

Nana

Thai-Indians own much of inner Sukhumvit, and Nana is named for a Muslim-Indian family. South Asian restaurants, budget inns and Sikh tailor shops proliferate between Sois 3-11. Arabs and North Africans make Sois 3 and 3/1 home, with kebab restaurants and frankincense shops frequented by Middle Eastern tourists, especially during the rains.

Opposite, geographically and culturally, Soi 4 is a red light district, emanating from **Nana Entertainment Plaza**. Souvenir stalls, travel agents and massage parlours (both healing and entrepreneurial) flank Sukhumvit up to Soi 12, where Koreans have turned Sukhumvit Plaza into Little Seoul. In a gentrifying trend led by **Q Bar** and **Bed Supperclub**, the Sukhumvit Soi 11 Association (www.sukhumvitsoi11.com) runs occasional bar crawls.

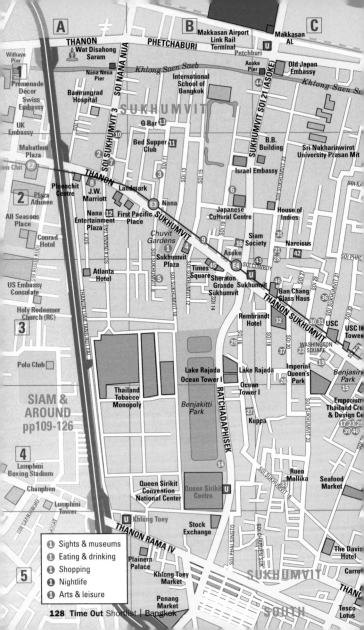

Sukhumvit

THANON PHETCHABURI TUD MAI

SUKHUMVIT

SOI 20 (CHAM CHAN)

SUKHUMVIT SOI 55 [SOI THONGLOR]

THANON SUKHUMVIT

SUKHUMVIT SOI 63 (SOI EKAMAI)

RCA Block S
RCA Block C
RCA Block D
RCA Block E
RCA Block F
RCA Block G
RCA Block H
Bangkok Hospital
Makro
Tops

Wat Maichonglom Pier
Wat Mai Chong Lom

© Copyright Time Out Group 2010

Thonglor Pier
H1 Complex

Police Station
Samitivej Hospital
Didyasarin International School
J. Avenue
RS Tower
Pridi Panomyong Institute
55th Plaza
Philippines Embassy
Thong Lo
Night Food Market
Face
UNESCO
Major Cineplex
Wat That Thong
Ekamai
Bangkok Planeturium
Ekamai Eastern Bus Terminal

SOI PROMPHIT
SOI PHROM KHAN
SOI 39
SOI PHROM SRI 1
SOI PHROMMIT
SOI 45
SOI 33
SOI 41
SOI 49
SOI 51
SOI 53
SOI 31
SOI 34
SOI 36
SOI 40
SOI 55
SOI 38
SOI 48
SOI YAEK 4
SOI SUKCHAI
SOI SAEN SUK
MA IV

SOI 49-17
SOI 49-14
SOI 49-15
SOI 49-12
SOI 49-10
SOI 49-8
SOI 49-6
SOI 25
SOI 23
SOI THONGLOR 19
SOI 17
SOI 13
SOI 9
SOI 1

SOI 19
SOI 11
SOI 9
SOI 12
SOI 10
SOI 5
SOI 10
SOI 8
SOI 6
SOI 4
SOI 2

hrom Phong
terlord

0   700 m
0   700 yds

Sights & museums

Chuvit Garden

Sukhumvit Soi 8. Nana BTS. **Open** 6am-7pm daily. **Admission** free. **Map** p128 B2 ❶

Its history means this small, elegant park is underused. Chuwit Kamonwisit, a moustachioed former massage tycoon known as Sia Ang ('bathtub godfather'), was assumed to have got off-duty 'men in uniform' to smash dozens of 'bar-beers' and stalls on this valuable plot by night in 2003. Cornered by public outrage, Chuvit exposed the bribes he'd paid police, reinvented himself as an anti-sleaze politician, and donated this park to the people, a generosity few public figures have matched.

Eating & drinking

Akbar

1/4 Sukhumvit Soi 3 (0 2253 3479/ 0 2255 6935). Nana BTS. **Open** 10.30am-1am daily. **BBB**. **Indian/ Persian**. **Map** p128 A2 ❷

Of all the Indian restaurants around Soi 3, this mish-mash of wooden ornaments, lanterns, coloured glass and Indian fabrics is the oldest. Unusually, it has a few good wines, plus Persian dishes.

Cheap Charlie's

1 Sukhumvit Soi 11 (08 7096 8444). Nana BTS. **Open** 4.30pm-1am daily. No credit cards. **Bar**. **Map** p128 B2 ❸

Microscopic yet infinitely expandable, this outdoor bar consists of just a few stools around a counter obscured by a thicket of eccentric ephemera. Post-work expats sup beers with Thai pals here. And, yes, it's very cheap.

Kaborae

1st floor, Sukhumvit Plaza, Sukhumvit Soi 12 (0 2252 5375/5486). Asoke BTS/ Sukhumvit MRT. **Open** 11am-10pm daily. **BB**. **Korean**. **Map** p128 B2 ❹

A family-style diner that's the pick of Little Seoul, where most outlets cater to Hermit Kingdom expats. Dishes include hot and sour soups, and the peppery noodle speciality *naingmyon*. Toast the table with the Korean rice whisky *soju*.

Le Banyan

59 Sukhumvit Soi 8 (0 2253 5556/ www.le-banyan. com). Nana BTS. **Open** 6.30pm-midnight (last orders 9.30pm) Mon-Sat. **BBBB**. **French**. **Map** p128 B3 ❺

A French institution with the theatricality required of silver service dining. The pressed duck and some of the other classic dishes are prepared at table by the maître d', Bruno Bischoff, or the eccentric chef, Michel Binaux – a charming double act. The old Thai house decor has faded, but few Bangkok restaurants are better, or better value.

Le Beaulieu

Sofitel Residence, 50 Sukhumvit Soi 19 (0 2204 2004/www.le-beaulieu.com). Asoke BTS/Sukhumvit MRT. **Open** 11.30am-2.30pm, 6.30-11pm daily. **BBBB**. **French**. **Map** p128 B2 ❻

The compact dining room of chef-patron Hervé Frerard, whose deft take on Gallic classics has a loyal following. Hervé tailors sensational signature courses with top-notch ingredients, from braised cheek of veal to sea urchin emulsion. His three-course set lunches are fantastic value.

Nasir Al-Masri

4/6 Sukhumvit Soi 3/1 (0 2253 5582). Nana BTS. **Open** 24 hs daily. **BB**. No credit cards. **Arab**. **Map** p128 A2 ❼

The pick of Soi Arab's eateries transports you to Cairo. Amid mirror-metal surfaces, men banter over Arabic music videos as they puff on shisha pipes. All the food is good, from kebabs to dips and the Egyptian national dish, *molokaya*. No alcohol.

New York Steakhouse

JW Marriott Bangkok Hotel, 4 Sukhumvit Soi 2 (0 2656 7700). Ploenchit/Nana BTS. **Open** 6-11pm daily. **BBBB**. **Steak**. **Map** p128 A2 ❽

Five-star food

Le Normandie, Mandarin Oriental

Dining in the confines of a hotel, in other cities, evokes all the cachet of a buffet. Not so at Bangkok's hotel eateries, where bright culinary stars cook some of the city's most rarified food.

No visit to the city is complete without strolling through Bangkok's original 'Grand Hotel', the **Mandarin Oriental** (p173). Dress smart casual for riverside cocktails, or dress up for elevated experiences like Le Normandie, an ode to a bygone, Escoffier-inspired era, or high tea in the fabled, white-wicker Author's Lounge.

Just downstream, the **Shangri-La** (p174), offers Angelini, a cavernous Italian restaurant that showcases seafood, pizzas and wine, or Sala Thai, refurbished teak pavilions serving Thai classics by the river. Across the Chao Phraya, the **Peninsula** (p173) serves premium Cantonese at Mei Jiang, Pacific rim fusion in Jesters and a spa sub-menu in the villagey Thai eatery Thip Tara.

Somewhat sexier, the **Metropolitan** (p173) shakes chic cocktails at the Met Bar, a branch of the London legend. Nearby, atop the **Dusit Thani** (p171), retro architecture meets modern French cuisine at **D'Sens** (p100), which is an offshoot of the Michelin-starred Pourcel brothers' fine dining empire.

Sunday brunch is an institution. The **Sukhothai** (p174) is as famed for its chocolate and champagne at the Colonnade as for its much-awarded haute-Thai restaurant Celadon, elegantly poised in pond pavilions. The **Sheraton Grande** (p178) started a trend for multi-outlet Sunday brunch, involving Rossini, a baronial-style Italian, and Basil, a suave setting for modern Thai delicacies. The **Four Seasons** (p177) also spreads its buffet between slick steakhouse Madison, sedate courtyard café Aqua, and the Spice Market, which resembles an old Siamese bazaar.

All river hotels have shuttle boats, but you get a lengthy cruise to the **Marriott Bangkok Riverside** (p178) for the jazz brunch at Trader Vic's. It also runs the pick of hotel dinner cruises aboard its converted teak rice barge, *Manohra Song*.

BANGKOK BY AREA

Nasir Al-Masri p130

A sensational, club-like restaurant that started a steakhouse boom, the New York flies in chilled American Angus beef and holds seafood live in tanks. The vegetables disappoint, but then this is melt-in-the-mouth carnivore territory. Many wines come by the glass, and there are around 20 Martinis. Booking is essential.

Shopping

Asia Books

221 Thanon Sukhumvit, between Soi 15 & 17 (0 2252 7277/www.asiabooks.com). Asoke BTS/Sukhumvit MRT. **Open** 9am-7pm daily. **Map** p128 B2 ⑨

The only non-mall branch of Thailand's biggest English book chain shelves magazines and tomes on Asian design, cooking and heritage, plus UK and US bestsellers, guidebooks, business advisories and lifestyle manuals.

Nightlife

Arabian Night

Ground floor, Grace Hotel, 12 Sukhumvit Soi 3 (0 2253 0651-75/ www.gracehotel.th.com). Nana BTS.

Open (except Ramadan) 11.30pm-2am daily. Bands midnight-2am daily. **Map** p128 A2 ⑩

An awesome Arabic band blasts souk rhythms to back mesmeric singers in a vast, ornate interior. From midnight onwards on some nights, bellydancers shimmy on the tables under a shower of bank notes.

Bed Supperclub

26 Sukhumvit Soi 11 (0 2651 3537/ www.bedsupperclub.com). Nana BTS. **Open** 7.30pm-2am daily. **BBBB**. **Fusion**. **Map** p128 B2 ⑪

Evolving far beyond the inspiration of Amsterdam's Bed bar, this brilliant venue keeps redefining itself via performance art, events, *Bedsheets* magazine, and top world DJs, plus an array of spin-off ventures. Divided into restaurant and bar-club, it's an all-white futuristic pod on stilts, with mattress seating, and look-at-me staircases leading to look-at-you balconies. The cocktails excel, as do Paul Hutt's inventive fusion dishes (the set menu changes each weekend). The club holds theme nights like Rehab. Note that there are strict ID checks on the door.

Nana Entertainment Plaza

Sukhumvit Soi 4 (0 2254 9347).
Nana BTS. **Open** 9pm-2am daily.
Map p128 A2 ⑫

Setting for many a genre 'Bangkok
novel' about the city's underworld, this
three-level complex gets racier the further the bar from the street. Locals
favour Soi Cowboy, but many a visitor
here ends up never leaving. See p104.

Q Bar

34 Sukhumvit Soi 11, on sub-soi to
Soi 3 (0 2252 3274/www.qbarbangkok.
com). Nana BTS. **Open** 8pm-1am
daily. **Admission** B400 (incl 2 drinks)
Mon-Thur; B600 (incl 2 drinks) Fri-Sun.
Map p128 B1 ⑬

Spawned from celebrity photographer
David Jacobson's original Q Bar
Saigon, this slick, New York-style conversion of a house takes off nightly.
Superbly trained bartenders mix an
astonishing range of imported spirits.
It was the Bangkok pioneer of themed
music nights, vari-colour lighting and
showcasing Thai DJs, while global leg-
ends guest on the decks.

Asoke to Phromphong

The **Siam Society** was built on
Soi 21 (Asoke) in 1933 amid fields.
Today, it's ringed by high-rises and
Asoke forms part of the inner ring
road, Thanon Ratchadaphisek,
which continues south past
Benjakitti Park, Queen Sirikit
National Convention Centre and
the port of Khlong Toei.

Aside from the red-light districts
at Soi Cowboy and Soi 22, the
residential sois off mid-Sukhumvit
are a smörgåsbord of international
dining, spas and boutiques. Among
affluent Thais, thousands of
expatriates live here, especially
Westerners and, in Sois 31-53,
Japanese. By Phromphong BTS, the
upmarket mall **Emporium** contains
the superb **Thailand Creative
& Design Centre** (TCDC).

Sights & museums

Benjakitti Park

Thanon Ratchadaphisek (0 2229 3000).
Queen Sirikit Centre MRT. **Open** 5am-
8pm daily. **Map** p128 B4 ⑭

Surrounding Lake Ratchada, this is the
first stage in converting the Thailand
Tobacco Monopoly into a park. It
offers jogging, cycling (with bike hire),
water features, a playground, boat hire,
an outdoor gym and a meditation zone,
although it lacks enough shade.
Thailand Segway Tours (0 2255 8463,
www.thailandsegwaytours.com) runs
Segway glides here daily.

Benjasiri Park

Thanon Sukhumvit, beside Emporium
(0 2262 0810). Phrom Phong BTS.
Open 5am-9pm daily. **Map** p128 C4 ⑮

Amid Benjasiri's fountains, ponds and
pavilions stand sculptures by Thai
artist Misiem Yipintsoi. The park hosts
festivals, and exercisers relish the
skate park, tiny pool and courts for
basketball and *takraw*.

Siam Society &
Baan Kamthieng

131 Sukhumvit Soi 21 (0 2661
6470-77/www.siam-society.org).
Asoke BTS/Sukhumvit MRT. **Open**
9am-5pm Tue-Sat. **Admission** B100;
B50 reductions. No credit cards.
Map p128 B2 ⑯

This handsome cultural centre has an
important library and holds Thursday
lectures, exhibitions and study trips,
and not just for members. In its well-
tended grounds, an allegedly haunted
150-year-old northern Thai wooden
house, Baan Kamthieng, is home to a
multimedia museum on Lanna culture.

Thailand Creative &
Design Centre (TCDC)

7th floor, Emporium, 622 Thanon
Sukhumvit (0 2664 7667). **Open**
10.30am-9pm Tue-Sun. **Admission**
free; some activities charge. **BB**. No
credit cards. **Thai**. **Map** p128 C4 ⑰

BANGKOK BY AREA

Siam Society & Baan Kamthieng p133

One of the world's best design centres, the Thailand Creative & Design Centre (more often, TCDC) inspires Thais with global design and showcases Thai creativity through superb exhibitions and talks. Accessed via this mall's cinema lobby, its stylish environs include a shop, an auditorium, Bharani restaurant, a massive library and the Material ConneXion resource archive.

Eating & drinking

Bo.Lan

42 Soi Picha Ranong Thanon Sukhumvit 26 (0 2260 2962-3/www.bo.lan.co.th). Phrom Phong BTS. **Open** 6.30pm-10pm Tue-Sun. **BBBB. Thai. Map** p128 C4 ⑱
Though a great food capital, Bangkok has a chink in its culinary armour: there are too few sublime, upscale Thai restaurants. This ambitious newcomer tries to redress that. Inside a secluded, wood-panelled house, Bo.lan aims high with smooth service, a wine list to pair with Thai food, and degustation menus to demonstrate their considerable kitchen skills, honed at David Thompson's Nahm in London. With some inconsistencies ironed out, Bo.lan will demand international respect.

Bourbon Street

Washington Square, Sukhumvit Soi 22 (0 2259 0328-9/www.bourbonstbkk. com). Phrom Phong BTS. **Open** 7am-1am daily. **BBB. Southern American. Map** p128 C3 ⑲
Amid the plaid-and-stetson bars of Washington Square, this New Orleans-themed bar/restaurant stands out for its long bar and Cajun-Creole food like jambalaya, pecan pie and crawfish from the owner's farm.

Bull's Head

Sukhumvit Soi 33/1 (0 2259 4444/ www.greatbritishpub.com). Phrom Phong BTS. **Open** 11am-1am daily. **BBB. British. Map** p128 C3 ⑳
Despite rivals within staggering distance, this wood-and-horse-brass tavern remains the city's most authentic British pub. The Bull's Head draws regulars with jukebox hits, pub grub, draught ale, games such as 'toss the boss', and, upstairs, internationally

known stand-up comedians headline the Punchline Comedy Club every two months (tickets cost B1,500).

Giusto

16 Sukhumvit Soi 23 (0 2258 4321/www.giustobangkok.com). **Open** 11.30am-2pm, 6pm-10.30pm daily. **BBBB. Italian.** Map p128 C2 ㉑
Chef-patron Fabio Colautti has Gucci-ised a house to create this power restaurant and its wine bar, Glass. The glazed octagon is the zone to book. Decent wines by the glass matched with dishes such as fish and spicy sausage soup, and spaghetti with sea urchin and sliced *bottarga*.

Govinda

6/5-6 Sukhumvit Soi 22 (0 2663 4970). Phrom Phong BTS. **Open** 11.30am-3pm, 6-11.30pm Mon, Wed-Sun. **BB. Italian Vegetarian.** Map p128 C3 ㉒
Despite the name, this excellent vegetarian restaurant is all Italian: thin-base pizzas, pastas and risottos, plus own-made bread. The interior has character, with a winding staircase and balcony. German beer too.

Greyhound Café

2nd floor, Emporium, Sukhumvit Soi 24 (0 2664 8663/0 2260 7149). Phrom Phong BTS. **Open** 11.30am-10pm daily. **BB. Thai/Fusion.** Map p128 C4 ㉓
Run by, and adjacent to, the hip Thai fashion store (p138), this chain retains its quirky minimalist style, handwritten menus and tailor-made crockery. The tried-and-tested menu features faultless Thai staples and inspired fusions. The Another Hound branch (1st floor, Siam Paragon, 0 2129 4409) applies that flair to finer dining. It's full of film, media and society types, yet good value.

Imoya

3rd floor, Terminal Building, 2/17-19 Sukhumvit Soi 24 (0 2663 5185). Phrom Phong BTS. **Open** 6pm-midnight daily. **BB. Japanese.** Map p129 D4 ㉔
In an area filled with sushi bars, Japanese bakeries, noodle outlets and fine Nipponese dining, this retro isakaya restaurant with bar, booths and shuttered rooms has a charm all its

own. Resembling a 1950s Tokyo diner, it serves small but good value dishes designed to accompany beer or sake.

Kalapapruek on First

1st floor, Emporium, Sukhumvit Soi 24 (0 2664 8410-2). Phrom Phong BTS. **Open** 11am-9.30pm daily. **BB**.
Thai/International. Map p128 C4 **25**
Friendly, trendy and spacious, Kalapapruek has park views and a menu strong on regional specialities, such as roti with curry and Chiang Mai's beloved *khao soi*, plus Western dishes and cakes. It's owned by the son of aristocrat Mom Chao Bhisadhet Rachanee, whose original restaurant is in the family house (27 Thanon Pramuan, Bangrak, 0 2236 4335).

Koi

26 Sukhumvit Soi 20 (0 2258 1590/koirestaurantbkk.com). Asoke BTS/Sukhumvit MRT. **Open** 6pm-midnight daily. **BBBB. Japanese. Map** p128 C3 **26**
LA celebrity hangout Koi opened this über-chic bar and California-Japanese restaurant, followed by an Italian eaterie in the artfully lit garden. On Tuesdays, Thursdays, Fridays and Saturdays a flock of models on free drinks and pheromones get into overdrive.

Kuppa

39 Sukhumvit Soi 16 (0 2663 0450). Asoke BTS/Sukhumvit MRT. **Open** 10am-11pm daily (closed 4th Mon of mth). **BBB** International. **Map** p128 B4 **27**
This hangar of blond wood and metal, which is dominated by a working coffee roaster, has the scale and feel of a major international restaurant, and the menu is consistently good, from duck pizza with hoi sin sauce to mighty desserts. Cultured urbanites relish the sofas and magazines all day till late.

Le Dalat Indochine

14 Sukhumvit Soi 23 (0 2661 7967-8). Asoke BTS/Sukhumvit MRT. **Open**
11am-2pm, 6pm-10pm daily. **BBB**.
Vietnamese. Map p128 C3 **28**
Oozing class, this adapted house is owned by the family of Mme Hoa Ly, daughter of a 1930s French governor to Indochina. Old photos line the lobby bar, while dining rooms brim with Asian antiques. Even Ladies peek in the gents to view the phallus collection. Consistently good specialities such as prawn on sugar cane come with a bouquet of herb-strewn leaves.

Long Table

25th floor, Column Building, Sukhumvit Soi 16 (0 2302 2557-9/www.longtablebangkok.com). Asoke BTS/Sukhumvit MRT. **Open** 5pm-2am; *Dinner* 6-11pm daily. **BBBB**.
Fusion/Bar. Map p128 B3 **29**
The views stretch even longer than the 24-metre teak shared table at this chic Thai-meets-Western concept, initially spawned from Bed Supperclub. Hi-so Thais and moneyed expats savour bespoke Asian fusion, like a crunchy salad of raw tuna with sprouts and crisped rice, and chicken breast stuffed with sausage in green curry. Service is smooth, the space sexy, and servings surprisingly large – so are their excellent long drinks, best sipped on the breezy terrace.

Maha Naga

2 Sukhumvit Soi 29 (0 2662 3060). Phrom Phong BTS. **Open** 6pm-midnight daily. **BBB. Thai/Fusion. Map** p128 C3 **30**
Exquisite decor qualifies this as a destination restaurant, despite the so-so food. Fusions like pork chop with green curry struggle for balance, so bask instead amid the Indian glass mosaics, Moroccan Ramadan lanterns, waiters' Moorish costumes, a fountain courtyard and an art nouveau house containing the bar.

Pizzeria Bella Napoli

3/3 Sukhumvit Soi 31 (0 2259 0405). Phrom Phong BTS. **Open** 11.30am-

Bo.Lan p134

2.30pm; 5-11.30pm Mon-Fri; 11.30am-
11.30pm Sat-Sun. **BB**. **Italian**.
Map p128 C3 ③①
Owner Claudio Conversi, who also
makes *gelato* for many of Bangkok's
top hotels and restaurants, opened
BKK's first stand-alone pizza parlour
in 2002. It was rammed from day one
and generates real buzz. Joining its
classic Neapolitan pizzas are pastas
and some trattoria mains.

Rang Mahal
*26th floor, Rembrandt Hotel, 19
Sukhumvit Soi 18 (0 2261 7100/
www.rembrandtbkk.com). Asoke
BTS/Sukhumvit MRT.* **Open** 11.30am-
2.30pm, 6.30-10.30pm daily. **BBBB**.
Indian. Map p128 C3 ③②
Superb city views and rich, north
Indian dishes make this palatial setting
worth a splurge, but do reserve a window table. The Moghul decor spreads
to the die-cut menu, while a loud, entertaining Indian band plays near the ban-
quet tables. There are good thalis and
a terrific-value Sunday brunch buffet
(B650, B325 6-12s, free under-6s). The
air-con is very cold.

Ruen Mallika
*189 Sukhumvit Soi 22, in sub-soi to Soi
16 (0 2663 3211/www.ruenmallika.
com).* **Open** 11am-11pm daily. **BBB**.
Thai. Map p128 C4 ③③
Servings are as huge as the wooden
menu, which features unusual dishes
such as deep-fried flowers, to the
recipes of mid 20th-century celebrity
chef ML Terb Chomsai. Opt for relaxed
garden seating amid fountains or triangular cushions at low tables inside this
Rama I-era teak stilt house. It runs the
Yantafo chain of retro noodle shops.

Spring Summer Winter
*199 Soi Promsri 2, off Sukhumvit Soi
39 (0 2392 2747-8).* **Open** 11am-
2.30pm, 5.30-11pm daily. **BBB**.
Asian seafood. Map p129 D3 ③④
Two striking 1960s houses dominate
this spacious compound. The inviting-
ly lit Spring serves good seafood with
Thai, Chinese and Japanese influences.
Summer café specialises in chocolate
desserts, while Winter is a dry-season
bar on the lawn where you can drink
or dine on beanbags. Sublime, but service can be so-so.

BANGKOK BY AREA

Shopping

Almeta

20/3 Sukhumvit Soi 23 (0 2258 4227/ www.almeta.com). Asoke BTS/ Sukhumvit MRT. **Open** 9am-6pm daily. **Map** p128 C2 ㉟

The first store to offer Thai silk 'à la carte', tailor-woven to request. It's top quality, and they haven't imposed a minimum spend, so order that silk hanky today.

Atelier Pichitra

43/27-28 Sukhumvit Soi 31 (0 2261 7553-5). **Open** 9am-6pm Mon-Sat. **Map** p128 C3 ㊱

Long before gracing Milan Fashion Week in 2005, Pichitra Boonyarataphan Ruksajit was a dame of Thai couture (she designed the Thai Airways uniforms). Society debs and doyennes snap up her cosmopolitan creations by the rack. Pricey, but with good reason.

Crystal Lounge

28 Sukhumvit Soi 20 (0 2258 1599/www.crystalevolution.com). Phrom Phong BTS. **Open** 11am-midnight daily. **Map** p128 C3 ㊲

Paris Hilton bought six Crystal Evolution navel rings by owner Bella. After founding the Bodysteel & Silver brand, with husband Robert she opened this jeweller-cum-lounge bar, where the bling includes a perfect wedding gift: Swarovski hand-cuffs.

Dasa

714/4 Thanon Sukhumvit, near Soi 26 (0 2661 2993/www.dasabookcafe.com). Phrom Phong BTS. **Open** 10am-8pm daily. No credit cards. **Map** p129 D4 ㊳

Over 10,000 second-hand titles fill two floors of well-organised shelves. There's also a coffee corner.

Emporium

622 Sukhumvit Soi 24 (0 2269 1000/www.emporiumthailand.com). Phrom Phong BTS. **Open** 10am-10pm daily. **Map** p128 C4 ㊴

Supremely successful, Emporium lures the well-off with Euro-couture and long-established Thai jewellers. Lesser mortals come for the local and imported fashion, opticians, books, hairstylists, travel agents and furnishings. It hosts catwalks, exhibitions, promos and concerts, and boasts a fine namesake department store and an excellent gourmet food hall.

Greyhound

2nd floor, Emporium, Sukhumvit Soi 24 (0 2664 8664). Phrom Phong BTS. **Open** 10am-9pm daily. **Map** p128 C4 ㊵

A legend among Thai labels, ex-ad guru Bhanu Inkawat offers understated essentials with characterful tweaks and vamped up suit fabrics. Bhanu recently entered couture territory with Grey (2nd floor, Siam Paragon, 0 2129 4358), while designer/artist Jitsing Somboon styles the street-cred offshoot Playhound. For Greyhound's hit restaurants, see p135 and p136.

Nightlife

Indus

71 Sukhumvit Soi 26 (0 2258 4900, 0 2661 5279/indusbangkok.com) Phrom Phong BTS. **Open** 11.30am-2.30pm, 6.30pm-11pm daily. **BBB. Indian Kashmiri.** **Map** p129 D4 ㊶

With India booming, this club-restaurant stages periodic arm-flailing Bhangra parties with live drumming plus star Indian DJs in its dance-bar. Out front, Chef Sonya Sapru concocts rich Kashmiri cuisine with fewer calories, so you're not too heavy to do your Bollywood moves. A large garden adds to the all-rounder quality.

Narcissus

112 Sukhumvit Soi 23 (0 2258 4805). Asoke BTS/Sukhumvit MRT then taxi. **Open** 9pm-late daily. **Admission** B200 (incl 1 drink). **Map** p128 C2 ㊷

Fronted by the pseudo-classical Pegasus hostess club, this temple to kitsch has a tourist-friendly attitude.

The fine sound system plays house and trance, periodically from DJs such as Tiësto or Paul Oakenfold. Three sparser renovated rooms offer hip hop, Thai rock bands and even a coyote theme.

Soi Cowboy
Sukhumvit Soi 23, Sukhumvit Asoke BTS/Sukhumvit MRT. **Open** 9pm-2am daily. **Map** p128 C3 ④③
Recent upgrades make this strip the most neon-intensive and least aggressive go-go strip, and so more favoured by expats. See box p104.

Arts & leisure

Bodhi & Holistic Medical Centre
20th floor, 253 Building, 253 Sukhumvit Soi 21 (0 2640 8090/ www.thebodhi.com/www.hmcthai.com). Asoke BTS/Sukhumvit MRT. **Open** 7am-9pm Mon-Fri; 10am-8pm Sat, Sun. **Map** p128 C1 ④④
A soothing, space-age spa offering hi-tech diagnostics and workouts for body-styling. Also does holistic rebalancing through tests and treatments, from chelation and colonics to nutrimedicine. Packages from B4,500.

Carpediem Galleries
4th floor, Times Square (0 2250 0898/ www.carpediemgallery.com). Asoke BTS/Sukhumvit MRT. **Open** 10.30am-6pm Mon-Sat. **Map** p128 B3 ④⑤
New location for Singaporean Delia Oakins' gallery for South-east Asian artists, including Symon and Krijono of Indonesia, Martin Loh of Singapore and Thai Thawun Pramarn, plus Italian Luigi Rincicotti.

Divana Massage & Spa
7 Sukhumvit Soi 25 (0 2661 6784-5/www.divanaspa.com). Asoke BTS/Sukhumvit MRT. **Open** 11am-11pm Mon-Fri; 10am-11pm Sat, Sun. **Map** p128 C3 ④⑥
A garden domain with ceramic jar showers and proper beds with pillows, geared to pampering couples and families. It uses scrubs, mud wraps, massages, steams, facials and milky baths. Divana favours ultra-modesty so ask if you need hip-area treatment.

Rasayana Retreat & Restaurant
57 Soi Prommitr, Sukhumvit Soi 39 (0 2662 4803-5/www.rasayanaretreat. com). Thonglor BTS then taxi. **Open** 9am-9pm daily; *Restaurant* 10am-8pm daily. **BB. Raw food. Map** p129 D3 ④⑦
This quiet detox centre is modern with Chinese touches. Having alkalised your diet, start with the low-stress, high-modesty colonics. Finish at the garden café, which serves juices and Californian-style raw food (which they can deliver). Cleansing/fasting programmes include emotional support, with hypnotherapy counselling for addicts. Pilates classes too.

Thonglor & Ekamai

From Sukhumvit Soi 39 to Soi 63 (Ekamai), old family compounds and shophouses are giving way to condominiums, restaurants, nightclubs and shopping villages. These cater to rich offspring departing the extended-family nest and to yuppies wanting to live near the glitziest social life (see box p140). Soi Ekamai and Soi Thonglor (Sukhumvit Soi 55) – have become highways in themselves, branching lanes labelled as Thonglor sois or Ekamai sois. Between chintzy wedding plazas and old-style family restaurants, sprout semi-outdoor retail plazas that build a sense of community.

Yet even hi-sos frequent the superior streetfood at the mouth of Sukhumvit Soi 38 (p79). Feeling more out of place at Ekamai, the proletarian Eastern Bus Terminal (p181) loads coaches for the coast, Pattaya and Ko Samet (p159).

BANGKOK BY AREA

Hi-So heaven

The parallel streets of Thonglor (Sukhumvit Soi 55) and Ekamai (Soi 63) frame Bangkok's most modish neighbourhood. From the ostentatious ladies-who-lunch to their partyboy offspring, the area's compounds, condos, spas, boutiques, furniture showrooms, bars, restaurants, and retail complexes function as a power magnet.

With bloodline no longer the sole factor in status, social climbers and new money have blurred the boundary between high repute and *hi-so*, slang for high society. While bouffant height may be lower these days, hi-so ladies still sport their trademark hairstyle, designer handbags and flamboyant jewellery. Spot them dining in groups within the four-storey J Avenue precinct, or buzzing along to bridal boutiques, stepping out of a Mercedes with a daughter called Benz and her Sino-Thai beau named Bank. No exaggeration.

After being primped at **Chalachol** salon (p142), younger hi-so browse through H1's understated, über-hip boutiques like **Basheer Graphic Books** (p142) or lounge in its courtyard at **To Die For** (p141). After dark, they head to nightclubs like **Muse** (p142) and Funky Villa (02 711 6970-1 beside **Demo**, p142), which often reach bursting point. (Doormen often ask foreigners for passports.) A more alternative genre of hi-so like to 'rough it' at hangouts like **Happy Monday** (p142), a creative Mecca for advertising folk, artists and musicians.

Sights & museums

Wat Maha But

749 Onnut Soi 7, Sukhumvit Soi 77 (0 2311 2183). Onnut BTS. **Open** 7am-6pm daily. **Admission** free. **Map** p129 F5 ⓽

This temple by Khlong Prakhanong holds a shrine to Mae Nak, who died in childbirth over 150 years ago while her husband was at war. In a much-filmed legend, he returned home, unaware his wife and child were ghosts. Conscripts and mothers come here to donate offerings such as dresses, wigs, make-up and toys to appease the vengeful spirits. It opens for 24 hours every 14th-15th and at the end of every month for *kor huai* ('seeking lucky numbers') for the state lottery.

Eating & drinking

Ana Garden

67 Sukhumvit Soi 55 (0 2391 1762/ www.anagarden.com). Thonglor BTS. **Open** 5pm-midnight daily. *Groove Kitchen 3pm-1am daily.* **BB**. **Thai**. **Map** p129 E4 ⓵

Garden bar-restaurants are getting rarer; this fine example with wooden decks within an (intentionally) broken wall can become a late-night affair. After a meat-oriented dinner, drinkers migrate to the Groove Kitchen bar shrouded in foliage at the back.

Baan Rai Café

Thanon Sukhumvit, at Soi 63 (0 2391 9783-5/www.banriecoffee.com). Ekamai BTS. **Open** 24hrs daily. **B**. No credit cards. **Thai/Coffee**. **Map** p129 F5 ⓾

This non-stop rustic wooden 'coffee garden' serves tea and coffee in modern and local styles, plus a full Thai menu. Inside are nine iMacs with internet, plus CDs and books.

Hazara

The Face, 29 Sukhumvit Soi 38 (0 2713 6048-9/www.facebars.com).

Muse p142

Thonglor BTS. **Open** 6-11pm daily.
BBBB. **Indian**. Map p129 E5 🟡
A giant Balinese *garuda* dominates an
interior of pan-Asian statuary, puppet
heads and carved doors. Hazara's rich
North Indian curries and creamy dals
includes enticing vegetarian options,
such as stuffed tandoor peppers. It's
better than the Lanna Thai restaurant
that shares this graceful Thai-style
complex. Try its spa before dining.

Khrua Vientiane
*8 Sukhumvit Soi 36 (0 2258 6171).
Thonglor BTS.* **Open** noon-midnight
daily. **BB**. **Thai Isaan**. Map
p129 E4 🟡
You feel almost upcountry in this soi
of Lao/Isaan eateries. The sprawling
wooden compound offers cushion or
table seating while dancers and musicians play *pong lang* nightly (7.30-
10pm). It may fill with farang, but the
food's authentic.

To Die For
*H1, 998 Sukhumvit Soi 55 (02 381
4714).* **Open** 5pm-midnight Mon-Thur,

Sun; 4pm-1am Fri; 4pm-1am Sat. **BBB**.
International. Map p129 F2 🟡
The gem of Thonglor's chic H1 complex,
To Die For has Greyhound-clad waiters
serving cocktails and inventive
European dishes with an Oriental zest to
hip young things. Courtyard sofas soft-
en the stark decor with a relaxed vibe.

Tuba
34 Ekamai Soi 21 (02 711 5500).
Open 10am-2am daily. **BB**. **Thai**.
Map p129 F2 🟡
An ever-changing mish-mash of funky
furniture, neon signs, robots, memorabilia and oil paintings, where regulars
play pool, use the free Wi-Fi, listen to
jazz, watch TV or snack on the cheap,
tasty Italian and Thai food. Like visiting a cool friend's home.

Xian Dumpling Restaurant
*10/3 Sukhumvit Soi 40 (0 2713 5288).
Ekkamai BTS.* **Open** 11am-11pm daily.
B. No credit cards. **Chinese**. Map
p129 E5 🟡
Amid good-bad taste decor, set in a
shadowy parking lot, the hearty Xian

food owes much to Mongolian, Muslim and Silk Road influences. Think shredded tripe and tofu with chilli oil, stewed aubergine, mutton soup and dumplings every which way.

Shopping

Basheer Graphic Books

H1, 998 Sukhumvit Soi 55 (0 2391 9815-6/www.basheergraphic.com). Thonglor BTS. **Open** 11am-8pm daily. **Map** p129 F2 ⑤⑥
The focus on graphic arts, design and photography titles rare elsewhere suits the fashion-forward H1 location. Browsing is encouraged.

Chalachol

205/13-14 Sukhumvit Soi 55 (0 2712 6481/www.chalachol.com). Thonglor BTS. **Open** 10.30am-7.30pm daily. **Map** p129 E3 ⑤⑦
Celebrity stylist Somsak Chalachol revolutionised Thai hairdressing with his chain of unisex designer salons. Get your hair washed sitting in a massage chair. Cut and blow dry from B400.

Nightlife

Demo

225/9-10 Sukhumvit Soi 63 (0 2711 6970-1). Ekamai BTS then taxi. **Open** 8pm-2am. **Map** p129 F3 ⑤⑧
A discerning, underground sister club to the gargantuan Funky Villa next door. Softly-lit girders, designer graffiti and plush seating conspire towards a 'demolition-chic'. Affluent Thai alternatives order bottles of spirits while shimmying to electro, house, hip-hop or indie.

Happy Monday

Corner of Ekamai Soi 10 (0 2714 3953/ www.myspace.com/happymonday). Ekamai BTS then taxi. **Open** 7pm-late night Mon-Sat. No credit cards. **Map** p129 F4 ⑤⑨
Daek naew (indie youth) are happy daily at this garden-bar tucked away at the front of a building housing the

pop culture mag *a day*. DJs spin eclectic Britpop-heavy mixes for the whisky-soda-coke-sipping ad folk, musicians and designer regulars.

Muse

159/8 Thonglor Soi 10 (0 2715 0998) Thonglor or Ekamai BTS then taxi. **Open** 6pm-2am daily. **Bands** 7pm-2am daily. **Map** p129 E3 ⑥⓪
Behind some gigantic black doors, upwardly mobile locals sing along to the live rock bands and huddle amid bottles of whisky. An elevator leads to the daybed tranquillity of the roof terrace, and a more intimate cocktail bar.

Nang Len

217 Sukhumvit Soi 63 (0 2711 6564). Ekkamai BTS then taxi. **Open** 6.30pm-2am Mon-Sat. **Bands** 8.30pm Mon-Thur; 9pm Fri, Sat. **Map** p129 F2 ⑥①
The name means 'lounge around' and a nubile student crowd crams around low tables in this dark, polished interior. MTV-style hip-hop DJs punctuate three indie/pop cover bands nightly. You'll need a passport as ID here.

Arts & leisure

Baan Chang Thai

38 Ekamai Soi 10 (0 2391 3807). Ekamai BTS. **Open** 8am-11pm daily. **Map** p129 F3 ⑥②
Baan Chang Thai is dedicated to preserving and teaching traditional crafts. There are courses on an ancient southern form of *muay thai*, plus puppet making and painting. Limited English, but bargain prices.

Sareerarom Tropical Spa

117 Thonglor Soi 10 (0 2391 9919/ www.thesareerarom.com). Thonglor BTS. **Open** *Spa* 10am-10pm daily; *Yoga* 8am-7pm daily. **Tea**. **Map** p129 F3 ⑥③
In a calming water garden, Sareerarom's pavilions and suites exude a pared-down Asian chic. The masseuses combine Balinese, Swedish and Thai strokes with essential oils. Dharma yoga available.

Chatuchak Weekend Market p144

Suburbs

Commuter train lines are reshaping BK's 'burbs and connecting this vast metropolis to downtown. The BTS accesses Chatuchak's must-see Weekend Market, bars and parks, and Aree's bohemian scene. Skytrain extensions southeast will make the suburbs of Further Sukhumvit less remote. The MRT arcs past nightlife strips off Ratchadaphisek inner ring road. Meanwhile, expressboats make Nonthaburi province a pleasant jaunt. Expressways also reach these hubs of unfiltered Thai life.

Chatuchak & Aree

When Bangkok's weekend market was moved from Sanam Luang to Chatuchak Park it seemed the back of beyond. Still, a quarter of a million visited weekly. Now JJ (from the alt spelling Jatujak) has spawned a creative subculture. As JJ winds down, huge bars just a saunter

down Thanon Kamphaengphet Road pump dance music or, at the far end, which plays host to an exuberant gay scene.

Many artsy JJ types and gays live or socialise around Aree and its restaurants-in-houses. In between, rough and ready Saphan Khwai is gaining cachet from **Reflections Hotel** (p179).

Sights & museums

Chatuchak Park

Thanon Phahon Yothin (0 2272 4575/08 1615 5776). Morchit BTS/ Chatuchak Park MRT. **Open** *Park* 4am-9pm daily. *Rail Hall of Fame* 6am-noon Tue-Fri; 6am-2pm Sat-Sun. *Butterfly Garden* 8.30am-4.30pm Tue-Sun. **Admission** free. No credit cards. This respite from market mayhem is branded a 'Learning Park', with sculptures and playgrounds. The small Rail Hall of Fame houses old locomotives and various vehicles, including London taxis and World War II Japanese patrol cars. Adjacent Suan Rotfai (Railway Park, 0 2537 9221), the old railway golf course, offers bike hire, a good pool, the Butterfly Garden and Insectorium (0 2272 4359-60), scale models of Bangkok landmarks and a Traffic Town where kids can test for a Junior Driving Licence. In more contiguous green space, Queen Sirikit Park hosts the Children's Discovery Museum and a botanical garden.

Eating & drinking

Chatuchak Weekend Market

Thanon Phahon Yothin, at Thanon Kamphaengphet (0 2272 4440-1). Morchit or Saphan Khwai BTS/ Kamphaengphet subway. **B**. **Thai**. **Open** 5am-6pm Sat, Sun.

Some foodies go to Chatuchak Weekend Market just to eat. Vendors, stalls and restaurants (most on the perimeter, a few with air-con) draw dishes from all Thai regions. Isaan food fans scoff from pottery plates at Foon Talob (Section 26, Soi 1, 08 1838 1146). Coffee and fresh juice outlets occur every few steps, while bars swell from mid-afternoon, with regulars lending buzz to Viva (Section 26, Sois 1-2, 0 2272 4783) and its sister Aviv (section 8, both open 7am-6pm Fri, 7am-9pm Sat, Sun). There are air-conditioned stalls in adjacent JJ Mall.

Pla Dib

1/1 Areesamphan Soi 7, at Thanon Rama VI (0 2279 8185). Aree BTS. **Open** 5pm-midnight Tue-Sun. **BBB**. **Seafood/pizza**.

Thai for 'raw fish', Pla Dib weds Thai, Japanese and European in dishes such as 'larb sashimi' and 'raw seafood ceviche', plus wood-fired pizza. Young professional and alternative Thais huddle around minimalist, candlelit tables at this restored house with a front yard. The warehouse aesthetic suits its small parties, gigs and exhibitions. Book on weekends.

Shopping

Chatuchak Weekend Market

Thanon Phahon Yothin, at Thanon Kamphaengphet (0 2272 4440-1). Morchit or Saphan Khwai BTS/ Kamphaengphet subway. **Open** 5am-6pm Sat, Sun. *Plants* daytime Wed, Thur.

This kaleidoscopic labyrinth of 8,000-plus stalls (see box p145) is well signed into numbered, colour-coded sections divided by *soi* and stall number, but is better navigated with *Nancy Chandler's Map*. Meeting points include the clock tower, the in-market subway station or tourist office/bank building (open weekends, with ATMs). Benches, trees, pedestrianisation and trolleybuses help ease the heat, while cafés and toilets dot the edges. Dress light, secure valuables and visit early on to pre-empt the heaving throngs.

Or Tor Kor (OTK)

Thanon Kamphaengphet (0 2279 2080-2). Saphan Kwai BTS/ Kamphaengphet MRT. **Open** 6am-10pm daily. **B**. **Thai**.

Across the road from Chatuchak Market (above), the Agricultural Market Organisation (OTK) sells some of Thailand's best fruit and veg, as well as prepared foods and sweets from across the country. An air-con Royal Projects shop sells fresh and preserved produce next door.

Nightlife

Bu Ngah Pub & Home

518 Thanon Kamphaengphet, left down parallel lane behind Cha Bar (0 2618 4916/08 1700 2087/08 9666 9404). Kamphaengphet MRT. **Open** 6pm-2am daily. **Admission** free. **B**. No credit cards. **Thai**.

Follow muffled music to an inconspicuous, white, wooden-walled forecourt with a Thai sign. It hides table after table of merry hipster students and

Treasure hunt

Asia's biggest bazaar, **Chatuchak Weekend Market** has transcended ethnic Asian knick-knack status to become a hive of Thai creatives. Young designers flog outfits and fabrics in Sections 5-6, among second-hand items, ethnic and bohemian clobber and uniforms. Bargain hard, as T-shirts or jeans can cost from B50. New clothes fill Sections 10, 12, 14, 16, 18, and 20-26. **Siam Ruay** pioneered retro Thai style (Section 4, Soi 3, 08 5907 4954). **Props Room** crowds two branches (Section 3, Soi 3, 0 1567 9025) with theatrical jewellery.

The boutiques in tree-shaded Sections 2-4 showcase Thai designers' work in materials from zinc and Lucite to mulberry paper. Aromatherapy and candle brand **Karmakamet** started from its stunning black stall (Section 3, Soi 3, 0 1564 0505). Pick of the jewellers, **Xistnz** (Section 3, Soi 2, 08 9891 4338) makes mounts for exotic beads and stones. The area bristles with cafés, plants, herbs,

seeds and flowers, plus the pots and charms that go with them. Bushes and trees take over the whole market mid week (7am-6pm Wed, Thur). More design goodies are in Sections 7-8 and 24-27.

Thai and hill tribe crafts are to be found in Sections 1, 24 and 26, among pricey antiques. In Section 1, you'll also find puppets, lacquerware, carvings, Isaan silk, bronzes, amulets and Buddhas. **Silpa Thai** arrays *khon* masks and puppets (Section 24, Soi 2, 08 9926 6530) from its Thonburi workshop. Workshops across Thanon Kamphangphet 2 recondition teak furniture and house parts or make-to-order. For discounted books and magazines browse Sections 1 and 27.

Mixed reactions abound in the animal area. Cages hold kittens, puppies, reptiles, birds and tanks of fish in Sections 8, 9, 11, 13, 15 and 17. Some trade in endangered species persists. You may even catch a cockfight or fighting fish duel. All Thai life is here.

fashionable Chutuchak market folk, singing along to Thai ska, reggae and *sam-cha*. Sporadic pockets of dancing break out throughout this converted fish shop-cum-speakeasy.

Chakran

Soi Aree 4 Tai, Phahon Yothin Soi 7 (0 2279 1359/5310/www.aboutg.net/ chakran). Aree BTS. **Open** 3pm-midnight Mon-Thur; 2pm-5am Fri-Sun. **Admission** B230 Mon-Thur; B250 Fri-Sun. No credit cards.

Meaning 'unquenched warrior desire', this opulent sauna features shadow-play showers, theme nights and intimate perches around the pool, rooms and restaurant.

Fake

359-360 Thanon Kamphaengphet (081 689 4166). Kamphaengphet MRT. **Open** 8pm-1am daily. **Admission** free before 10pm; B100 Fri, Sat after 10pm (incl 1 drink). No credit cards.

Fake attracts a more mature, moneyed set of well-coiffed young men than its rivals on either side, El Nin-Yo or Obama (formerly Mogue, then Celebrity). Lasers and a glitterball bounce light from bubbled purple walls as the regulars sway to electro and house music. It's a real squeeze inside, but that's the point.

Arts & leisure

Luang Pradit Phairoh Foundation

47 Thanon Setsiri (0 2279 1509/ www.thaikids.com).

You're free to hear and join in practice sessions at this school of *phiphat* Thai classical music (9am-5pm Sat, Sun), founded by the subject of the film *Hom Rong* (The Overture). Its *wai khru* ceremony is in August.

Numthong Gallery

Room 109, 1129/29 Bangkok Co-op Housing Building, opposite Samsen Station, Thanon Toeddamri (0 2243 4326). **Open** 11am-6pm Mon-Sat. No credit cards.

Numthong Tang champions artistic individuality at this gallery with a magnificent roster of works by modern masters like Natee Utarit, Niti Wuttuya, Chatchai Puipia, Kamin Lertchaiprasert and Montien Boonma.

Ratchada & beyond

The Ratchadaphisek inner ring road arcs past nondescript towers, stores and housing, but hosts two of Bangkok's three official nightlife zones – disco barns and beer halls around Sois 4 to 8, and swisher clubs at RCA (Royal City Avenue) – as well as gaudy massage parlours.

Ratchada's hinterland has some cultural draws and stretches down residential Lad Prao to the unpretentious youth hub of Thanon Ramkhamhaeng, an artery packed with malls, shops, bars (many gay) and Na Ram Market (between Sois 43-53, 4pm-midnight daily) – all frequented by students of Ramkhamhaeng University.

Sights & museums

Bangkok Sculpture Centre

4/18-19 Nuanchan Soi 56, near Thanon Ramindra expressway exit (0 2559 0505 ext 119, 232/www.thaiart project.org). **Open** 10am-4pm Tue-Sat. **Admission** free.

Museums of modern Thai art are rare, but this private collection houses 120 major works, which are displayed on lawns, ledges, warehouse gantries and the fountain terrace of this airy, dramatic edifice.

Kwan Im Shrine

Chokchai Soi 39, Lad Phrao Soi 53 (Chokchai 4) (0 2514 0715). **Open** 6.30am-8pm Mon-Fri, Sun; 6.30am-11pm Sat; 6.30am-2am Chinese religious holidays. **Admission** free.

Bangkok Sculpture Centre

The cult of Kuan Im (aka Kuan Yin, the Chinese *bodhisattva* of mercy) prompted this massive, gaudy sculpture garden, embellished with wagon wheels, barrels and a modern pagoda. Eye-popping offerings crowd the basement museum. It holds a procession nine days after Chinese New Year.

Origin Cultural Programs

Lad Prao Soi 60 (0 2259 4896-7/ www.alex-kerr.com/www.origin-asia.com). No credit cards.
Authentic cultural experiences of one day or longer, with Thai experts offering a hands-on insight into arts like dance, *lai Thai* design, cooking and martial arts. The programmes are held in English at a teak compound, with branches in Chiang Mai and Japan.

Prasart Museum

9 Krung Thep Kreetha Soi 4A (0 2379 3601). **Open** by appointment 1 day ahead 9am-3pm (last entry) Tue-Sun. **Admission** B1,000; B500 per person groups of 2 or more. No credit cards.
It's worth the hassle (but perhaps not the price) to luxuriate amid these antiques housed in replicas of a European-style mansion, a Khmer shrine and Northern and Central Thai teak houses, plus Thai- and Chinese-style temples. Prasart Vongsakul's shop in Peninsula Plaza (153 Thanon Ratchadamri, 02253 9772) sells reproductions of his collection.

Eating & drinking

Old Leng

29/78-81 Royal City Avenue (0 2203 0972-3). **Open** 6pm-1am daily. **B. Thai**.
This survivor of the original RCA explosion looks like a cowboy saloon stranded in ancient China. 'Songs for Life' (Thai blues) fans flock here for live bands; smoochers gather on the quieter front deck. The clientele are mostly older, and hard-drinking.

Shopping

Ratchada Night Market

Thanon Ratchadaphisek at Thanon Lad Prao (Superhit Bar 08 5936 0693). Lad Prao MRT. **Open** 6pm-midnight Sat. No credit cards.

DudeSweet at 808

A Saturday bike meet has ballooned into a huge hip retro night market, with vintage cars, bikes and clothing, loungey stalls, creative knick-knacks and the makeshift Superhit Bar.

Nightlife

808

29/53-64, Block C, Royal City Avenue (02 622 2572). **Open** 9pm-2am Tue-Sun. **Admission** free; events may charge.

Besides local talent, 808's glowing industrial interior imports world famous DJs, from Grandmaster Flash to Goldie to Steve Aoki. Often home to hipster club nights such as DudeSweet (see box p149), 808 attracts an active jumble of Thai and *farang* party people. A balcony offers some respite from the impenetrable dancefloor.

Hollywood Awards

72/1 Thanon Ratchadaphisek Sois 8 (0 2246 4311-3). Thailand Cultural Centre MRT. **Open** 9pm-2am daily. *Bands* 10pm-midnight daily. **Admission** free.

An Oscar-themed disco show hall held together by neon. Street-dressed youth

raves to live *luuk grung* T-pop among tiny tables piled with whisky mixer sets and chicken knuckles.

Isaan Tawandaeng

484 Thanon Pattanakarn, east of Khlong Tan intersection (0 2717 2320-3). **Open** 6pm-2am daily. *Shows* 8.30pm-2am daily. **BB**. **Thai Isaan**. **Admission** free.

There's a diverse roster of *morlam/luuk thung* (daily), from dancing girl revues to formation crooners in Day-Glo tuxedoes, at this comfortable venue. It has branches that (from 8pm nightly) offer *pleng puer cheewit* bands instead.

Khrua Yaa Jai

15/8 Lad Phrao Soi 71 (0 2542 4147). **Open** 3.30pm-1am daily. *Shows* 8pm-1am daily. **B**. **Thai Isaan**. **Admission** free.

Folk star Mike Piromporn owns this *luuk thung* and *pleng puer cheewit* ('songs for life'), named 'Kitchen of Medicine for the Heart' after his album.

Snop

58/5 Ratchada Soi 4 (0 2612 2459). Rama IX subway. **Open** 7pm-2am daily. **Admission** free. No credit cards.

Soi 4 bars are getting fewer, bigger and smarter. Snop's huge new building keeps its toy-decorated, low-table dish shape surrounding the acoustic/indy bands. Staff costumes change quarterly, from superheroes or toons to chainmail or French revolution. Weirdly cute.

Slim & Flix
29/22-32 Block S, Royal City Avenue (0 2203 0226-8/08 1645 1177). **Open** 6pm-2am daily. **Admission** free.
Book a table in advance, as the chance of getting one on arrival is, ahem, slim. Still, it's more fun to roam the three zones catering to live Thai rock under chandeliers, hip hop and, in a white area branded Flix, local and imported pop-dance. Black leather sofas and low tables dot the interior, while the outdoor terrace has no-nonsense doormen demanding to see your ID.

Zeta
29/67-69 Royal City Avenue (08 0211 1060/www.zetabangkok.com). **Open** 9pm-2am daily. **Admission** free.
Zeta reflects RCA's young weekend crowds, but only lets in women. Vast prints of female figures along the mezzanine set the tone, while cute waitresses serve *toms* and *dees* dancing around whisky tables to Thai/Western pop from the all-girl band and DJ.

Arts & leisure

House
3rd floor, UMG Cinema, Royal City Avenue (0 2641 5177-8/www. houserama.com). **Tickets** B100. No credit cards.
Comfy and modern, Bangkok's main art-house cinema offers niche and festival films, some with gay themes.

Muang Thai Ratchadalai Theatre
Rear of Esplanade Mall, 99 Thanon Ratchadaphisek, near Soi 5 (0 2669 8288/www.rachadalai.com). Thailand Cultural Centre MRT. **Tickets** vary.

Party people

Sometimes, knowing where to go out in Bangkok is less important than knowing when to go. Clubland's disillusionment with burnt-out superstar DJs and anonymous whisky barn hip-hop hegemony has fuelled cult followings for a series of nomadic 'one-nighters' orchestrated by home-grown DJs and creatives.

Online networkers populate intimate, scene-building venues such as **Café Democ** (p69), **Pla Dib** (p144) and Copper (Royal City Avenue, 08-6327 0787). These provide a sense of community for the new club nights notified on flyers, Facebook, MySpace, and websites like BangkokRecorder. com as well as via email/SMS shots by party hosts.

Building a loyal clan of hipsters since 2002, Bangkok's original indie night, DudeSweet (www.dudesweet.org), remains the most popular one-nighter. Not buying the self-started rumours of DudeSweet's demise, a thousand-plus *daek naew* (indie kids) cram into either **Club Culture** (p126) or **808** (p148), to bounce to 'indietronica' DJs, video installations, international star showcases and live acts like Gene Kasidit and the Diet Pills. Founder, DJ Note, paces the wittily themed parties every couple of weeks, stoking clubber anticipation. Its success inspired a second wave of indie nights, spearheaded by the youthful Club Soma (www.myspace.com/ clubsomabkk) and Mind The Gap (www.myspace.com/mindthe gapbkk), which provides a platform for emerging bands like Samurai Loud.

BANGKOK BY AREA

Bangkok's first purpose-built theatre for Broadway-style shows hosts touring productions and concocts melodramatic Thai musicals.

Siam Niramit (Magical Siam)

Ratchada Grand Theatre, 19 Thanon Tiam Ruam-mit (0 2649 9222/ www.siamniramit.com). Thai Cultural Centre MRT then taxi. **Shows** 8pm daily. **Admission** B1,500. **BBB. Thai.**

This B1.5-billion, 2,000-seat theatre has one of the world's widest and tallest sets. It presents an 80-minute cultural spectacular with special effects, 150 performers, 500 costumes – and no soul. The outdoor crafts village is more authentic, and you can eat here too.

Thailand Cultural Centre

Thanon Thiam Ruam-mit (0 2247 0028/www.thaiculturalcenter.com). Thailand Cultural Centre MRT. **Tickets** vary. No credit cards.

Built by the Japanese, this state-run concert hall also has a small hall, but suffers from uncomfortable seating, a poor cafeteria, ageing facilities and being a long trek from the MRT. It's home to the Bangkok Symphony Orchestra and most visiting dance and music performances (including September's International Festival of Music & Dance; p36). The site will eventually gain a new national theatre and an art gallery.

Nonthaburi

Suburbia extends 33 kilometres (20 miles) upriver into this fruit-growing province, though flood damage and heedless building scar its semi-rustic charm. Expressboats terminate at **Nonthaburi Pier**, where the canal tours start. The esplanade fronting the sublime wooden fretwork of Nonthaburi Provincial Office ends at a simple pier restaurant.

Sights & museums

Canal tours

From Nonthaburi Expressboat pier (from B500/hr) or travel agency tour. **Open** around 9am-5pm daily.

Tours or hired longtail boats go to Koh Kred (below). Others ply the picturesque canals, viewing daily waterborne lifestyles around wooden stilt houses on a two-hour loop via Khlong Om or Khlong Bangkok Noi (p69).

Koh Kred

Tour from Nonthaburi Expressboat pier (around B300 a head for 2hrs), full day tour by Chao Phraya Expressboat (0 2623 6001-3) from Saphan Thaksin Pier (10am Sun, B300), agency tour or ferry from Pakkred Pier (B10). **Open Market** 9am-5pm Sat, Sun. **B. Thai.**

This rustic car-free island dotted with temples and wooden cottages makes for a languid half-day trip, though it gets busy on weekends. Legend says its ethnic Mon residents can return to Burma upon the collapse of the tilting *chedi* of Wat Poramai (Wat Mon), which houses a small museum (9am-4pm Mon-Fri, 0 2584 5120). Like another Wat Chimphlu on the northern side it displays Mon banners shaped like millipedes. The village lane between them has pottery workshops, the endearingly haphazard Khwam Aman Pottery Museum (9am-5pm daily, 0 2584 5086, 0 2583 4134), massage *salas*, restaurants and, on weekends, a packed market of speciality foods. An 8km path loops the island via farms and a traditional candy shop, taking two hours to stroll, but most go round by boat.

Eating & drinking

Suan Thip Baan Chao Phraya Thai Cultural House

Thanon Chaengwattana-Pakkred 3 (Soi Wat Koo) (0 2583 3748/www. suanthip.com). **Open** 11am-11pm daily. **BB. Thai.**

Mambo p152

A riverside dining retreat worth travelling for, or combining with Ko Kred or canal tours. It serves genteel presentations of authentic Thai dishes, notably *kaeng kii lek* and *kaeng born* curries, plus international options, either in air-conditioned teak rooms, traditional *salas* or at garden tables, all with lush riverscape view. Suan Thip also runs cultural programmes, cooking classes and parties.

Arts & leisure

IMPACT
Muang Thong Thani, 99 Popular Road, Thanon Chaengwattana, Pakkred (0 2833 4455/www. impact.co.th).
Most major rock/pop concerts – Thai and inter – hire the 12,000-seat IMPACT Arena in Asia' vast complex. Book via Thai Ticket Major (www.thaiticketmajor.com). Challenger Hall, the world's largest column-free hall, also hosts Fat Festival (early-Nov, see p38) and its trade fairs' public days draw bargain hunters. GEMS (late-Feb, mid-Sept) deals in jewellery, TIFF (mid-Mar) focuses on furniture, BIG (late Apr, mid-Oct) features design, housewares and gifts, THAIFEX (mid-May)

does food, and BIFF exhibits Thai fashion (Aug). Though distant, its fast to reach by expressway.

Yannawa & the Port

South of Thanon Sathorn the river girds the bulbous peninsula of Yannawa. This low-rise district will doubtless grow once it's served by the new BRT (Bus Rapid Transit) line. Temples and seafood restaurants fringe the river, which is packed with ships towards the port of Khlong Toei. The Khlong Toei Fresh Market (Thanon Na Ranong, open dawn to dusk) offers a safe glimpse of community life at Thailand's biggest slum. This is the access point for Bangkok's green lung, Bang Kra Jao.

Sights & museums

Bang Kra Jao
Ferry from Tha Wat Khlong Toei Nok, Thanon Kasemrat, Khlong Toei.
This protected wooded peninsula formed by an oxbow in the river lies in Samut Prakarn province. It feels like the countryside yet lies just 15 mins by road and ferry from Khlong Toei MRT.

Frequent boats from Wat Khlong Toei Nok Pier (B5, speedboat B10) meet a pierside shop with rental bicycles at B100/hr and motorcycle taxis to Ban Nam Pueng Floating Market or to quiet, semi-wild Suan Si Nakhon Keun Kan (Thanon Phetchachueng, 6am-7pm daily, free), with its mangroves, nipa palm boardwalks and lookout tower. You can explore Bang Kra Jao's plantations and sights on tours by bicycle (SpiceRoads, 0 2712 5305, www.spiceroads.com) or Segway (SegwayTour Thailand, 0 2221 4525, 0 8 5476 791, www.SegwayTourThailand.com).

Eating & drinking

Baan Klang Nam

3792/160 Rama III Soi 14 (0 2292 2037-8). **Open** 11am-10pm daily. BB.
Thai seafood.
Down a narrow soi, the pick of Yannawa's waterfront seafood restaurants serves every seafish, shell and crustacean combo in the Thai repertoire. Set simply in an old teak stilt house on a pier, it harbours views of ocean-going ships.

Ban Nam Pueng Floating Market

Wat Ban Nam Pueng, Thanon Phetchachueng, Bang Kra Jao (0 2819 6762). **Open** 7am-3pm Sat, Sun. **B**.
No credit cards. **Thai**.
This revived *talad nam* (floating market) is quick to reach, yet very local. Thais prize the local speciality sausages, elephant ear curry and potted desserts, and savour the clean conditions. The stalls loop past the canalside vendors and back via plantation paths to Wat Ban Nam Pueng, which has parking and taxis. Combine it with a boat or bike tour round Bang Kra Jao.

Le Lys

148/11 Nang Linchi Soi 6 (0 2287 1898-9/0 2675 4474-5/www.lelys.info). **Open** 11.30am-10.30pm daily. BB. **Thai**.

The French-Thai owners lure the young and the old alike with Gallic sensibilities and oh-so-Thai dishes: pickled bamboo shoot soup, red curry with duck and lychee, salmon in the Thai yum, and squid with tamarind sauce. Vintage French posters hang amid Lanna textiles and, as a final touch, there's even a pétanque court.

Nightlife

Tawandang German Brewhouse

462/61 Thanon Narathiwat Ratchanakharin, at Thanon Rama III (0 2678 1114-6/www.tawandang 1999.com). **Open** 5pm-1am daily.
Shows *Fong Nam* 7pm-1am Mon-Sat.
Bands 7pm-1am Sun. **BB**.
Thai/German.
For a decade, this 1,600-diner microbrewery has served Thai and German fare with yard-tall tabletop kegs under a barrel-shaped dome. Nightly (excepting Sunday night covers), it witnesses extraordinary Moulin Rouge extravaganzas from avant-garde *phiphat* group Fong Nam, fusing every Thai musical style with dancing girls, film, shadow puppets, ladyboys, Godzilla, Elvis, and riffs from Led Zeppelin to Carabao. It's Sgt Hanuman's Lonely Hearts Club *phiphat wong* and he wants you all to sing along.

Arts & leisure

Mambo

59 Thanon Rama III, between Sois 57 & 59, near the Sathupradit intersection (0 2294 73181-2/ www.mambocabaret.com). **Shows** 7.15pm, 8.30pm, 10pm daily.
Tickets B100; VIP B800.
Just moved from Sukhumvit, this ladyboy cabaret has toured the UK. They primp and grin through feathered extravaganzas designed to tick the nationality boxes of each coach party present. After teasing audience members, the stars charge to pose for photos.

Prachuap Khiri Khan p160

Excursions

Samut Prakarn

Thanon Sukhumvit continues all the way to Cambodia, and the BTS is extending above this highway – past Bangna's housing estates, industry, golf courses and outsize theme restaurants – into suburban Samut Prakarn province. You can combine its sights located at the Chao Phraya estuary into a half- or full-day trip.

Sights & museums

Erawan Museum

99/9 Moo 1, Bang Muang Mai, Thanon Sukhumvit (0 2371 3135-6/www.ancientcity.com). **Open** 8am-6pm (5pm last entry) daily. **Admission** B150; B50 reductions; English guide B300. No credit cards. A monument to religious harmony by the founder of Muang Boran, this huge 150-tonne metal statue depicts Erawan, the three-headed elephant mount of

Hindu god Indra. From a kitschy museum, steps and a lift up the rear legs take you to a multi-faith chapel in the body. Oddly deep and deeply odd.

Muang Boran (Ancient City)

Sukhumvit Sai Kao km33, Bangpu Mai (0 2709 1644-8/www.ancientcity.com). **Open** 8am-5pm daily. **Admission** Thais B150; B75 reductions. Foreigners B300; B150 reductions. No credit cards. The visionary Lek Viriyaphant created this open-air architectural museum, reconstructing salvaged masterpieces and scale versions of landmarks in a park shaped like Thailand. It's a sublime, relaxing half-day jaunt by car or tour. Bicycles are for hire. Lunch in the floating market here or bring a picnic.

Samut Prakarn Crocodile Farm

555 Thai Baan (0 2703 5144-8). **Open** 7am-6pm daily. **Admission** Thais B60; foreigners B300; B30-B200 reductions.

Wat Si Sanphet

The world's biggest croc farm, with 100,000 occupants, includes the near-extinct Siamese species and the longest crocodile at 6m (20 ft). Hourly shows feature wrestling and head-in-jaw stunts, plus elephant shows and rides.

Ayutthaya & Bang Pa-In

For the best historical day trip, head 55km (34 miles) north to **Bang Sai**, another 17km (11 miles) to the 19th-century **Bang Pa-In** summer palace, and 21km (13 miles) further to the ruined Siamese capital of **Ayutthaya**. Tours tend to engulf Bang Pa-in before lunching in Ayutthaya, and boating back, or breaking the return at Bang Sai. The reverse order is quieter, but start early.

Centred on an artificial island, Ayutthaya is a World Heritage Site. Not only are the former capital's remains impressive, but its fall in 1767 is a historical hinge that still reverberates here. Most of its 400 temples razed and 90% of its people gone, the scorched red-brick ruins were abandoned (and much looted) until Prime Minister Phibun made it into a showpiece in the 1950s. He cleared the 20m-high, 5m-thick city walls for a ring road; during excavations treasures that weren't looted were displayed in museums. A Historical Park covers the main sights.

The conch-shape island – formed by the Lopburi, Pasak and Chao Phraya rivers and a canal – is ringed by Thanon U-thong and criss-crossed by avenues, with businesses, food and accommodation to the east side towards the modern city, beyond Pridi Thamrong Bridge.

Sights & museums

Bang Sai Folk Arts & Crafts Centre
59 Moo 4, Bang Sai, Ayuthaya (0 353 66 252-4/www.bangsaiarts.com). **Open** 8.30am-4.30pm Tue-Sun. **Admission** Thais B50; foreigners B100; reductions B30-B50. No credit cards.
Under Queen Sirikit's patronage, resuscitated court crafts help diversify the incomes of farmers trained at this tranquil riverbank centre reachable on boat tours. Visitors tour the workshops; a vast shop sells the handiwork.

Bang Pa-In Palace
(0 3526 1044/www.palaces.thai.net). **Open** 8am-4pm daily. **Admission** Thais B30; foreigners B100. No credit cards.
This river island has since 1632 been a summer royal retreat. In 1872, Rama V turned it into an eclectic palace named after a drowned princess. Flanked by lawns and topiary – and surveyed from a candy-striped pagoda – it's a collage of Baroque, Gothic and Chinese, with a copy of the Phra Thinang Aporn Phimok Prasat from the Grand Palace in

a reflecting pool. The dazzling Chinese Wehat Chamrun Palace contrasts with the simple houseboat and English Gothic-style Wat Nivet Dhammaparvat.

Chao Sam Phraya Museum

108/16 Thanon Rotchana, Ayutthaya (0 3524 1587). **Open** 9am-4pm Wed- Sun. **Admission** Thais B50; foreigners B100; reductions B20-B50. No credit cards.

During excavations, royal regalia was stolen from the frescoed crypt of Wat Ratchaburana and the old ritual centre, Wat Mahathat. Remnants of the gilded cache – plus marvellous statuary – fill this lamentably labelled hoard.

Chandra Kasem Palace Museum

Thanon U-Thong, Ayutthaya (0 3525 1586). **Open** 9am-4pm Wed-Sun. **Admission** Thais B20; foreigners B100. No credit cards.

This 'palace of the deputy king' typifies Rama IV's taste for European and Chinese design, and features his astronomical observatory tower and decaying photographs of Ayutthaya when entangled by jungle. Other treasures occupy the fretworked galleries.

Historical Study Centre

Thanon Rotchana, Ayutthaya (0 3524 5123-4). **Open** 9am-4pm daily. **Admission** Thais B20; foreigners B100; reductions B5-B50. No credit cards.

This Japanese-built centre looks empty, but does display dioramas and models of what Ayutthaya lost, amid hi-tech displays on its social, cultural, economic and diplomatic importance. It's scanty but offers more perspective than the TAT tourist office, which is housed in an old city hall.

Phra Nakhon Si Ayutthaya Historical Park

Nestled around the old town (0 3524 2284). **Open** 8am-6pm daily. **Admission** Thais B10; foreigners B50 per site. *All sites* Thais B40; foreigners B220. No credit cards.

Island remains

Only foundations – and the **Trimuk Pavilion**, built by Rama V for ceremonies – indicate the presence of the old Grand Palace, though the iconic triple *chedi* (built in 1492) of its temple, **Wat Si Sanphet**, remain. Engravings popularised the vast vine-clad, roofless Buddha image of **Vihaan Phra Mongkhon Bophit** next-door, and its 1975 'as-new' revamp is most appreciated by Thais as a focus for offerings. Beyond a market and the exquisite teak 1894 **Khun Phaen's House**, you can get elephant rides (08 1869 9520, B200 10mins, B400 20mins, B500 30mins). Opposite is **Beung Phra Ram**, a park of lily ponds and a lone *prang*. Behind it, **Wat Mahathat** draws photographers to its root-encased Buddha head.

Outer-bank remains

Outer bank remains are easiest seen on separate detours, but we follow them anti-clockwise from the southeast access point. Built by a Ceylonese sect,

Wat Yai Chaimongkhon p156

Wat Yai Chaimongkhon boasts a 60-metre (197-foot) bell *chedi*, a reclining Buddha and a shrine to toys. East on Highway 3058, **Wat Maheyong** retains stucco elephants around a Sri Lankan-style *chedi*. To the north, the restored **Kraal** was where elephants were trained, and **Wat Phramane** (Thanon U-Thong) is the only surviving original temple. Contrast its regalia-adorned Ayutthayan Buddha with the serene white Mon Dvaravati image in a side *vihaan*. Dominating the west is the five-*prang* **Wat Chaiwattanaram**, which hosts **boat races** at Loy Krathong. To the south, King U-Thong stayed at **Wat Phuttaisawan** before making Ayutthaya the capital. En route you pass **St Joseph's Church** in the old French settlement, which was one of many foreign quarters then housing, among others, Portuguese, Japanese, Dutch and Malays.

Getting there & around

By boat
Most hotels and tour companies run one-way cruises to/from Bang Pa-in/Ayutthaya, with the other leg by road or train. Si Phraya Boat Trip & Travel (0 2235 3108) goes by bus to Bang Pa-in then by boat to Ayutthaya and cruises back to Bangkok on the *Pearl of Siam* (B2,000). River Sun Cruise (0 2266 9125-6) does similar with a smaller boat (B2,100). Both start and end at River City. Benjarong (0 2943 4047-9, www.thaicruises.com) runs overnight cruises aboard a converted teak barge.

From Bang Pa-In Palace, longtail boats ply the scenic 45-minute trip to Ayutthaya. In Ayutthaya you can hire longtail boats at piers by Chandra Kasem Museum or Wat Phanan Choeng (from B500/hr).

By road & rail
Most tours combine 90min minibus rides with train or boat (above) and call at Bang Pa-In. Otherwise, buses leave Bangkok's Northern Bus Terminal every 20mins, 5.40am-8.40pm daily (B65), taking 90mins. Trains to Bang Pa-In and Ayutthaya leave 4.20am-11.40pm daily from Hualumphong station (B12-B54, 90mins).

In Bang Pa-In, pedal rickshaws and *tuk-tuks* ply the short, walkable road to the palace. In Ayutthaya, you can hire *tuk-tuks* (B200/hr), and bicycles from the tourist police (B50/day) or near the train station (B40/day).

Tourist information

TAT *Old City Hall, 108/22 Thanon Si Sanphet, Ayutthaya (0 3524 6076-7).* **Open** 8.30am-4.30pm daily.

Floating markets

Siam's oldest city and the entry point of Buddhism, Nakhon Pathom was a centre of the Mon-influenced Dvaravati culture two millennia ago. Its huge **Phra Pathom Chedi** and **Sanam Chan Palace** make it a drop-in destination on the way west or south, or on a day trip to canal communities in this province, and neighbouring Amphawa. Amphawa retains some bygone lifestyles and markets, which are usually best viewed in the early morning. Before the evening **Amphawa Floating Market** tour the estuarine attractions of Samut Songkram, including mangroves, fireflies, plantations, homestays, and **Rama II Memorial Park**. On the way view the salt pans flanking the highway at Samut Sakhon.

The district bordering Bangkok features **Putthamonthon**, a vast Buddhist theme park. Look out for its 40-metre (131-foot) Buddha and Utthayan Avenue, which shimmers with ornate bridges, fountains, flora and lampposts. It makes a good half-day trip with the nearby **House of Museums** and **National Film Archive**.

Sights & museums

Amphawa Floating Market

Near Wat Amphawan, Samut Songkram. **Open** 6am-6pm daily. **Admission** free.

The old wooden market of Samut Songkram (aka Amphawa) has been revived, with boats selling food and produce. On weekends it overflows with young Bangkokians drawn by the bohemian vibe and many quirkily designed products – and of course the speciality foods. At dusk myriad boat tours take people to view fireflies, though many overnight here in plantations, boating to one of many stilt-house homestays, like Baan Tha Kha (0 3476 6170, double B350) or Baan Hua Had (0 3473 5073, double B350). Day boat tours take in Dickensian caramel factories in sugar palm groves.

Don Wai Floating Market

Near Wat Rai King, Tha Nakhon Chaisri. **Open** 6am-noon daily.

A revival and expansion of an old wooden orchard port on the Tha Chin, Don Wai is authentic, untacky and very clean. It's busiest on weekends as Thai tourists drive 30km west of Bangkok for its speciality foods. The Rose Garden (0 3432 2544, www.rosegardenriverside.com), which has accommodation and tourist shows, makes it the focus of a half-day teak barge cruise (Sat, Sun).

National Film Archive

94 Thanon Puttha Monthon Sai 5, Putthamonthon (0 2482 2013-5/www.nfat.org). **Open** 10am, 2pm & 4pm Sat, Sun. **Tickets** free.

This vital repository of decaying celluloid heritage hosts free informal screenings of Thai and foreign films (Sat, Sun 4pm), some subtitled. Its retro-style museum includes dioramas and Thai movie memorabilia.

Phra Pathom Chedi

Nakorn Pathom town (0 3424 2143). **Open** 6am-8pm daily. **Admission** Thais free; foreigners B40.

Don Wai Floating Market

You can't miss what is reputedly the world's tallest *stupa* at 120 metres (414 feet). It's constantly busy wth pilgrims. Since 1853, its bell shape has clad a Khmer *prang* that encased a Mon *stupa*. There's also a reclining Buddha, a circular cloister, and Dvaravati treasures in Phra Pathom Chedi National Museum (Thais B20; foreigners B100; open 9am-4pm daily). Artefacts in the free Phra Pathom Museum (closed Mon, Tue) are less organised.

Rama II Memorial Park

Amphawa, Samut Songkram (0 3475 1666). **Open** 9am-6pm daily. *Museum* 9am-4pm daily. **Admission** B20; B5 children.

A riverside park beside Amphawa Floating Market features replicas of sumptuous teak stilt houses used by King Rama II, who was born here. They contain traditional instruments, bonsai-like Thai topiary and other fine objects. You can hire bikes to tour the grounds and their sculptures of characters by the king's poet, Sunthorn Phu.

BANGKOK BY AREA

Sanam Chan Palace

*6 Thanon Rajamankha Nai, Nakorn
Pathom town (0 3424 4236-7).* **Open**
8.30am-4pm daily. **Admission** Thais
B30; foreigners B50. **Performances**
10am, 2pm Sat, Sun.

Across town, the leafy grounds of King
Rama VI's palace contain fretworked
museums in timber residences, plus a
theatre resembling a *wat*.

House of Museums

*Baan Phipitaphan, Khlong Pho
Soi 2, Thanon Sala Thammasop,
Putthamonthon (08 9200 2803).*
Open 10am-5pm Sat, Sun. **Admission**
B30; B10 reductions. No credit cards.
Historian and author Anake
Nawigamune displays his vast popu-
lar culture collection in interactive retro
reconstructions of mid-20th century
Thai lifestyle, including a schoolroom
and pharmacy.

Samphran Elephant
Ground & Crocodile Farm

*Km30 Thanon Phetkasem, Samphran
(0 2429 0361-2/www.elephant
show.com).* **Open** 8.30-5pm daily.
Admission Thais B90; foreigners
B500; reductions B50-B300.
Located near Rose Garden, this landscaped attraction offers elephant rides,
croc wrestling, and mock battles.

Getting there

By road & rail

Most hire a car/van and driver (p183).
To Nakhon Pathom buses depart the
Southern Bus Terminal (daily every
15mins, 5.30am-8.30pm, B38), while
13 trains leave 8.05am-10.50pm daily
from Hualumphong station (B14-B60),
and five 3rd-class trains run daily from
Thonburi station (B10).

To Samut Songkram, buses depart
the Southern Bus Terminal (daily every
20mins, 4.45am-5.30pm, B52), while 12
3rd-class trains leave hourly 5.30am-
8.10pm daily from Wongwian Yai
station (B10), changing for the
ferry at Samut Sakhon.

Tourist information

*2nd floor Amphawa Municipality
City Hall, 2/1 Amphawa (0 347 2847-
8/www.tourismthailand.org/samutsongk
ham.com).* **Open** 8am-4pm Mon-Fri.

Ko Samet

When Bangkokians go on
long beach weekends, the more
conservative head for Hua Hin,
while the sparkier, younger set
zooms southeast to this dagger-
shaped islet in Rayong province.
Without getting on a plane, this
is the easiest place to test the
brochures' 'forested isle in an
emerald sea' claims. The sand is
fine and the water is clear, but for
coral, take a diving or snorkelling
tour to the offshore islets.

Chic resorts are now gentrifying
a shambolic fringe of formerly basic
resorts, but pricing out its young
regulars. Boats from Baan Phe dock
at Na Dan, near the squeaky white
sand of Had Sai Kaew. Its jetskis
and inflatable banana rides start the
string of quieter, pretty east coast
bays where the calm is disturbed
only by beach massages,
snorkelling and a mellow party
scene focused on populist Had
Sai Kaew and groovier Ao Phai.
Look out for the fire-jugglers.

Resorts get sparser as the coccyx-
bruising road judders to Ao Phai
and Ao Tubtim. A direct boat is
the best way to reach the busy half
moon of Ao Wong Deuan, which is
full of seafood restaurants. A short
hike further lies rockier Ao Thian.
In high season and at weekends,
booking is essential.

Sights & museums

Phra Aphai Manee Statue

On rocks near Naga, Had Sai Kaew.
Siam's UNESCO-listed literary lion,
Sunthorn Phu, immortalised Ko Samet
in his epic ballads during the reigns of

Kings Rama II and III. The folkishly styled cement statue of his mermaid from Phra Apai Manee here, is outdone by the bronzes of his most famous characters at the Sunthorn Phu Memorial Park in Klaeng on the mainland, though it's hardly worth a detour.

Kao Laim Yaa & Samet National Park

Baan Kon Ao, Rayong (0 3865 3034). **Admission** Thais B40; foreigners B200. The forested interior slopes are National Park, a protection that's arguably worsened the inevitable development by confining it to a coastal sliver. Speedboats bypass the park gate, but you need to show a ticket for pick-up bus trips to Na Dan and back.

Resorts

Ao Phrao Resort

Ao Phrao (0 384 4100-3/ www.kohsametaoprao.com). **BBB**. This upmarket resort with its own ferry is located in the only bay on the more humid west coast, and is a snazzy and romantic place to stay.

Lung Dum

Ao Thian (0 3864 4331). **B**. Eccentric shoreline huts offer a budget bohemian vibe amid the yellow sand and rocks of long, narrow 'Candlelight Beach'. The journey here requires a minor trek after a hilly drive or ferry via Ao Wong Deuan.

Moo Ban Talay

Ao Noi Na (0 3864 4251/08 1838 8682/www.moobantalay.com). **BBB**. Facing the mainland across a gravelly beach too shallow for swimming, this sleekly minimalist resort has a pool, spa, watersports and great food. The villas have outdoor showers with upward views of lofty trees.

Paradee

Ao Kiew (0 2438 9771/www. kohsametparadee.com). **BBBB**. Samet's poshest resort commands the southern tip – and a B6,000 fee for the speedboat from Ban Phe. In terms of food, you're a captive, but in luxury!

Samet Villa

Ao Phai (0 3864 4094/www. samedvilla.com). **BBB**. Handsome wooden lodges dot the shaded slope at the north end of this bay, not quite out of earshot of the disco, but far enough.

Tubtim Resort

Ao Tubtim, (0 3864 4025-7/ www.tubtimresort.com). **BB**. If Koh Samet is Silom-on-Sea, then Ao Tubtim is Silom Soi 4-on-Sea, where clubbers, fashionistas and independent young expats, many gay, chill out and dine on superior seafood, before padding up the beach to party.

Vongduern Villa

Ao Wong Deuan (0 3864 4260/08 1863 9868/www.vongduernvilla.com). **BB**. Retro-chic bungalows on the southern headland survey the bay. Trendier types don their dancing shoes and kick back to DJs at its bar/dancefloor.

Eating & drinking

Restaurants and bars are located in resorts. The finest dining is at the upmarket resorts like Paradee (left) and Moo Ban Talay (left). The best beach seafood restaurant is at Tubtim Resort (above), which has a chill-out bar.

Naga

Had Sai Kaew (0 8 1218 5832). **B**. An eccentric guesthouse set atop a rocky outcrop known for its bakery, beachside disco and *naga* serpents of painted cement.

Silver Sand

Ao Phai (0 3864 4074). **BB**. A plain resort that hosts the grooviest beachside disco around.

Getting there

By road

Buses from Ekamai Bus Station (almost hourly, 7am-8.30pm daily, B157) reach Baan Phe port in four hours, cars in three. Call Taxis (p181) will go for B2,300, return B3,500. On Samet, open *songtaews* and hired motorcycles ply rutted tracks.

By boat

Ferries to Na Dan (B100 return; 30mins) depart Baan Phe bus station pier (hourly, 9am-5pm daily) and Nuan Thip pier 500m into town (hourly 24hrs, return hourly 8am-6pm daily, plus waiting). A few serve Wong Deuan (45mins). Pricey speedboats (0 3865 1999) go direct to beaches. Boats rarely run after dark.

Tourist information

Minimal leaflets at piers. Try www.kohsamet.com.

Hua Hin & Cha-am

The former fishing village of Hua Hin in Prachuap Khiri Khan province owes its prestige to King Rama VI building Marukhathaiyawan Palace between here and Cha-am, a resort catering to raucous Thai *sanuk* that's rapidly going upmarket. High society and Thailand's first golf course followed. Overcrowding can be a problem on weekends, but the many world-class resorts have more tasteful architecture, while there's less sleaze than in Pattaya or Phuket.

Hua Hin's 5km of beaches have reasonable sand, but the water is often murky and there are many jellyfish, particularly in the monsoon season. Still, you can always ride its famous ponies.

Outside the busy Thanon Naretdamri lanes, where most of the restaurants beer bars and tailors are

located, it becomes quieter north towards Cha-am or 4km south to Hat Khao Takiap, a hill with a standing Buddha and fine views. Enterprising locals offer rental deck chairs and cold drinks along the way.

Sights & museums

Kaeng Krachan National Park

Petchaburi province (0 3245 9251). **Open** daily. **Admission** Thais B20; foreigners B200.

The broken-tooth mountain horizon behind Cha-am harbours this crucial animal habitat in Thailand's vast western forest park complex. Tours and hikes are possible.

Khao Sam Roi Yod National Park

Kuiburi, Prachub Khiri Khan (0 3282 1568). **Open** daily. **Admission** Thais B20; foreigners B200.

Some 58 kilometers south of Hua Hin, this park's 98 square kilometers are dominated by an undulating mountain range that hugs some of the area's most pristine coastline. It's all littered with an extensive network of caves (King Rama IV built a *sala* in one) and home to one of the most diverse bird populations in Asia.

Phra Ratchaniwet Marukhathaiyawan

Rama VI Army Camp, Cha-Am, Petchaburi (0 3250 8233). **Open** 8am-4pm Mon-Fri; 8am-5pm Sat, Sun. **Admission** Thais B30; foreigners B90. Visitors swoon over these teak pavilions and a galleried theatre, connected by long open corridors, all built on stilts at the beach by King Rama VI in 1923. Now in an army camp, the palace has been restored and its artfully themed gardens contain other attractions reflecting aspects of his reign and 1920s Siamese culture, from literature, theatre and scouts to food, flowers and fashion. A magical place.

Hua Hin

Ploen Waan

Thanon Phetchkasem, between Hua Hin Sois 38 & 40, Hua Hin (0 2712 6891/0 3253 0312/www.plearnwan. com). **Open** 10am-10pm Mon-Thur; 10am-midnight Fri; 9am-midnight Sat; 9am-10pm Sun. **Admission** free.
Bangkokians adore this surreal new attraction, a 'vintage village' evoking old Hua Hin through recycled wood, retro everything and stores channelling bygone market culture, complete with temple fair-style sideshows on weekends. It's basically about shopping, eating and photographing friends, with guest rooms on the upper level.

Eating & drinking

Baan Itsara

7 Thanon Naebkehat (0 3253 0574/0 3251 1673/www.itsara-huahin.com). **Open** 11am-10pm daily. BB. **Thai**.
One of the better beach view restaurants set in a converted old wooden home. Succulently fresh seafood.

Brasserie de Paris

3 Thanon Naresdamri (0 3253 8999). **Open** noon-2pm, 6-10pm daily. BBB. **French**.

One of the several good European restaurants here, this French place is a good place to eat at the waterfront.

Chao Ley

15 Thanon Naretdamri, near Soi 57 (0 3251 3436). **Open** 11am-10pm daily. BB. **Thai seafood**.
Hua Hin is famed for its seafood, and the best places to sample it are the restaurants clustered on fishing piers at the north end of Thanon Naresdamri, providing breezes and scenic views. All serve fresh fish, crab and gargantuan shrimp at reasonable prices. This is the pick of the bunch.

Jae Keao (Madame Green)

Moo Baan Takiab, Hua-Hin (0 3253 6899/0 3253 6900). **Open** 9am-10pm daily. BB. **Thai seafood**.
Thais pack-out this famous, simple seafood restaurant. Its upper floor overlooks the beach.

Jeh Pia

51/6 Thanon Dechanuchit, Hua Hin. **Open** 6.15am-9pm daily. No credit cards. B. **Coffee/Thai**.
Meet locals of note who breakfast in this institution of a Thai-style coffee

house in a timber corner building. Arrayed around the edge (which stays open later) is a rotating cast of vendors who sell sublime dishes for pennies, from pork *sate* to seafood rice soup, which can be eaten inside.

Sang Vean Seafood
Thanon Mung Talae, Cha-am (0 32547 2280/08 6096 4799). **Open** 10am-9pm daily. **B**. **Thai seafood**.
Auntie Vean sells the most famous seafood in Cha-am from a simple, open-sided hall facing the beach near the Veranda, often visited by Princess Sirindhorn. Mountains of crab and delicacies for bargain prices mean that it's always packed.

Resorts & spas

Aleenta
Pranburi (0 3261 8333, 0 2508 5335/ www.aleenta.com). **BBB**.
Visitors such as the Beckhams and hip hotel mavens gush about the remote, all-white villas.

Anantasila Villa
33/15 Soi Mooban Huadon, Takiab, Hua Hin (0 3251 1879/www. anantasila.com). **BBBB**.
Hidden away from the crowds on Takiap Beach, a short walk from a traditional fishing village, is this luxurious hotel with arty touches and a rugged rocky backdrop to ocean views.

Baan Bayan
119 Thanon Phetchkasem, Hua Hin (0 3253 3544/www.baanbayan.com). **BBB**.
Aristocrats have turned their old wooden beach house into this conservation award-winning resort half way to Takiab. Luxuriate in the authentically unfussy mansion or in spacious rooms built to the side.

Ban Somboon
13/4 Soi Kasemsamphan, Thanon Damnoen Kasem (0 3251 1538). **B**.

A cheaper, antiquey home-conversion with cosy rooms and artworks.

Casa Papaya
810/04 Thanon Petchkasem, Cha-am (0 8 6607 1431/0 3247 0678/ www.casapapayathai.com). **BB**.
Guesthouses don't come much funkier than this orange Mexican adobe garden compound. Quirky, good value rooms with rooftops, a pool and beach access. Close to Sang Vean Seafood.

Sofitel Central Hua Hin
1 Thanon Damnoen Kasem (0 3251 2021-38/www.centralhotelsresorts.com). **BBBB**.
The former 1920s Railway Hotel retains its air of nobility with modern five-star comforts and colonialesque lounges framed by frangipanis and prime central beachfront. One of Asia's storied grand hotels.

Veranda Resort & Spa
737/12 Thanon Mung Talay, Cha-am (0 3270 9000-099/www.veranda resortandspa.com). **BBBB**.
One of the sleek designer hotels that's raising Cha-am's profile. Elegantly modernist low-rise blocks with Thai timber touches flank a long, shape-shifting pool from the dramatic lobby to the expansive sands.

Getting there

By road & rail
Frequent buses from the Southern Bus Terminal take 3hrs (B160), hired cars 2hrs, taxis B2,500. Rail is a historic (ie slow) way to arrive (12 daily, 5hrs, B44-B1,522). Most hotels arrange Bangkok airport transfers. Charter flights only land at the small Hua Hin Airport. Cha-am, Hua Hin and Pranburi are strung out. Local *songtaews* cost from B50, depending on the route.

Tourist information
TAT *500/51 Thanon Phetkasem, Cha-am (0 3247 1005-6).*

Essentials

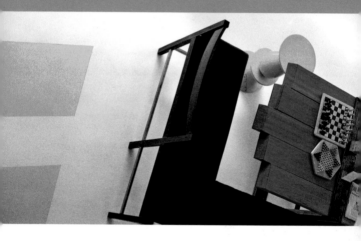

Mandarin Oriental p173

Hotels

Beds are one of Bangkok's strengths. The Big Mango has long excelled at grand hotels, with some of the best value luxury rooms in the world even earning splurges from those on a budget. When the likes of Joseph Conrad steamed in a century ago there was only one place to stay: the Oriental (p173). It has been joined by others along the river and up the business district of Bangrak to Siam and Sukhumvit. Grand hotels are social city institutions, too, notably with regard to haute cuisine (see box p131), rooftop skyscraper bars (see box p96) and destination spas (see box p172).

For people with less money, there are guesthouse options spread from the traveller ghetto of Banglamphu, and its extension up Samsen to the original traveller's hub, Soi Ngam Duphlee/Soi Sri Bumphen, which is now more a place for long-term stayers, who enjoy its frisson and tolerance for night guests.

The boutique hotel boom has transformed the mid-range, which was dowdy and limited to blocks, inns above tailors around Nana, or faded, no-frills, no-smiles Chinese hotels. Now all manner of compact hotels offer quirky surroundings, artist-commissioned decor, minimalist chic or comforting ambiences. The trend for converting old buildings has greatly broadened choice near the major sights.

The latest trend is in hip hostels (see box p175). Sharing a dorm or bunking on a shoestring has never been so chic or clean, with innovative hostels carving out a savvy new category.

Rooms and rates

Single rooms can often sleep two, while doubles may have two double beds. Some beds could even sleep three. So ask to view rooms first. In guesthouses and cheap Chinese hotels, rates can vary widely by the room's size, or whether it has a fan or air-conditioning, and en suite or shared bathrooms.

We rate hotels by price for a standard double room: **BBBB** (deluxe, from B7,000), **BBB** (expensive, B3,500-B6,999), **BB** (moderate, B1,200-B3,499) and **B** (budget, under B1,200). Rates given are for high season (November-March), but off-season discounts can be huge. Given Thailand's recent travails and a glut of swish new openings, getting a deal is easier than ever.

Big hotels add service and VAT (known as 'plus plus' or '++'). All hotels below have air-conditioning, unless we mention fan-cooled rooms. Thailand's ban on smoking in all public buildings includes hotels, but permits hotels to have some guest rooms that allow smoking. Bangkok has a habit of snaring visitors, and if you decide to stay longer, monthly rates start as low as B10,000, with studios and apartments from B13,000. At the other extreme, discreet motels charge by the hour.

Bookings and background

Booking in advance avoids traipsing around suitcase-unfriendly Bangkok streets. The better hotels fill up at busy times, but you should always be able to find a room. Rates at major hotels may be higher if booked within Thailand.

The **Thailand Hotels Association** (www.thaihotels.org) provides information and reservations, and has a stall at the airport. The best website for cheaper prices is **www.hotelsdirect.com**, while other good online booking sites are **www.asia-hotels.com/**

ESSENTIALS

RUEN URAI

FINE THAI CUISINE

Discover a century-old traditional Thai house of a herbalist hidden in a secret oasis right in the heart of Bangkok. Experience exotic flavours of fine Thai cuisine. **Savour exquisite dishes from classic creations to new inspirations.** Open from 12 noon to 11 p.m.

10% off for Time Out readers. Please show this ad until 31st December 2011.

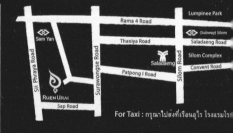

For Taxi : กรุณาไปส่งที่เรือนอุไร โรงแรมโร

Ruen Urai at the Rose Hotel
118 Soi Na Wat Hualumphong, Surawongse Road
Tel. +662 266 8268-72 Fax +662 266 8096
www.ruen-urai.com

thailand, www.asiarooms.com,
www.bookingthaihotel.com,
www.hotelthailand.com,
www.sawadee.com,
www.siam.net and
www.tripadvisor.com. For
hostels run to IYHA standards,
contact the **Thai Youth Hostels
Association** (0 2628 7415,
www.tyha.org) and check
www.hostelworld.com, which
also lists good guesthouses.

Serviced apartments

Many residential blocks let rooms
short-term at very good rates.
Hotels have won a restriction on
apartment stays under a week,
despite the evident demand for
domestic ambience, kitchenettes
and multi-room layouts.
Apartments are coy about daily
rates, but may quote them if asked.
Compare and reserve apartments
online at www.sabaai.com.

Phra Nakorn & Thonburi

Deluxe

Chakrabongse Villas

*396 Thanon Maharat (0 2622 335
6-8/www.thaivillas.com). Tha Tien.*
BBBB.
The 19th-century mansion of Prince
Chakrabongse opens three Thai-style
villas to guests. Exquisitely furnished
with teak, silk and modern amenities,
they offer seclusion, a garden pool and
views of Wat Arun across the river
from the dining *sala*. Expect a warm
welcome and Thai meals bought and
cooked to order. Outside the gate lies
Wat Pho, the flower market, the
apothecaries of Tha Tien and
Expressboat piers (although the villas
also have their own boat). Book well in
advance. Tailored dinners can be
booked separately.

Expensive

Aurum: The River Place

*Soi Pansook, 394/27-29 Thanon
Maharat (0 2622 2248/www.aurum-
bangkok.com). Tha Tien.* **BBB.**
A three-storey corner landmark in the
Tha Tien community, Aurum affords
guaranteed views: three rooms overlook the old town, nine the adjacent
river. Its stuccoed Parisian feel continues inside, with tall windows, dark
floorboards and white marble ensuites
in rooms that make up in practical,
tasteful touches what they lack in size.

Ibrik Resort

*256 Soi Wat Rakang, Thanon Arun-
Amarin (0 2848 9220/www.ibrikresort.
com). Boat from Tha Chang or Tha
Prachan Pier to Tha Wat Rakang.* **BBB.**
A trio of unique balconied rooms –
River, Sunshine and Moonlight – fea-
ture pared-down design and oriental
touches. With boats functioning as the
main transport, this retreat boasts
unmatched riverscapes of the Grand
Palace. A branch has rooms at 235/16
Thanon Sathorn (0 2211 3470).

Old Bangkok Inn

*607 Thanon Phra Sumen (0 2629
1787/www.oldbangkokinn.com).* **BBB.**
This charming boutique inn has won
awards, so it books out fast. Beside the
Queen's Gallery, it occupies a shophouse on the site of a palace that has
been in the Tulyanond family for seven
generations. The compact, colour-
themed rooms and suites recreate a
bygone Thai/Burmese urban ecology,
with matching salvaged-wood bathrooms and fittings with in-room com-
puters and CFC-free coolers. A dollar a
night goes to a community charity.

Moderate

Arun Residence

*36-38 Soi Pratoo Nok Yoong,
Thanon Maharat (0 2221 9158/
www.arunresidence.com).* **BB.**

ESSENTIALS

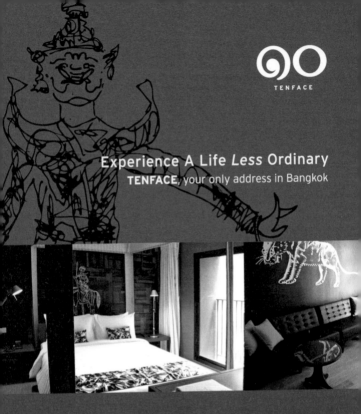

This old corner shophouse has been sleekly converted but reflects the neighbourhood's retro charms. There are views of Wat Arun from its superb Franco-Italian-Thai bistro the Deck, its rooftop bar Amoroso, its riverbank patio, and some of its five rooms. The loftiest room has a garden.

Baan Dinso
113 Trok Sin, Thanon Dinso (02 622 0560-3/www.baandinso.com). **BB**.
Within walking distance of bustling Khao San Road, this peaceful two-storey golden teakwood house has been lovingly renovated as a nine-room colonial 'boutique hostel'. Decorated in a 1950s style, rooms are clean and comfortable. Complimentary American and continental breakfasts are served at outdoor tables.

Banglamphu & Dusit

Moderate

Buddy Lodge
265 Thanon Khao San (0 2629 4477/ www.buddylodge.com). **BB**.
Buddy Lodge's red brick façade hides modern rooms with wooden floors, writing desks, old-fashioned lamps and white timber walls. The balconies in the deluxe rooms are bigger than the standard rooms, and are good spots for a nightcap. The first boutique hotel in Khao San, it also has a pool.

Phra Nakorn Norn Len
46 Thewet Soi 1 (0 2628 8188-9/ www.phranakorn-nornlen.com). **BB**.
This cosy guesthouse melds bygone styles of Thai wooden-house living with art and a sense of community. It encourages guests to use a nearby laundry or breakfast in the market instead of the hotel's lovely coffee corner. In the tranquil garden, they sell products from their Rabbit in the Moon foundation, which teaches children arts and nature appreciation. Every room has its own characteristics, like a bath-room mosaic, or an old door turned outsize window. The rooftop area looks towards the giant Buddha of Wat In.

Budget

My House
37 Soi Chanasongkhram (0 2282 9263-4). **B**.
The area behind Wat Chanasongkhram risks becoming a cheap drinking substitute for Khao San refugees, but its old tranquillity remains intact at this tidy, five-storey guesthouse. The Thai-style entrance and lounge/restaurant give way to rooms that are a touch generic, but perfectly clean and comfy.

Nakorn Pink Hotel
9/1 Samsen Soi 6 (0 2281 6574/ fax 0 2282 3727). **B**.
Of the many old Chinese-style hotels off Thanon Samsen, this pastel-coloured one is the plum. Rooms are well decked out, with clunky old wooden furniture and small fridges. There's no restaurant, but the *soi* mouth has a fine seafood eatery.

Peachy Guesthouse
10 Thanon Phra Arthit (0 2281 6471/6659). **B**.
This converted school offers large double beds, wardrobes and a beer garden/ restaurant serving breakfasts, crêpes and real coffee. If that seems homely, remember that it's rumoured to be haunted by the ghosts of an old lady and a handyman.

Phiman Water View
123 Samsen Soi 5 (08 3130 0101/ 08 6353 1942/www.phimanwater view.com). **B**.
Feeling creative? Guests at this bohemian waterfront 'art guesthouse' are invited to paint and re-decorate their rooms. Some have. Concealed within the winding alleys of a temple neighbourhood, Phiman was conceived by its English-fluent proprietor, artist Vee, as a participatory community, com-

ESSENTIALS

Metropolitan p173

plete with creative workshops, gallery and exhibitions. Rustic rooms range from stilted bamboo huts to a locker-equipped 'love shack'. The kooky 'a(r)tmosphere' and stunning private riverbank views of Rama VIII Bridge compensate for the odd mosquito.

Chinatown

Moderate

Grand China Princess

215 Thanon Yaowarat (0 2224 9977/www.grandchina.com). **BB**.
Large rooms, some with balconies, overlook the city and river. The top floor has Bangkok's only revolving club lounge (open in the evenings). Facilities are a bit worn and the decor rather haphazard, but it rewards those who like character.

Shanghai Inn

479-481 Thanon Yaowarat (0 2221 2121/www.shanghai-inn.com). **BB**.
It's little overstatement to say this boutique hotel is electrifying, and it's not just the acidic colour scheme: it has a real buzz to it. The rooms are beautiful and come with mod cons. This is oriental kitsch at its best.

Budget

Baan Hualampong

336/20 Chalong Krung Soi 21 (0 2639 8054/www.baanhualampong.com). Hualamphong MRT. **B**.
Basic but delightful, this semi-wooden guesthouse near the main station has a friendly atmosphere and a comfortable lounge, kitchen and laundry. The owner speaks English and German. See box p175.

New Empire Hotel

57 Thanon Yaowarat (0 2234 6990-6/ www.newempirehotel.com). **B**.
In Chinatown's main drag, the Empire is clean, cheap and comfortable, with well-equipped rooms, and carpets and wallpaper straight out of a Wong Kar Wai movie. The staff speak enough English for essential exchanges.

Riverview Guesthouse

768 Thanon Songwad (0 2235 8501/fax 0 2237 5428). **B**.
Basic, but great value, quiet and clean, the Riverview offers a chance to experience 'old' Bangkok. The higher rooms overlook the Chao Phraya, as does the top-floor restaurant. The largest air-con room has a fridge and (Thai) TV.

ESSENTIALS

Train Inn
*428, Thanon Rong Meuang (0 2215
3055/08 1819 5544/www.thetrain
inn.com). Hualamphong MRT.* **B**.
Next to the Italianate terminus, this
simple shophouse plays with the idea
of staying aboard a train with rooms
classified as First, Second and Third
Class. Touches of bright colour and
nicely arranged furniture make for an
enjoyable stay. See box p175.

Bangrak & Riverside

Deluxe

Ascott Sathorn
*187 Thanon Sathorn Tai (0 2676
6868/www.the-ascott.com). Chong
Nonsi BTS.* **BBBB**.
Ringed by bank towers, these fabulous
serviced apartments are flush with modern comforts stimulating design, plus an
outstanding gym, the well-regarded
Aldo's Café and Hu'u Bar (p107).

Banyan Tree Bangkok
*21/100 Thanon Sathorn Tai (0 2679
1200/www.banyantree.com).* **BBBB**.
This all-suite hotel with stylish rooms
and great service occupies a distinctive, wafer-thin tower with an enormous central atrium. The Singaporean
chain provides its signature spa treatments over six levels of spa facilities,
an outdoor 'sky deck' and two pools.
The rooftop alfresco grill Vertigo and
its Moon Bar (p107) have great views
at correspondingly high prices.

Dusit Thani
*946 Thanon Rama IV (0 2236 9999/
www.dusit.com). Saladaeng BTS/
Silom MRT.* **BBBB**.
Dignitaries and royalty favour this triangular, spired institution, which soars
above Lumphini Park and Patpong. Its
angular 1970 architecture has been
newly re-accentuated, from the chic
MyBar, offering garden views, via nice-
enough rooms, to haute cuisine D'Sens
(p100) in the penthouse and meditative
haven, Deverana Spa (see box p172).

Le Meridien Bangkok
*40/5 Thanon Surawong (0 2232 8888/
www.lemeridienhotelbangkok.com).*
BBBB.
Opening opposite Patpong is a risk for
a five-star, but it may instead rebrand
grubby Surawong. The frisson suits
the arty aims of a hotel 'curated' by
French artist Jerome Sans, who
installed an 'official photographer',

Mandarin Oriental p173

Knead to know

Devarana Spa

Bangkok's hotels are home to some of Asia's most luxurious destination spas. Local therapies apply native healing traditions to release blocked energy, relieve sore muscles and stimulate the circulation and respiration.

Bangrak is home to the best of them, many by the river. You are literally transported to another realm on the **Mandarin Oriental** (p173) ferry to the Oriental Spa. Evoking the interior of a Thai teak house, the spa provides classic Thai therapies along with Turkish Rassoul steam and Moorish mud wraps. An Ayurvedic doctor supervises the penthouse devoted to ancient Indian treatments.

Next door, the name **Shangri-La** (p174), the mythical, age-defying Himalayan kingdom, inspired the theme of Chi Spa. Amid vast, meditative spaces and medicine shop motifs, Tibetan and Chinese treatments are prescribed based on your particular Chinese element. Look for specialities such as a Tsampa (Tibetan barley flour) body scrub and Tibetan chimes for *chakra* clearing.

Opposite, the **Peninsula** (p173) built its Spa in a lovely garden building reassembled from old northern Thai houses. Oozing luxury in treatments, service and style, it encompasses classic Asian and European therapies. One highlight is the relaxation room with chaise longues equipped with iPods and mags.

The airy pampering rooms overlooking the garden courtyard at the downtown **Dusit Thani** (p171) are named after the mythical Thai garden of heaven. Devarana Spa builds upon its Thai holistic repertoire with more unusual treats like Indian head massage using medicated oil, and creative body indulgences using ingredients like chocolate.

Nearby, the **Metropolitan** (p173) maintains its contemporary minimalist aesthetic at Shambala Spa, with Spartan, white-on-white treatment rooms. Offering just a handful of purist treatments, the emphasis is on quality, not quantity or novelty. In-house Shambala home-spa products make a popular souvenir or gift.

Ralf Tooten. A hit of assertive contemporary design, the tower has already won awards. Every space feels huge, but the rooms are a bit neutral; not so the sculpted steel-benched lobby, the sixth floor SPA centre (with round rooms for couples) or the spectacular Bamboo Chic bar restaurant serving Sino-Thai-Japanese food and Asian fusion martinis. Impressive, but less so for those who prefer comfy to curated.

Mandarin Oriental
48 Charoen Krung Soi 38 (0 2659 9000/www.mandarinoriental.com). Saphan Taksin BTS. **BBBB.**
One of the world's grandest hotels, this river landmark started life as a lodge for European traders, which burnt down in 1865. Two Danish naval captains, Jarck and Salje, rebuilt it 11 years later and soon attracted the cultured guests for which it's famed. In 1887 another Dane, HN Anderson, upgraded the hotel into what is now the Authors' Wing, containing suites named after writer-guests from an unknown Joseph Conrad to Somerset Maugham, Noel Coward, Graham Greene, John le Carré and, er, Barbara Cartland.

Although the Oriental feels a tad dated, little beats its superior dining and drinking places: Le Normandie's silver service French cuisine, sublime seafood at Lord Jim's, China House (p94) and the jazzy Bamboo Bar (p97). Two venues count as city sights: high tea in the Author's Lounge, and cocktails on the riverbank terrace. Ferries shuttle you to the BTS, River City and the Oriental Spa (see box p172) and Sala Rim Nam restaurant (p98), which stages Khon dance nightly. There are no sandals allowed, so dress up for this piece of living history.

Metropolitan
27 Thanon Sathorn Tai (0 2625 3333/ www.themetropolitan.com). **BBBB.**
Owner Christina Ong forged a sleek, oriental look from the former YMCA, birthing a sister hotel to London's pioneering minimalist icon. Staff in Yohji Yamamoto uniforms whisk guests off to a lofty reception where iMacs offer free internet. Also in pared down style, the rooms are by far the city's biggest, and boast wonderful desks. The two-storey suites come complete with kitchenette and full-height windows, and the terrace rooms have a balcony shower. The poolside Cy'an has innovative cuisine, while Glow café is health-oriented, taking its cue from Shambhala Spa (see box p172). Only guests and members (from BKK's elite) can enter the exclusive Met Bar (see box p131).

Millennium Hilton Bangkok
123 Thanon Charoen Nakorn (0 2442 2000/www.hilton.com). Hilton ferry from Tha Saphan Thaksin or Tha River City. **BBBB.**
A ferry ride from River City opposite, this white landmark contains striking interior halls, while all rooms have river views, open-plan bathrooms and Thai accents like golden lacquer. Pick of the restaurants, the café/buffet Flow surveys the Chao Phraya through vast windows and its deck. At the pool, loungers rest in the water, and on a sandy beach, several floors up. Bar 360 looks over the city from the discus-shaped penthouse.

Peninsula
333 Thanon Charoen Nakorn (0 2861 2888/www.peninsula.com). Saphan Taksin BTS then shuttle boat. **BBBB.**
This stylish tower in many ways outdoes the Oriental opposite, even in meticulous service. The large, well-equipped rooms exude sophistication, with contemporary Thai art and river vistas. Restaurants Mei Jiang (Cantonese) and Jester's (Pacific Rim fusion) are among the city's best, while the teak-market style Thip Thara serves Thai cuisine with a healthy special menu for those treated at the Spa (p172). Beyond a canal, a five-pool deck cascades towards the river. Shuttleboats serve the BTS pier and River City.

ESSENTIALS

Shangri-La

89 Soi Wat Suan Plu, Thanon Charoen Krung (0 2236 7777/www.shangri-la.com). Saphan Taksin BTS. **BBBB.**

Bangkok's largest river hotel – with two wings, two pools, leafy grounds and direct BTS/Expressboat access – has won many awards. The newly refurbished rooms have either city or river vistas. The Shangri-La has first-rate service, facilities and dining options, notably Italian cuisine at Angelini, Thai food at the palatial teak Sala Thai (see box p131), and family Sunday brunch at refurbished NEXT2, plus river trips on its luxury cruiser. For Chi Spa, see box p172.

Sofitel Silom

188 Thanon Silom (0 2238 1991/www.sofitel.com). Chong Nonsi BTS. **BBBB.**

Decorated in contemporary Thai design, this business high-rise also exudes French 'art de vivre', with harmonised hues, smart furnishings and flamboyant artwork. The possibilities for refreshment are excellent, notably at a branch of LeNôtre and in the penthouse wine bar V9 (p95).

Sukhothai

13/3 Thanon Sathorn Tai (0 2344 8888/www.sukhothai.com). **BBBB.**

Designed by Ed Tuttle in an influential Siamese minimalist fashion – which showcases extraordinary floral installations by designer Sakul Intakul – the Sukhothai is arguably Bangkok's most beautiful hotel. Most rooms look out on to the six acres of peaceful grounds and pools containing brick *chedi*, although the owners are endangering the view by erecting a massive tower behind. However, this is a classy retreat, offering exquisite service. Locals love the Thai food at Celadon, the Italian restaurant La Scala and the indulgent champagne brunch at the Colonnade, and many join the first-rate health club for its tennis, squash and people-watching pool.

Expensive

Luxx

6/11 Thanon Decho (0 2635 8800/www.staywithluxx.com). **BBB.**

Tucked away off busy Silom, this slim five-floor boutique hotel keeps things Zen, with refreshing scents, wooden floors, reclining Japanese bathtubs, pool and an intriguing use of space; bathroom partitions can extend the rooms.

Tarntawan Place Hotel

119/5-10 Thanon Surawong (0 2238 2620/www.tarntawan.com). Saladaeng BTS. **BBB.**

Right by Patpong, yet quiet, this small hotel forgoes chic for other qualities: cosiness, convenience and efficiency. It's very gay-friendly.

Triple Two Silom

222 Thanon Silom (0 2627 2222/www.tripletwosilom.com). Saladaeng BTS/Silom MRT. **BBB.**

Bangkok's first boutique hotel (2002) hit just the right attitude and service to earn that mantle. The vibrant mixture of colours and textures involves unusual materials: marble floor mosaics, striking woven rugs on wooden boards, collaged panels of old photos. Some of the finely appointed rooms overlook a garden. The pool, fitness facilities and new Dalah Spa are in the drab adjoining parent hotel, the Narai.

Moderate

Baan Pra Nond

18/1 Thanon Charoenrat (02 212 2242/www.baanpranond.com). **BB.**

Friendly owner and operator, Tasma Cotsmire, converted her grandfather's colonial-style house into a grand nine-bedroom bed-and-breakfast with the family's original furniture. Rooms are charming, spacious and comfortable, especially in the main house. However, the serenity can be broken by the noise of 21st-century traffic. Walking distance to Saphan Taksin BTS and pier.

La Résidence

173/8-9 Thanon Surawong (0 2266 5400-2/www.laresidencebangkok.com). Saladaeng BTS/Silom MRT. **BB**.

This small modern hotel is out of earshot but within reach of Patpong and has many repeat visitors. Each room has a theme, with colour schemes, wallpaper and art conjuring up different moods, whether cosy living room, grand European salon or dramatic red-walled suite. It's clean and friendly, and fairly good value, but has no leisure facilities save for a small library.

Rose Hotel

118 Thanon Surawong (0 2266 8268-72 www.rosehotelbkk.com). **BB**.

This handy hotel has had a retro facelift but retained its atmosphere and friendly staff. The rooms are compact but feel new and come with a big bath. Just don't expect a view. A gorgeous pool abuts the teak house restaurant Ruen Urai (p101).

Budget

Malaysia Hotel

54 Soi Ngam Duphli, Thanon Rama IV (0 2679 7127-36/www.malaysia hotelbkk.com). **B**.

An old GI R&R joint, this block became Bangkok's first backpacker hotel in the 1970s. Today, many guests return time and again, including many gays, due to the hotel's value, location and the people-watching quotient in the 24-hour coffeeshop, notorious as a clearing house for creatures of the night. You get a lot for the 10% service charge: a pool, travel booking, rooms with phones, air-con and hot-shower bathrooms; some rooms with a television, video and fridge.

Sala Thai Daily Mansion

15 Soi Saphanku, off Soi Sri Bamphen (0 2287 1436). Lumphini MRT. **BB**.

Tucked down a quiet sub-*soi*, Khun Anong's guesthouse remains popular with journalists, models and English

Hip hostels

The gap between boutique hotel and youth hostel is being filled by a rise in hostels with a sense of style that bring designer decor, free Wi-Fi and air-con to budget bunking. Exemplifying this trend, **Lub-D** (p176) couples minimal furnishings with colourful, hi-tech amenities. Room types vary from private en-suite doubles to shared dorms for 8 people. Guests get their own reading lights, power sockets and safety boxes, but communal bathrooms.

Train Inn (p171) echoes that functional-and-fun aesthetic. Inspired by nearby Hualumphong Station, it splits no-frills lodging into three cabin classes. Some hostels, like **Take-a-Nap** (p176), also offer 'sleeping rooms' with a family-style array of king-size and single beds. Most dorms offer stowage space underneath beds, while some can store bags for a limited time.

Hostels function as online/offline hubs for travellers. They're more social than many guesthouses and English-fluent staff happily share insider tips on the city. See the growing choice of budget lodgings at www.hostelworld.com.

Among hostelesque guesthouses, the semi-wooden **Baan Hualampong** (p170) has a dorm with a traditional ambience. The courageous can share the 8-bed 'love shack' of bamboo and thatch at the inimitable **Phiman Water View** (p169) 'art guesthouse'. A measure of how the categories blur, **Baan Dinso** (p169) bills itself as a 'boutique hostel'.

Lub-D

teachers. The rooms are clean, basic and small, with shared bathrooms, TV area and rooftop garden. Alone among the Ngam Duphli area's flophouses, it refuses night visitors.

Lub-D

4 Decho Road, Silom Area, Suriyawong Bangrak (02 634 7999/ www.lubd.com). **B**.
This friendly industrial-chic hostel was named one of the 17 coolest in the world by *The Observer*. Electronic cards grant access to four floors, two communal, with both co-ed and women-only quarters, or 'No Men's Land'. Private rooms come with bunks and spotless shared bathrooms; or with queen-size beds, flat-screen TVs and en-suites. Guests lounge in the beanbag strewn movie theatre and mingle in the lobby until midnight.

Take-a-Nap

920-926 Thanon Rama IV (02 637 0015/www.takeanaphotel.com). **B**.
At this hip hostel, each of the 30 air-conditioned, brightly-walled 'sleeping rooms' has a different artistic theme. The private rooms and dorms come

with individual safety boxes. Guests get acquainted at the pool table. It has a large gay following due to the vibrant nearby nightlife.

Siam & around

Deluxe

Chateau de Bangkok

29 Ruamrudee Soi 1 (0 2651 4400/ www.chateaudebangkok.com). Ploenchit BTS. **BBB**.
Accor's serviced apartment tower gets much repeat business due to flexible stays, luxury decor, daily cleaning, king-size beds, full kitchens, Italian restaurant, rooftop pool/gym and jacuzzis in all but the smallest studios.

Conrad Bangkok

All Seasons Place, 87 Thanon Witthayu (0 2690 9999/www.conradbangkok. com). Ploenchit BTS. **BBBB**.
This elegant tower hotel brandishes its chic attitude. The warm, luxurious decor features vibrant carpets, and backlit silk and flower installations by Sakul Intakul. The Diplomat Bar (p119) sets a suave jazzy note, and Liu Chinese

restaurant was designed by Zhang Jin Jie of Beijing Green T House. Facilities include the spa/pool/gym, situated amid roof gardens, 87-Plus nightclub and All Seasons mall.

Four Seasons

155 Thanon Ratchadamri (0 2254 9999/0 2251 6127/www.fourseasons. com). Ratchadamri BTS. **BBBB**.
An impressive spot for meetings, the lobby wows with its murals and back-lit marble columns. The rooms employ craftsmanship while retaining contemporary style and functionality, and generous bathroom/dressing areas. The stunning i.sawan spa villas crown the roof. The Tony Chi-designed restaurants include the impeccable Biscotti (Italian; p119), Madison (grill), Shintaro (Japanese) and Aqua, a bar sharing the water garden with a pâtisserie, shops and photo exhibitions.

Grand Hyatt Erawan

494 Thanon Ratchadamri (0 2254 1234/www.bangkok.hyatt.com). Chidlom/Ratchadamri BTS. **BBBB**.
Behind the brash façade, welcoming, business-like rooms offer spacious mar-

ble bathrooms, modern Thai art and sleek furnishings. Locals frequent Spasso (p123), You & Mee noodle shop, the cavernous ballroom, and the crackled-glass encased Chinese Restaurant. The Hyatt abuts the Erawan Shrine (p119) and Erawan mall, where it serves Thai in the Erawan Tea Room.

Nai Lert Park Hotel

2 Thanon Witthayu (0 2253 0123/ www.swissotel.com/EN/Destination/ Thailand). Ploenchit BTS. **BBBB**.
All rooms of this canalside Swissôtel have balconies overlooking the unusually expansive grounds and pool, and the bathrooms are bright and airy. High society flocks here for functions, and to the designery bar Cyn and swanky arcade Promenade Décor (p122). At the Soi Somkid entrance there stands the phallic Chao Mae Tubtim Shrine (p118).

Expensive

Pathumwan Princess

444 Thanon Phayathai (0 2216 3700-29/www.pprincess.com). National Stadium BTS. **BBB**.

Connected to MBK mall and the BTS, this family-friendly if pricey hotel has all conceivable amenities, large comfy rooms and helpful staff. The Olympic Health Club is famed for its gym and pool, while the Korean restaurant comes well rated.

Budget

Golden House

1025/5-9 Thanon Phloenchit (0 2252 9535-7/www.goldenhouses.net). Chidlom BTS. **B**.

Tucked away in a quiet yet still ultra-convenient *soi*, this guesthouse provides good services and bright, clean standard-sized rooms.

Reno Hotel

40 Kasemsan Soi 1, Thanon Rama I (0 2215 0026-7). National Stadium BTS. **B**.

The makeover of the crisply styled lobby and hip Reno Café hangout has not yet reached all of the rooms, but they're still clean and great value. The pick of several budget digs in this *soi*, and, to make it an even more attractive place to stay, it has a pool too.

Sukhumvit

Deluxe

JW Marriott Bangkok

4 Sukhumvit Soi 2 (0 2656 7700/ www.marriott.com). Ploenchit/Nana BTS. **BBBB**.

During a state visit by the previous president of the USA, George W Bush, this award-winning business hotel served as the temporary White House (well, it is white). Designed by modernist Thai architect Sumet Jumsai, it stands on Sukhumvit Soi and has the airy Bangkok Baking Company café, a Japanese restaurant called (gasp) Tsu-Nami, and New York Steakhouse (p130) serving prime beef upstairs. Great health club and a spa, but the pool is small and shallow.

Sheraton Grande Sukhumvit

250 Sukhumvit Soi 12 (0 2649 8888/ www.sheratongrandesukhumvit.com). Asoke BTS/Sukhumvit MRT. **BBBB**.

Despite the haughty 'e' on the name, this impressive hotel earns loyalty through charming service, large luxurious rooms, an intimate pool with attached spa and great F'n'B outlets that combine in an awesome Sunday brunch, like Basil (contemporary Thai), Rossini (Italian) and Bar Su. The Living Room hosts top jazz players.

Expensive

Eugenia

267 Sukhumvit Soi 31 (0 2259 90179/ www.theeugenia.com). **BBB**.

This stuccoed colonial mansion dates from, oh… 2006. Taiwanese designer Eugene Yu-Cheng Yeh has blended French Indochinoise with British Burma tiffin-ness in 12 bright, massive bedrooms where soft Belgian linens snuggle four-poster beds, as well as in the lounge, reading room and the emerald pool in the lawn. Compounding the Merchant-Ivoryness, the limos are vintage Daimler, Jaguar and Merc.

Moderate

Majestic Suites

110 Thanon Sukhumvit, between Sois 4 & 6 (0 2656 8220/www.majesticsuites. com). Nana BTS. **B**.

This small, friendly, Indian-run inn offers great value, especially the comfy deluxe double. It includes breakfast in the lobby bar and free use of the pool and parking at the owners' luxury, 251-room Majestic Grande nearby.

Seven

3/15 Sawasdee 1, Sukhumvit 31 (02 662 0951/www.sleepatseven.com). Phrom Phong BTS. **BB**.

The six stylish rooms (and lobby) in this converted townhouse are mural-painted according to the Thai tradition of colours for each weekday, offset by white furniture. Some guests move room each day, so book ahead! The lobby functions as a reception, gallery, bar and library. Perks include balconies, iPod docks, free Wi-Fi and mobile phone with pre-paid SIM-card. Despite being convenient, Seven is surprisingly tranquil.

Budget

Atlanta Hotel

78 Sukhumvit Soi 2 (0 225 21650). Nana BTS. **B**.

This one-time beau-monde haunt has hosted Jim Thompson and Scandinavian royalty, and a cult following of creatives and Asia obsessives. Moralistic literary notices dot the bookshelves, walls and even the menu at its superb, mainly vegetarian Thai restaurant. The exterior may be plain and the bathrooms basic, but it retains the original 1952 art deco lobby, Bangkok's first hotel pool (24-hour), writing desks in the garden and Thai dancing on Saturdays. A legend… but behave!

Honey Hotel

31 Sukhumvit Soi 19 (0 2253 0646-9). Asoke BTS/Sukhumvit MRT. **B**.

Superbly kitsch, the Honey's long, low, black granite foyer and aqua pool will suit anyone who thinks crimplene and cocktail frankfurters are 'faaabulous'. The 75 rooms are unglamorous and slightly musty, but good value. Honey has tons of atmosphere, plus a cast of generic middle-aged white men and Thai girls lounging poolside.

Miami

2 Sukhumvit Soi 13 (0 2253 0369). Nana BTS. **B**.

The Miami has seen better days, but has retro motel cachet (check out the pale blue pool) and large, functional, if somewhat on the plain side, rooms. There are quieter rooms away from the street bustle, and the friendly *kathoey* staff will discount long stays.

Suk11 Guesthouse

1/33 Sukhumvit Soi 11 (0 2253 5927-8/www.suk11.com). Nana BTS. **B**.

A rarity in Sukhumvit, this guesthouse spreads charmingly over four shophouses disguised by old wooden fittings. Rooms are smallish, but pleasant and clean, and there are dorm beds too. All come with air-con and breakfast in a café you can't help lingering in. Its spa transports you to an imagined village apothecary.

Suburbs

Deluxe

Marriott Bangkok Resort & Spa

257/1-3 Thanon Charoen Nakorn, Khlong San (0 2476 0022/www.marriotthotels.com/bkkth). Saphan Taksin BTS then hotel boat. **BBBB**.

Guests relish the teak shuttle boat trip downstream from Saphan Taksin Pier/BTS to this elegant yet unpretentious resort, which frames a vast pool garden. It may be remote, but it has a Mandara Spa, a mini-mall and several dining options such as Trader Vic's, renowned for its Sunday jazz brunch. The teak barge, *Manohra*, hosts dinner and overnight cruises.

Moderate

Baan Waree by Reflections

24 Sailom Soi 1, Thanon Phahonyothin Soi 8, Phyathai (02 272 6300/www.reflections-thai.com). Ari BTS. **BB**.

Now in its third location, this colourful (and we might bright) hotel dares to think differently. Guru of Thai kitsch, Anusorn 'Nong' Ngernyuang applies the sensibility behind the fabulously camp Global Trash Chic products he makes. Each of the 27 rooms has a different concept, designed by a different artist. A restaurant roof terrace and bar add to the quirky spaces. Though not central, Baan Waree is just a 10-minute walk to the BTS and expressways.

ESSENTIALS

Getting Around

Arriving & leaving

Trains from Singapore via Malaysia, and from Laos, terminate at Hualumphong Station (p182). Buses terminate at regional Bus Stations (p181).

Airports

Don Muang Airport

Thanon Wiphawadi Rangsit (0 2535 1111/www.airportthai.co.th).
The old airport is used only by some budget airlines.

Suvarnabhumi Airport

Thanon Bangna-Trad km15 (0 2132 1888/help desk 0 2132 3888/flight information 0 3212 000/www.bangkok airport.co.th/www.suvarnabhumi airport.com).
Bangkok's new airport.

Airport transit

Road 25km (15.5 miles) east of downtown, 30-60mins via either of two expressways.
Car parks *(0 2132 9171).* **Open** 24hrs daily. **Fee** B30 for 1hr up to B220 for 7-24hrs.
Public Taxi-Meter *Outside arrivals (0 2132 9199).* **Open** 24hrs daily. Desks *outside* arrivals manage taxi-meters, and write your destination on a card. You keep the part carrying the driver's number in case of complaints or lost property. At journey's end, you pay the meter fare (B200-B250 to downtown), plus a B50 airport surcharge; en route you pay tolls.
Airport Associate *(0 2391 8100/www. aaclimousine.com).* **Open** 24hrs daily. Reliable rental firm.
AOT Limousine *Inside arrivals (0 2132 2323).* **Open** 24hrs daily. The airport's limo service charges B4,400 for a Merc to downtown.

Airport Bus *(0 2132 9171).* **Times** 5am-midnight Mon-Sat; 5.30am-12.30am Sun & hols. **Fare** B100. Four routes: **AE1** (to BTS Saladeang via Oriental Hotel), **AE2** (Thanon Khao San via Phyathai), **AE3** (Nana via Sukhumvit/New Petchaburi) and **AE4** (Hualumphong via Ploenchit/ Siam).
Airport Rail Link *(0 2535 7481 2).* See p182 Trains.

Navigation & maps

Bangkok's infamous traffic gets worse in rush hours (7am-9am, 4-8pm), the rainy season, school terms and holiday weekends. So travel at quieter times and favour the expressways, boats and trains. *Thanon* (roads) have branching *soi* (lanes), usually numbered, sometimes named. Building numbers can be non-contiguous, and one-way systems are common. Taxi routes can seem strange, but may be following traffic radio advice. Venues and hotels often provide directions in Thai.

Many signs are in English, which is widely spoken, but transliterations often differ between signs, guides and maps. The best maps are *Nelles: Bangkok* and *Periplus Bangkok Street Atlas*; Thinknet maps are bilingual. The hand-drawn *Nancy Chandler's Map of Bangkok* excels for shopping and Chinatown. The *Groovy Map* also covers nightlife.

Public transport

Bus services

BMTA Buses

0 2246 0973/hotline 184/ www.bmta.co.th.
Bangkok Mass Transit Authority and private firms run over 13,400

buses on 442 routes. It's cramped and chaotic, with new and old buses, air-con and fan, having the same number but different colours and prices. Signs are all in Thai. Minibuses cover routes unserved by buses.

Air-conditioned buses are blue with a white stripe or white and articulated (5am-11pm). Fares: B8-B16. Orange buses (5am-11pm) charge B12-B20.

Non-air-conditioned buses are red/cream (5am-11pm, B7). Red/cream ones using expressways cost B9; running as nightbuses (11pm-5am) it's B8.50.

Bus Rapid Transit (BRT)
0 2354 1224-7.
The BRT will have dedicated central bus lanes with stations every 700m. The overdue first line will feed Chong Nonsi BTS (16.5km, from Rama IX Bridge via Thanon Rama III-Thanon Narathiwat Ratchankharin).

Long-distance buses
Rot tour (inter-provincial buses) are the mainstay of ordinary Thais and often sell out well ahead of time, so book ahead through travel agents, hotels or bus terminals. *Rot air* (air-con buses) are roomier; VIP buses serve food and drink. Drivers can be reckless. Be alert to your bag security. Minibuses run upcountry routes.
www.transport.co.th provides information on all bus terminals.
Eastern Bus Terminal (Ekamai)
Sukhumvit Soi 42 (0 2391 8097). Ekamai BTS. **Open** 4am-midnight daily. **No credit cards.** .
Northern & North-eastern Bus Terminal (Morchit 2, also serves Central region) *999 Thanon Kamphaengphet 2 (0 2936 2852-66).* **Open** 24hrs daily.
Southern Bus Terminal (Sai Tai Mai, also serves the West) *147 Thanon Boromratchachonnani (0 2435 5605).* **Open** 5am-11pm daily.

Songtaew
Local roads and *soi* often have pick-up truck buses called *songtaew* ('two rows', after the bench seating), *seelor* (four-wheeler) or *hoklor* (six-wheeler). Often gaily painted, they cost B5-B10 and stop at will. Hail and hop in; pay when you buzz to alight.

Taxis

Taxi-meters
With radios and meters, air-con taxis are cheap, plentiful and comfy. Those with a red light are vacant and stop for you instantly. Signal by flapping your hand, palm *down* (up is rude). Taxis are coloured by company. Decline drivers refusing to use the meter. Poor maintenance often indicates a dodgy driver. Front seatbelts are compulsory. Directions in Thai (especially written) help more than showing maps. From B35, rates rise at B2 increments with a traffic jam surcharge, but no night-time increase. Round up fare for a tip. For safety and ease, 24hr radio taxis collect within 20mins (B20 surcharge) or offer full-day hire (from B1,500).
Bangkok Taxi Radio Centre
0 2880 0888.
Community Radio Taxi *1681.*
Nakornchai *0 2878 9000/ www.taxithai.com.*
Siam Taxi *1661.*

Taxi motorcycles
For a quick pillion ride, *rot motocy* serve most *soi*. Short runs cost B5-B20, longer rides mirror taxi fares (agree the rate first). For a helmet, say *ow muak garn knock*; they're compulsory, but often not worn.

Tuk-tuks
The open-air tuk-tuk (or *samlor*, three-wheeler) is customised from Japanese motorised rickshaws. The

ESSENTIALS

bench may fit three slim *farang*. You get rain, fumes, soot and sweat en route, and even the *sanuk* (fun) may fade if you get haven't agreed the unmetered fare.

Train services

Airport Link City Line

(0 2535 7481-2). Times, frequency and fares to be announced.

Due by 2010, Airport Link (AL) trains to Suvarnabhumi will run from Makkasan check-in terminal (accessing MRT Phetchburi). Parallel commuter trains will run from BTS/AL Phyathai to AL Lad Krabang.

BTS SkyTrain

BTS Tourist Information Centre (0 2617 6000/www.bts.co.th). **Open** 6am-midnight daily every 5mins (3mins peak). New Year 24hrs.

This safe, private train has two lines that intersect at Siam: the dark green Sukhumvit line (Morchit to Onnut, extending to Baring); and light green Silom line (National Stadium to Wong Wien Yai, extending to Phetkasem). It connects to the MRT, Airport Link, Expressboats, and by SkyBridges to many malls. Machines issue **Single-journey** tickets (B15-B40), but people queue for B5 and B10 coins from the counter. The **Sky Card** (refillable, minimum B100 plus B30 deposit, valid 5yrs) depletes by distance. The **1-Day Pass** (B120), **30-Day Adult Pass** (20 trips B440, 30 trips B600, 40 trips B800) or **30-Day Student Pass** (20 trips B340, 30 trips B450, 40 trips B600) have no distance limit.

Hualumphong Station

1 Thanon Rong Muang (0 2225 6964/booking 0 2220 4444/schedule 1690/www.srt.or.th). **Open** *Trains* 4.20am-11.40pm daily. *Booking* (3-60 days ahead) 8.30am-4.30pm daily. *Tour desk* 8.30am-4pm daily.

The State Railway of Thailand (0 2621 8701) runs all long-distance trains.

Most depart from this Italianate terminus, some from **Bangkok Noi station** (0 2411 3102) or **Wong Wian Yai station** (0 2465 2017) for the quaint line to Mahachai.

MRT Subway

Bangkok Metro (0 2354 2000/www. bangkokmetro.co.th). **Open** 5am-midnight daily; 4-6mins (2-4mins peak).

The underground blue line arcs 20km (12 miles) from Hualumphong railway station to Bang Sue railway station, and connects to the BTS and Airport Link. Fares are B17-B41 from station counters and machines. Top-up cards (refillable, minimum B100 plus B50, valid 5yrs) deplete by distance. The 30-day pass costs B1,000. Entrances open a metre above the highest flood level.

Water transport

Canal boats

Quick, exhilarating, but cramped and awkward, covered longtail boats ply Khlong Saen Saeb, an east–west canal from Tha Saphan Phan Fah (Golden Mount, for old town) taking 15-17mins to Tha Pratunam (change boats) and 40mins to Tha Bang Kapi, with many useful stops.

Family Transport *(0 2375 2369).* **Boats** every 2-11mins, 5.30am-8.30pm Mon-Fri; every 5-11mins 6am-6.30pm Sat, 6am-7pm Sun. **Fare** B8-B18.

River boats

Chao Phraya Expressboat

78/24-9 Thanon Maharaj, Phra Nakorn (0 2623 6143). **Open** 8am-6pm Mon-Sat.

The private river bus service covers 18km (11 miles). Buy tickets from boat conductors or at one of the 35 piers, which are signed in English, with Tha Sathorn ('Central Pier') linking to Saphan Taksin BTS. Flags on the roof identify boat types:

Yellow flag (rush-hour express)
*Few stops Tha Nonthaburi-Tha Sathon
(45-50mins).* Mon-Fri every 10mins
6.10-6.30am, every 4mins 6.30-8.40am,
every 15mins 4.30-6.20pm. Returns
every 10 mins 3.45pm-7.30pm.
Fare B18-B27.

**Green & Yellow flag (rush-hour
express)** *Few stops Tha Pakkred-Tha
Sathon (1hr).* Mon-Fri every 15mins
6.05-8.05am. Returns every 15mins
4pm-5.30pm Mon-Fri. **Fare** B12-B30.

Orange flag (express) *Major piers
Tha Nonthaburi-Tha Wat Rajsingkorn
(1hr).* Mon-Fri every 5mins 5.50-
9.15am, every 15mins 3-5.50pm.
Returns every 12mins 6.30-8.45am,
every 20mins 2-4pm, every 10mins
4-6pm, every 15mins 6-7pm. On Sat
every 15mins 6.45-8.40am, 4-6.20pm;
no Sun service. **Fare** B13.

No flag (local) *All piers.* Mon-Fri
every 15mins 6-8am, every 20mins
8am-6.40pm. On Sat and Sun every
20-25mins 6am-6.40pm. **Fare** B9-B13.

Tourist Boat *From Sathorn Pier to
piers at sights.* Daily every 30mins,
9.30am-3pm. **Day pass** B150. Also to
Koh Kret 10am-4.30pm Sun. **Fare**
B300 adults, B250 children.

River ferries

Dumpy ferries (*kham fahk*) cross
the Chao Phraya from many piers
(every 5mins 5am-midnight, some
until 9pm, daily) for just B3. River
hotels' ferries serve Tha Saphan
Taksin, Tha Oriental and Tha Si
Phraya (River City).

Driving

Drivers need an international
licence (foreign licences aren't
accepted). Thais drive on the left,
front seatbelts are compulsory
and speed limits are 80kmh in
Bangkok, 90kmh outside. Fines
can resemble arbitrary extortion.
Expect bad drivers, expressway
tolls, narrow *soi* and many 'one-
way'/'no right turn' detours.

Car & van hire

Rental firms provide cars from
B900 per day (most including
insurance); most offices close
Sunday. Along with travel agents,
many also rent a car/van with
driver (B1,500-B2,000 per day,
overnight B2,500 per day, plus
tip). All exclude petrol and tolls.
For problem assistance try the
Transportation Safety Centre
(0 2280 8000, hotline 1356,
www.mot.go.th) or Highway
Police (0 2354 672/hotline 1193).

Avis (0 2255 5300-4/www.avis.co.th).
Budget (0 2203 9200/
www.budget.co.th).
Highway Car Rent (0 2266 9393-8/
www.highway.co.th).
Japan Rent (0 2259 8867-70/
www.japanrenthailand.com).
Krung Thai Car Rent (0 2291
8888/www.krungthai.co.th).
Lumphini Car Rent (0 2255 1966-8).
Tranex Services (0 2874 1174/
www.tranex.yellowpages.co.th).
Thai Prestige Rent-A-Car (0 2941
1344-8/2231-3/www.thaiprestige.
yellowpages.co.th).

Parking & services

Street parking is limited (and
banned 5am-10pm on some
highways and bus lanes); pay
attendants a B10-B20 tip. Malls,
hotels and offices charge from
B40/hr, often with a free period if
you get the ticket stamped at a
venue on site. Double parking is
normal, so to enable shunting,
park in neutral, wheels straight,
handbrake off. Petrol is cheap
at plentiful stations. In case of
breakdowns try:
B-Quik Service *16th floor, 253
Sukhumvit Soi 21* (0 2620 0900/www.
b-quik.com). **Open** 8am-9pm daily.
Carworld Club *2/1 Thanon Rama IV*
(0 26121 9999/www.cwc.co.th). **Open**
Breakdown service 24hrs daily.

ESSENTIALS

Resources A-Z

Accident & emergency

Erawan Centre
514 Department of Medical Services, Bangkok Metropolitan Administration, Thanon Luang (0 2223 9401-3/hotline 1646/1554). **Open** 24hrs daily.
Free emergency medical treatment and despatch of ambulances and doctors, plus health advice.

International SOS Services Thailand
11th floor, Diethelm Tower, 93/1 Thanon Witthayu (0 2205 7755/www.internationalsos.com). **Open** 24hrs daily.
Tackles any emergency, emphasising speedy ambulances and police contact.

Tourist Police
TAT, 4 Ratchadamnoen Nok Avenue (24hr hotline 1155/0 2308 0333). **Open** 8.30am-4.30pm. *Hotline* 24hrs daily.
This English-speaking force is best for empathy, efficiency, perseverance and familiarity with non-Thai concerns. Or call **Tourist Assistance Centre** (0 2281 5051). If necessary, try the 24-hour **Police Hotline** (191) or police stations, where procedures can be stressful. Road casualties often get sent to the Police Hospital, Thanon Ratchadamri, by Chinese charities like Poh Tek Tung.

Customs

On arrival, fill in Passenger Declaration Form 211 for Customs (hotline 1164, www.customs.go.th). Duty-free import limits include 200 cigarettes; 1 litre of spirits; 1 litre of wine; B10,000 of perfume. Prohibited imports/exports include drugs, pornography, protected wild animals or related products. Items requiring permits include Buddha images and antiques (Fine Arts Department, 0 2221 7811).

Disabled

Contact the **Association of the Physically Handicapped** (0 2951 0445/www.apht.or.th/ www.flyingwheelchairs.org).

Electricity

The standard current is 220V, 50 cycles/sec, but plugs are unearthed two-pins (round or parallel flat), so beware of shocks.

Embassies

American Embassy *120-122 Thanon Witthayu (0 2205 4000/www.usa.or.th).*
Australian Embassy *37 Thanon Sathorn Tai (0 2287 2680/ www.austembassy.or.th).*
British Embassy *1031 Thanon Witthayu (0 2305 8333/www.british embassy.gov.uk/thailand). Ploenchit BTS.*
Canadian Embassy *15th floor, Abdul Rahim Place, 990 Thanon Rama IV (0 2636 0540/www.bangkk.gc.ca). Saladaeng BTS/Silom MRT.*
New Zealand Embassy *14th floor, M-Thailand Building, 87 Thanon Witthayu (0 2254 2530/www.nz embassy.com/thailand). Ploenchit BTS.*

Health

Dentists
Asavanant Dental Clinic *58/5 Sukhumvit Soi 55 (0 2391 1842/ www.asavanant.com). Thonglor BTS.*
Dental Hospital *88/88 Sukhumvit Soi 49 (0 2260 5000-15/www.dentalhospitalbangkok.com).*

Hospitals

State hospitals range from the humble to teaching institutions. The good value private hospitals listed have multilingual clinics and handle medical tourism and medevacuations.

Bangkok Hospital *2 Soi Soonvijai 7 (0 2310 3000/www.bangkokhospital.com).*

BNH Hospital *9/1 Thanon Convent (0 2686 2700/www.BNHhospital.com). Saladaeng BTS/Silom MRT.*

Bumrungrad Hospital *33 Sukhumvit Soi 3 (0 2667 1000/www.bumrungrad. com). Nana BTS.*

Police Hospital (state) *492/1 Thanon Ratchadamri (0 2252 8111-25/www.policehospital.go.th). Chidlom/Ratchadamri BTS.*

Sirirat Hospital (state) *2 Thanon Prannok (0 2419 7000/www.si. mahidol.ac.th). Tha Sirirat.*

Pharmacies

Plentiful branches of Boots and Watsons have pharmacies open till 9pm. *Kai yaa* (drug stores) are commonplace, especially near hospitals, and open late night around Patpong and Nana. Many sell medicines without prescriptions, except those with major impact. Hospitals dispense in-house at inflated prices.

STDs & HIV/AIDS

Anonymous Clinic*1871 Thanon Ratchadamri, Pathumwan (0 2256 4107-9/www.redcross.or.th). Ratchadamri BTS.* Thai Red Cross HIV/AIDS testing, counselling and treatment.

Internet

Many shops stock prepaid online packages, including CS Loxinfo (0 2263 8222, www.csloxinfo.com), KSC (0 2979 7000, www.ksc.net), Pacificnet (0 2618 8088/8688, www.pacific.net.th) and Qnet (0 2377 0555, www.qnet.co.th). Terminals are common in business and tourist areas, most cheaply in

Banglamphu, while CATNET at selected post offices costs B0.12/min using CATNET cards (B100, B300, B500). All cafés by True (www.truecorp.co.th) and the following centres have net access:

Olavi *53 Thanon Chakrabongse (0 2629 2228-9/www.olavi.com).* **Open** 10am-8pm Mon-Sat. **Rate** B40/hr.

Time *2nd floor, Times Square, Thanon Sukhumvit (0 2653 3636-9). Asoke BTS/Sukhumvit MRT.* **Open** 9am-midnight Mon-Sat; 10am-midnight Sun. **Rate** B1/min.

Money

ATMs & currency

ATMs are plentiful at banks, malls, petrol pumps and many shops. They're open 24 hours, and most accept credit cards.

Thai currency is the *baht* (B). B1 equals 100 *satang*. Coins are 25 satang, 50 satang, B1, B2, B5 and B10. Bank notes are B20, B50, B100, B500 and B1,000.

Credit cards

Most air-conditioned hotels, restaurants, shops, bars and malls accept Visa, MasterCard and American Express; Diners Club less often. To report lost or stolen cards, call these 24-hour hotlines:

American Express *0 2273 5500/5522.*

Diners Club *0 2238 3660.*

MasterCard *ASEAN countries 001 800 11 887 0663.*

Visa Contact issuing bank.

Post

Letters not over 20g cost B3 within Thailand; postcards and letters abroad B12-B19; aerogrammes B15. Post Offices (hotline 1545) have parcel packaging, express and registered mail, and internet terminals, usually opening 8.30am-4.30pm Mon-Fri, 9am-noon Sat. The CPO holds poste restante mail for up to a month (bring ID, fee payable). Stamps are sold at convenience stores and souvenir shops.

Central Post Office (CPO)

Thanon Charoen Krung, at Sois 32-34 (0 2614 7455/call centre 1545). **Open** *Packing* 8am-4.30pm Mon-Fri; 9am-noon Sat. *Post* 8am-8pm Mon-Fri; 8am-1pm Sat, Sun. *Postal orders & money services* 8am-5pm Mon-Fri; 8am-noon Sat. *Poste restante* 8am-8pm Mon-Fri; 8am-1pm Sat, Sun.

Prohibitions

Fines include B2,000 for littering, B200 for jaywalking and the acts itemised below. Alcohol is sold only 11am-2pm and 5pm-midnight. You must be 18 to drive, buy cigarettes and alcohol, or have sex (straight or gay), while under-20s aren't allowed in bars or clubs, which request picture ID of all customers (sometimes a full passport). Prostitution is technically illegal, but openly tolerated.

Drugs

Those in possession of illicit drugs face one to ten years' jail and fines of B10,000-B100,000. Punishment for drug dealing or trafficking is severe, with the death penalty enforced. Occasional nightclub raids may enforce urine tests.

Smoking

Draconian new rules prohibit smoking in all air-conditioned buildings and public places (including streets, parks, transport, hotel lobbies and restaurants), except bars, clubs and places with signed smoking rooms or zones (fine B2,000). Cigarettes are legally on sale, but cannot be displayed.

Taboos

■ Criticism of anyone or anything (including Thailand) causes offence. Show respect for royalty, Buddhism, monks and Buddha images. Stand for the King's Anthem at the start of performances and the national anthem. Committing lese-majesty may result in prison.

■ Don't touch or point at the head, which is sacred. Never use feet, the lowest body part, to move or point at things, nor step on money as it bears royal imagery.

■ Inside temples, wear polite clothing (cover shoulders and knees). Monks must not touch women.

■ Remove shoes before entering rooms in temples, palaces, homes and some museums.

■ Anger loses face, and prevents the resolution of problems. Jollying Thais along is more effective.

■ Presentable, clean clothing, footwear and hair gain you respect and help, particularly from officials.

■ Eat and pass things with your right hand as the left is used for cleaning after defecating.

Telephones

Dialling & codes

You must dial the area codes, even within the area. Bangkok landlines start 0 2 plus 7 digits, provincial landlines have 3-digit codes (eg Samet 0 38) before 6-digit numbers. Local calls cost B3 (unlimited). Calling upcountry is cheaper if you dial 1234 before the 0. Mobiles start 7-digit numbers with the prefix 08 1, 08 5, 08 6, 08 7 or 08 9.

To call Thailand, dial the country code 66, omit the 0, then dial the remaining 8 digits (or 9 digits for a mobile phone). To call outside Thailand, dial 007 or 008, or the pricier 001, before the country code and number.

For operator assisted calls, dial 100 and let the operator call (including 3mins surcharge before you speak).
Directory inquiries *Hotline 1133 Bangkok; 183 regional.* 24hrs; free.
Talking Yellow Pages *Hotline 1188.* 24hrs; B6/min.

Public phones

Call boxes require B1, B5 or B10 coins and/or a phone card (sold at post offices or convenience stores). Some accept credit cards for international calls. Bangkok 0 2 area calls cost from B1 for 3mins, B5 for 15mins. Dialling a mobile costs B3 for 1min.

Mobile phones

Visitors can use roaming, buy a cheap local phone (*meur teur*, from B3,500 including some calls) or, if sharing the Thai GSM 900 or 1800 systems, buy a local prepaid SIM card from corner stores or phone shops in most malls. SIMs by AIS One-2-Call, DTAC's D-Prompt, True Move or Hutch's Say Prepaid include some free calls. 1900 GSM users should consult service provider.

Time

Thailand is seven hours ahead of Greenwich Mean Time, 12 hours ahead of US Eastern Standard Time, and three behind Sydney. The Thai calendar is 543 years ahead of the Gregorian calendar; 2010 AD is 2553 BE (Buddhist Era).

Tipping

Tips are small (B20-B50), but some places levy 10 per cent. Tip guides, maids and drivers, but not hairdressers or food vendors. Round up taxi fares. Masseurs get low piece rates so tip B100 or so.

Toilets

Public conveniences (*hong nam* or *suka*) are rare, and may charge (B2-B5) in markets, stations and public places. So use the generally cleaner ones in gas stations, department stores, hotels, temples or (asking politely) pubs, restaurants or shops where you're not a patron.

Squat pans are common, with a plastic dipper and a water trough for cleaning yourself and flushing. Flush toilets usually have a spray hose. Toilet paper is often not provided (carry some) and must go in the basket to not block the pipes.

Tourist information

Bangkok Tourist Bureau
17/1 Thanon Phra Athit (0 2225 7612-5/www.bangkoktourist.com). **Open** 9am-7pm daily.
BTB offers good advice, maps and brochures on Bangkok attractions, tours and its own trips, including online listings. BTB booths are found at tourist, hotel and shopping areas.

Tourism Authority of Thailand (TAT)
TAT Building, 1600 Thanon Petchaburi Tud Mai (0 2250 5500/www.tat.or.th). **Open** 8.30am-4.30pm Mon-Fri.
TAT covers the whole country. Branches include one at Suvarnabhumi Airport (0 2132 1888).

Visas

US, UK, Australasian and most European nationals can get a visa on arrival for 30 days (15 days at land borders), extendable twice to a maximum of 90 days in any six months, enforcing a 90-day gap before returning.
Immigration Department
507 Soi Suan Plu, Thanon Sathorn Tai (0 2287 3101-10/www.imm.police. go.th). **Open** 8.30am-4.30pm Mon-Fri.

ESSENTIALS

Vocabulary

Pronunciation

Transliterations of Thai vary as it's syllabic, hierarchical and tonal: high (ó), falling (ô), even (no mark), rising (ō), low (ò). However, the language has no articles or tenses; adjectives follow the noun, but numbers go before a 'counting' word like *un* (small thing).

Consonants: **j** (ch or tch), **kh** (as in karma), **k** (hard g), **ng** (as in sing), **p** (bp), **ph** (pine, not f), **r** (trilled, or like l), **t** (dt), **th** (as in Thai, not the/three), **v** (w). At end of syllable: **-j**, **-ch** and **-s** become **-t**; **-r** becomes **-orn**; **-l** becomes **-n**. Vowels: **a** (as in pun), **aa** (barn), **ae** (air), **ai** (high), **ao** (how), **aw** (awe), **e** (hay), **eu** (fleur), **i** (hit), **ii** (teeth), **o** (hot), **oe** (earn), **oh** (so), **oo/u** (book), **uu** (pool), **uay** (oo-ay).

Useful phrases

Politely end sentences with *khâ* for females or *krúb* for males (like 'please'), as in **thank you** *khòb khun khâ/krúb*.

Thais put titles with first names not surnames, but go mostly by nicknames. **I** *chán* (female)/*phŏm* (male); **Mr/Mrs/Miss/you** *khun*; **he/she** *khǎo*; **wife** *mia*; **husband** *samee*; **child** *dek*; **girl/boyfriend** *faen*; **friend** *puêan*. **hello/goodbye** *sàwàsdee*; **what's your name?** *khun chêu arai?*; **my name is...** *chán/phŏm chêu...*; **yes** *châi*; **no** *mâi châi*; **can** *dâi*; **cannot** *mâi dâi*; **please** *pròd*; **sorry** *sîa jai*; **never mind** *mâi pen rai*; **ask/can I have...** *kŏr...*; **excuse me** *kŏr thôd*; **(don't) like...** *(mâi) chôrp...*; **good** *dee*; **bad** *mâi dee*; **big** *yài*; **small** *lék*; **little** *nói*; **very/much** *mâak*; **enough** *por láeo*; **without** *mâi mee*; **help**

chûay; **do you speak English?** *khun phôod pasǎa angìd dâi mái?* **I don't understand** *mâi khâo jai*; **please speak slower** *pròd phôod chá nòi*; **do you have a double/single room?** *mee hông khôo/hông dêow?*; **I have a reservation** *jong hông láeo*; **open/close** *pèrd/pìd*; **where?** *têe nǎi?*; **the way to...?** *thang pai...máii?*; **right** *khwǎ*; **left** *sáai*; **straight** *dtrong*; **turn** *líi-o*; **return** *pai klàb*; **where's the toilet?** *hông nám yoo nǎi (khâ/krúb)*; **stop here/there** *yùut tîi-nîi/tîi-nán*; **...hospital** *rong phaya bâan...*; **embassy** *sàtǎan tôot*; **where?** **entrance** *thang khâo*; **exit** *thang ôkk*; **near** *klâi*; **far** *klaai*; **ticket** *tua*

Timings

when? *mûea rài?*; **what time?** *kèe mong?*; **now** *torn níi*; **today** *wan níi*; **yesterday** *mêua wan níi*; **tomorrow** *wan prôong níi*; **week** *aa-thít*; **Mon** *wan jun*; **Tue** *wan ankarn*; **Wed** *wan phúd*; **Thur** *wan páréuhàt*; **Fri** *wan sùk*; **Sat** *wan sǎo*; **Sun** *wan athít*; **month** *deuan*.

Numbers & money

0 *sǒon*; **1** *nèung*; **2** *sǒng*; **3** *sǎm*; **4** *sìi*; **5** *hâa*; **6** *hòk*; **7** *jèd*; **8** *pàed*; **9** *kâo*; **10** *sìb*; **11** *sìb-èt*; **12** *sìb-sǒng*; **20** *yî-sìb*; **21** *yî-sìb-èt*; **30** *sǎm-sìb*; **100** *nèung-rói*; **101** *nèung rói nèung*; **200** *sǒng rói*; **1,000** *phun*; **10,000** *nèung mèun*; **100,000** *nèung sǎen*; **1,000,000** *nèung láan*; **1st** *tée nèung*; **2nd** *tée sǒng*; **last** *tíi sòod*; **how much?** *thâo rai?*; **price** *raakha*; **expensive/cheap** *paeng /tòok*; **discount** *lód raakha*; **free** *free*; **check/bill** *chék bin*; **do you have change?** *khun mee torn mái?*

Menu Glossary

General terms

phet spicy; **mai phet** non-spicy; **phet nit noi** a bit spicy; **aa-roi** delicious; **iik neung** one more; **im laew** full; **bpuu** crab; **hoi** shellfish; **kai** chicken; **koong** shrimp; **moo** pork; **muu daeng** red-roasted pork; **neua** meat/beef; **ped** duck; **pla** fish; **pla meuk** squid; **talay** seafood; **phak** (vegetables); **tua pluu** winged bean; **taohuu** tofu; **kin jeh** vegan; **mung sa virat** meat-free; **kreung prung** seasonings; **sord si racha** chilli ketchup; **nam pla** fish sauce; **nam tan** sugar; **si-ew** soy sauce; **phrik Thai** white pepper; **phrik Thai dum** black pepper; **kratiam** garlic; **nam phrik** chilli dip.

Cooking styles

neung steamed; **ping/phao** grilled; **thord** deep fried; **yaang** roasted/grilled; **op** baked; **tom** boiled; **khem** salty; **waan** sweet; **priao** sour; **jeud** bland; **sub** minced; **sod** fresh/uncooked.
Kaeng curry: **kaeng khiao-waan** sweet green curry; **kaeng phet** red curry; **kaeng karii** mild yellow; **kaeng Matsaman** mild curry; **kaeng pa** jungle curry; **kaeng panaeng** thick red curry with peanuts; **kaeng som** sour tamarind soup; **kaeng jeud** bland soup; **tom yum** hot-and-sour soup; **tom kha** coconut soup with galangal; **khao tom** boiled rice soup.
Phat stir-fried; **phat khing** with ginger; **phat kaphrao** with basil; **phat nam-man hoey** with oyster sauce; **phat pong karii** with curry powder; **kai phat med ma-muang** chicken with cashew nuts; **pad ka-na muu krob** kale with crispy pork; **phak boong fai** daeng stir-fried morning glory; **pad phak ruam-mit** vegetables. **Yum** spicy salad; **yum pla dook foo** fluffy catfish; **yum maa-kheua yao** eggplant with pork; **som tam** shredded papaya; **larb** warm Isaan-style; **muu nam tok** Isaan-style with pork.

Rice & noodles

khao plao plain rice; **khao niao** sticky rice; **khao phat** fried rice; **khao kaeng** curry over rice; **khao mun kai** oily chicken rice; **khao na ped** roast duck rice; **khao mok kai** Muslim chicken biryani. **ba mee** egg noodles; **kuaytiao** rice noodles; **sen lek/yai/mee** narrow/wide/fine; **haeng** dry; **nam** in soup; **look chin pla/moo** fish/pork balls; **phat thai** stir-fry with prawns; **phat si-ew** fried in soy sauce; **rad na** in gravy; **kuaytiao reua** 'boat' rice noodles with herbal broth; **woon sen** clear noodles.

Dessert & drinks

Khanom dessert: **kluay buat chii** banana in coconut milk, **sangkhayaa** Thai custard; **foy thong** duck egg yolks spun with sugar; **khao niao ma-muang** sticky rice with mango.
Fruit ponlamai: **ap-peun** apple; **cantaloup** melon; **farang** guava; **kluay** banana; **malakor** papaya; **ma-muang** mango; **mangkut** mangosteen; **maphrao** coconut; **ngo** rambutan; **sapparot** pineapple; **som** orange; **som-o** pomelo; **taeng mo** watermelon.
Deum drinks: **nam plao** water; **nam soda** soda water; **nam manao** lime juice; **nam ponlam ai bun** iced fruit shake; **kafae** coffee; **cha** tea; **yen** cold; **rorn** hot.

Index

Sights & Areas